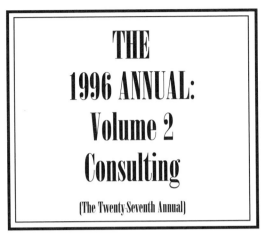

THE
1996 ANNUAL:
Volume 2
Consulting

(The Twenty-Seventh Annual)

Edited by
J. William Pfeiffer, Ph.D., J.D.

Johannesburg • London
San Diego • Sydney • Toronto

PREFACE

The Pfeiffer & Company *Annual* series has been a success since its inception in 1972. One key to this success has been how well the *Annuals* meet the needs of human resource development (HRD) practitioners. The contents of each *Annual* focus on increasing a reader's professional competence by providing materials of immediate, practical use.

In 1995, Pfeiffer & Company began to publish two *Annuals* each year. Volume 1 is focused on training, and Volume 2 is focused on consulting. For the purposes of the *Annuals*, we consider training to be that which has an impact on individuals and consulting to be that which has an impact on organizations. Obviously, it is difficult in some cases to place materials strictly in one category or another, so there will be some overlap in what the two volumes cover.

Results have shown that our readers need and use both volumes. We are delighted to have the opportunity to showcase twice as much of the finest materials available in the HRD field.

The 1996 Annual: Volume 2, Consulting is the twenty-seventh volume in our *Annual* series; its contents reflect our intention to continue to publish materials that help our readers to stay on the cutting edge of the field. In keeping with this objective, users may duplicate and modify materials from the *Annuals* for educational and training purposes, as long as each copy includes the credit statement that is printed on the copyright page of the particular volume. However, reproducing Pfeiffer & Company materials in publications for sale or for large-scale distribution (more than one hundred copies in twelve months) requires *prior written permission*. Reproduction of material that is copyrighted by some source other than Pfeiffer & Company (as indicated in a footnote) requires written permission from the designated copyright holder. Also, reproduction on computer disk or by any other electronic means requires prior written permission.

For the *Annual* series, we actively seek materials from our readers as practicing professionals in the field. We are interested in receiving presentation and discussion resources (articles that include theory along with practical application); inventories, questionnaires, and surveys (paper-and-pencil inventories, rating scales, and other response tools); and experiential learning activities (group learning designs based on the five stages of the experiential learning cycle: experiencing, publishing, processing, generalizing, and applying). Contact the Editorial Department at the San Diego office for copies of our guidelines for contributors, and send submissions to the *Annual* editor at the same address.

I want to express my heartfelt appreciation to the dedicated people who produced this volume. First, I offer my genuine thanks to Dr. Beverly L. Kaye, who served as an acquisitions editor for the 1996 volumes. Her contacts and her talent enabled us to have many submissions from which to choose the pieces that are published here. Also, I am very grateful to Dr. Beverly Byrum-Robinson, who once again has reviewed all of our experiential learning activities. Her perspective as a facilitator and her insightful recommendations are irreplaceable in our quest to publish activities that meet the high standards of Pfeiffer & Company. I recognize and applaud the efforts and accomplishments of our Pfeiffer & Company staff: project manager Marian K. Prokop; graphic designer and page compositor, Judy Whalen; cover designer, Lee Ann Hubbard; and the members of our editorial and graphics staff, Arlette C. Ballew, Dawn Kilgore, Shana Lathrop, Marion Mettler, Carol Nolde, and Susan Rachmeler. Finally, as always, I extend my sincere gratitude to our authors for their generosity in sharing their professional ideas, materials, and techniques so that other HRD practitioners may benefit.

About Pfeiffer & Company

Pfeiffer & Company is engaged in human resource development (HRD) and business book publishing. The organization has earned an international reputation as the leading source of practical publications that are immediately useful to today's facilitators, trainers, consultants, and managers. A distinct advantage of these publications is that they are designed by practicing professionals who are continually experimenting with new techniques. Thus, readers benefit from the fresh but thoughtful approach that underlies Pfeiffer & Company's experientially based materials, resources, books, workbooks, instruments, and tape-assisted learning programs. These materials are designed for the HRD practitioner who wants access to a broad range of training and intervention technologies as well as background in the field.

The wide audience that Pfeiffer & Company serves includes training and development professionals, internal and external consultants, managers and supervisors, team leaders, and those in the helping professions. For its clients and customers, Pfeiffer & Company offers a practical approach aimed at increasing people's effectiveness on an individual, group, and organizational basis.

Contents

---

*See Experiential Learning Activities Categories, p. 5, for an explanation of the numbering system.

General Introduction
to the 1996 Annual

The 1996 Annual: Volume 2, Consulting is the twenty-seventh volume in the *Annual* series. Each *Annual* has three main sections: twelve *experiential learning activities;* three *inventories, questionnaires, and surveys;* and a series of *presentation and discussion resources.* Each of the pieces is classified in one of the following categories: Individual Development, Communication, Problem Solving, Groups, Teams, Consulting, Facilitating, and Leadership. Within each category, pieces are further classified into logical subcategories, which are explained in the introductions to the three sections.

The *Annual* series is a collection of practical and useful materials for human resource development (HRD) practitioners—materials written by and for professionals. As such, the series continues to provide a publication outlet for HRD professionals who wish to share their experiences, their viewpoints, and their procedures with their colleagues. To that end, Pfeiffer & Company publishes guidelines for potential authors. These guidelines, revised in 1996, are available from Pfeiffer & Company's Editorial Department in San Diego, California.

Materials are selected for the *Annuals* based on the quality of the ideas, applicability to real-world concerns, relevance to current HRD issues, clarity of presentation, and ability to enhance our readers' professional development. In addition, we choose experiential learning activities that will create a high degree of enthusiasm among the participants and add enjoyment to the learning process. As in the past several years, the contents of each *Annual* span a range of subject matter, reflecting the range of interests of our readers.

A list of contributors to the *Annual* can be found at the end of the volume, including their names, affiliations, addresses, telephone numbers, facsimile numbers, and e-mail addresses (if available). Readers will find this list of contributors useful if they wish to locate the authors of specific pieces for feedback, comments, or questions. Further information is presented in a brief biographical sketch of each contributor that appears at the conclusion of his or her article. These elements are intended to contribute to the "networking" function that is so valuable in the field of human resource development.

The editor and the editorial staff continue to be pleased with the high quality of materials submitted for publication. Nevertheless, just as we cannot publish every manuscript we receive, readers may find that not all of the works included in a particular *Annual* are equally useful to them. We invite comments, ideas, materials, and suggestions that will help us to make subsequent *Annuals* as useful as possible to our readers.

Introduction
to the Experiential Learning Activities Section

Experiential learning activities should be selected based on the participants' needs and the facilitator's competence. A good way to begin to select an activity is with the goal in mind: What do I want to accomplish with the participants as a result of this activity? Many activities address similar goals and can be adapted to suit the particular needs of a group. However, in order for the activity to meet the needs of the participants, the facilitator must be able to assist the participants in successfully processing the data that emerge from that experience.

All experiential learning activities in this *Annual* include a description of the goals of the activity, the size of the group and/or subgroups that can be accommodated, the time required to do and *process*[1] the activity, the materials and handouts required, the physical setting, step-by-step instructions for facilitating the experiential task and discussion phases of the activity, and variations of the design that the facilitator might find useful. All of these activities are complete; the content of all handouts is provided.

The 1996 Annual: Volume 2, Consulting includes twelve activities, in the following categories:

Individual Development: Diversity

Fourteen Dimensions of Diversity: Understanding and Appreciating Differences in the Work Place, by Sunny Bradford (#557, page 9)

Problem Solving: Generating Alternatives

PBJ Corporation: Using Idea-Generating Tools, by Phil Ventresca and Tom Flynn (#568, page 131)

---

[1] It would be redundant to print here a caveat for the use of experiential learning activities, but HRD professionals who are not experienced in the use of this training technology are strongly urged to read the "Introduction" to the *Reference Guide to Handbooks and Annuals* (1994 Edition). This article presents the theory behind the experiential-learning cycle and explains the necessity of adequately completing each phase of the cycle to allow effective learning to occur.

Problem Solving: Action Planning

Ideal Work Place: Creating a Team Vision, by M.K. Key, Glenn Head, and Marian Head (#561, page 45)

Groups: Competition/Collaboration

The Egg Drop: Using Human Resources Effectively, by Douglas Bryant (#564, page 77)

Teams: How Groups Work

Team Interventions: Moving the Team Forward, by Chuck Kormanski (#558, page 19)

Teams: Conflict and Intergroup Issues

Performance Unlimited: Solving Problems As a Team, by James W. Kinneer (#566, page 113)

Consulting and Facilitating: Consulting: Diagnosing/Skills

Walking the Talk: Identifying and Eliminating Organizational Inconsistencies, by Peter R. Garber (#559, page 27)

The MPM Scale: Identifying Beliefs About the Study of Organizations, by Ernest M. Schuttenberg (#563, page 67)

Consulting and Facilitating: Facilitating: Blocks to Learning

Taking Your Creative Pulse: Enhancing Creativity at Work, by Stephen R. Grossman (#567, page 119)

Leadership: Interviewing/Appraisal

Calloway Power Station: Assessing Team-Leader Effectiveness, by William N. Parker (#562, page 57)

Leadership: Motivation

The Flip-It Company: Exploring the Impact of Work Quotas, by James I. Costigan (#560, page 39)

Leadership: Diversity/Stereotyping

Under Pressure: Managing Time Effectively, by Glenn H. Varney (#565, page 87)

Other activities that address goals in these and other categories can be located by using the "Experiential Learning Activities Categories" chart that follows, or by using our comprehensive *Reference Guide to Handbooks and Annuals.* This book, which is updated regularly, indexes all of the *Annuals* and all of the *Handbooks of Structured Experiences* that we have published to date. With each revision, the *Reference Guide* becomes a complete, up-to-date, and easy-to-use resource for selecting appropriate materials from *all* of the *Annuals* and *Handbooks.*

EXPERIENTIAL LEARNING ACTIVITIES CATEGORIES

6

Pfeiffer & Company

557. FOURTEEN DIMENSIONS OF DIVERSITY: UNDERSTANDING AND APPRECIATING DIFFERENCES IN THE WORK PLACE

Goals

- To help participants understand that diversity is multidimensional and applies to everyone.
- To assist participants in exploring which of the dimensions of diversity have special relevance to their own identities.
- To stimulate appreciation of the value of diversity in the workplace.

Group Size

Fifteen to thirty participants in groups of approximately five members each.

Time Required

One hour and ten minutes to one and one-half hours.

Materials

- A copy of the Dimensions of Diversity Diagram for each participant.
- A copy of the Dimensions of Diversity Work Sheet for each participant.
- A pencil for each participant.

- An overhead transparency or a flip chart drawing of the Dimensions of Diversity Diagram.[1]

- An overhead projector (if a transparency is used).

Physical Setting

A room large enough for subgroups to work without disturbing one another. A writing surface and movable chair should be provided for each participant.

Process

1. The facilitator begins by showing an overhead transparency or flip chart drawing of the Dimensions of Diversity Diagram and gives a copy of the Dimensions of Diversity Diagram and a pencil to each participant. The following explanatory comments are made:

   - Diversity is a multidimensional phenomenon. Its dimensions represent major aspects of people's backgrounds and identities, which make them similar to and different from one another. In the workplace, diversity refers not only to race and gender but to many other significant characteristics as well. These different dimensions represent an array of contributions that people can make because of their various outlooks and differences.

   - Each person is a complex mix of many dimensions. We all have other characteristics that are not in this diagram, but the ones that do appear in the diagram are some of the most fundamental aspects of who we are and how we experience the world.

   - The six dimensions in the center circle are called "primary" because they are central aspects of our identities and greatly impact our values and perceptions. Some of them are present at birth, and some have a significant impact on how we are socialized as children. Also, other people frequently respond to or make judgments about us based on their assumptions regarding "who we are" in terms of these dimensions. Most of the major "isms" are based on the elements in the center: racism, sexism, ageism, etc.

   - The dimensions in the outer circle are called "secondary" because they are characteristics that we can modify and because their

---

[1] Diagram from *Workforce America! Managing Employee Diversity As a Vital Resource* by M. Loden and J. Rosener, 1991, Burr Ridge, Illinois: Irwin, p. 20. Used with permission.

presence or absence does not usually change our core identities. However, for some people, certain dimensions in the outer ring exert a fundamental influence on their identities and world views (e.g., their incomes, religious beliefs, and military experiences).

- The diversity dimensions are significant in an organizational context. For example, consider how the work expectations and priorities of a twenty-three-year-old, first-time employee might compare to those of a fifty-five-year-old employee who has worked for the organization for eighteen years. Or consider the work-related goals and experiences of a recent immigrant to the United States who speaks English as a second language and has worked in several countries, compared to those of a native-English speaker who has not worked or traveled outside the United States.

- Because people all are unique, each of us could draw a personal diversity diagram showing which of these fourteen dimensions are especially relevant to his or her core identity at this time in life. For one person, his or her gender or race might be very significant; to another person, such factors may be less important than sexual orientation or physical characteristics. For some people, characteristics on the outer circle of the diagram might be central to their identities today. Respecting differences means recognizing that the individual coworkers, customers, and clients with whom we interact will have different perceptions, values, concerns, and life experiences based on the various dimensions of diversity that have been salient in their lives.

(Ten minutes.)

2. The participants are formed into subgroups of approximately five members each, with each subgroup representing as much gender, race, culture, and age diversity as possible.

3. The facilitator announces the goals of the activity and hands out a Dimensions of Diversity Work Sheet to each participant. The facilitator briefly reviews the three questions on the work sheet. (Option: To establish an atmosphere of openness, the facilitator may give brief examples of how he or she would personally answer one or two of the questions.) The participants are told that they will have ten minutes in which to fill out the work sheets individually. *[Note to the facilitator:* Be sure to be familiar with the fourteen dimensions and be prepared to answer questions that might arise, such as how race and ethnicity overlap or how generational differences can shape people's perceptions.] (Fifteen minutes.)

4. When all participants have finished filling out the work sheet, the members of each subgroup are invited to report their answers to their subgroup. One person in the subgroup gives his or her answer to question 1, another person gives his or her answer to question 1, and so on, until all group members have explained their answers to all work sheet questions. Before the participants start their reporting, the facilitator provides the following suggestions:

- There are no right or wrong answers; each person will have unique responses to the questions.

- When you share your answers, please explain the reason that you said what you did.

(Thirty to forty-five minutes.)

5. The facilitator calls time and reassembles the total group. Some of the following questions can be used to elicit the participants' reactions to the experience:

- Was it easy or difficult for you to select the three most important aspects of your core identity? What made it easy? What made it difficult?

- How did some of you respond to the first question? Which three dimensions did you identify as part of your core identity?

- How many of you found that some dimensions of diversity are more (or less) salient to you now than they were ten years ago? Why was this?

- What did some of you list as special contributions you bring to the workplace because of your diversity? What have you come to appreciate about the special contributions of others?

- What have you learned about diversity? What have you learned about diversity in the workplace?

- How might you apply the understanding you gained about diversity at work?

(Fifteen to twenty minutes.)

Variations

- In Step 1, examples relevant to the organization's employee-diversity or customer-diversity mix may be used to illustrate the organizational significance of the diversity dimensions.

- In Step 1, the material may be presented as an interactive lecturette by asking the group a few questions. For instance, before explaining the primary/secondary distinction, the facilitator may ask participants what the six elements in the center have in common or why they might be considered "primary."

- If the group consists of people who work together (an intact work group or committee), the activity may be used to help members move to greater trust and a deeper appreciation of their differences. For such a group, questions such as the following may be added to the work sheet or used in the debriefing:

  - What dimensions of your own diversity do you think others at work (peers, clients, customers) see first when they interact with you? Why is this?

  - What aspects of your own diversity do you wish your coworkers understood better? Why are they important to you?

  - What diversity dimensions or aspects of yourself do you express most fully (authentically) at work? What aspects are not fully expressed or are masked?

Reference

Loden, M., & Rosener, J. (1991). *Workforce America! Managing employee diversity as a vital resource.* Burr Ridge, IL: Irwin.

Submitted by Sunny Bradford, Ph.D.

Sunny Bradford, Ph.D., *is an organization development consultant and principal of Bradford Consulting Associates. Working with private and public organizations, she consults, trains, and conducts research in the areas of managing strategic change, workforce diversity, team effectiveness, conflict resolution, and business ethics. In addition, she is an active member of ASTD, former president of the Los Angeles Organization Development Network, and an associate faculty member of Antioch University in the Masters in Organizational Management Program.*

FOURTEEN DIMENSIONS OF DIVERSITY DIAGRAM[1]

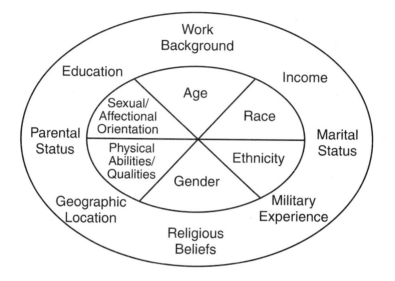

Primary Dimensions of Diversity

The primary dimensions of diversity are those basic characteristics that are inborn and/or that greatly affect how you are socialized. These dimensions shape your self-image, your world view, and how others perceive you. At the core of your identity and life experience, they continue to exert powerful impacts throughout your life.

Age: the number of years you have been alive and the generation in which you were born.

Race: the biological groupings within humankind, representing superficial physical differences, such as eye form and skin color. Race accounts for .012 percent difference in a person's genetic heredity.

---

[1] Diagram from *Workforce America! Managing Employee Diversity As a Vital Resource* by M. Loden and J. Rosener, 1991, Burr Ridge, Illinois: Irwin, p. 20. Used with permission.

The 1996 Annual: Volume 2, Consulting.
Copyright © 1996 by Pfeiffer & Company, San Diego, CA.

Ethnicity: identification with a cultural group that has shared traditions and heritage, including national origin, language, religion, food, customs, and so on. Some people identify strongly with these cultural roots; others do not.

Gender: biological sex as determined by XX (female) or XY (male) chromosomes.

Physical Abilities/Qualities: a variety of characteristics, including body type, physical size, facial features, specific abilities or disabilities, visible and invisible physical and mental talents or limitations.

Sexual/Affectional Orientation: feelings of sexual attraction toward members of the same or opposite gender, such as heterosexual, gay/lesbian, or bisexual.

Secondary Dimensions of Diversity

The secondary dimensions of diversity are those characteristics that you acquire and can modify throughout your life. Factors such as income, religion, and geographic location may exert a significant impact in childhood, but most of the others are less salient than the core dimensions. However, all of these characteristics add another layer to your self-definition and can profoundly shape your experiences.

Education: the formal and informal teachings to which you have been exposed and the training you have received.

Work Background: the employment and volunteer positions you have held and the array of organizations for which you have worked.

Income: the economic conditions in which you grew up and your current economic status.

Marital Status: your situation as a never-married, married, widowed, or divorced person.

Military Experience: service in one or more branches of the military.

Religious Beliefs: fundamental teachings you have received about deities and your internalized experiences from formal or informal religious practices.

Geographic Location: the location(s) in which you were raised or spent a significant part of your life, including types of communities, urban areas versus rural areas, and so on.

Parental Status: having or not having children and the circumstances in which you raise your children (single parenting, two-adult parenting, and so on).

FOURTEEN DIMENSIONS OF DIVERSITY WORK SHEET

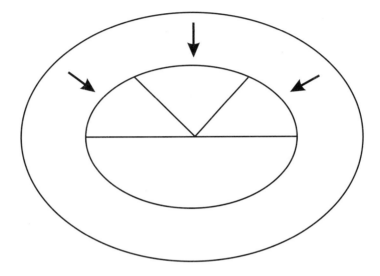

Review the Dimensions of Diversity Diagram. Then fill out the blank diagram above by responding to the following:

1. Which dimensions of diversity are part of your core identity? In other words, which of the fourteen dimensions belong in *your* inner circle? Place the three most central aspects on the top row of the inner circle above. Why are these three dimensions especially important aspects of your identity?

---

2. For many people, aspects of identity change over the years. Would you have selected the same three dimensions ten years ago? If not, what has changed?

3. Now think of yourself at work. What are two or three special contributions that you bring to the workplace becaue of your own diversity? Think in terms of any of the fourteen dimensions of diversity.

558. Team Interventions: Moving the Team Forward

Goals

- To present a team-development model for team leaders and supervisors.
- To provide an opportunity for participants to analyze team performance and assess team needs.
- To provide an opportunity for participants to suggest leader interventions that are based on stages of team development.

Group Size

Ten to thirty team leaders/supervisors in subgroups of five to seven members each.

Time Required

Two to two and one-half hours.

Materials

- A copy of the Team Development Summary Sheet for each participant.
- A copy of the Team Development Intervention Sheet for each participant.
- A copy of the Team Development Vignettes Sheet for each participant.
- A newsprint flip chart and felt-tipped markers for each team.
- Masking tape for each team.

Physical Setting

A room large enough for teams to work without disturbing one another. Movable chairs and tables are suggested.

Process

1. The facilitator presents the goals of the activity and forms subgroups ("teams") of five to seven members each. Each team is given a newsprint flip chart, felt-tipped markers, and masking tape. (Five minutes.)

2. The team members are requested to get acquainted by sharing their names, job information, and two or three suggestions about how the group might work together as a team. (Five to ten minutes.)

3. The facilitator delivers a lecturette on stages of team development, then gives each participant a copy of the Team Development Summary Sheet and reviews the contents. (Ten to fifteen minutes.)

4. The facilitator explains that certain interventions by the team leader can assist the team in completing the outcomes for each stage of development and moving into the next. The facilitator gives each participant a copy of the Team Development Intervention Sheet and reviews the contents. (Five to ten minutes.)

5. The facilitator gives a copy of the Team Development Vignettes Sheet to each participant and reads the instructions aloud. Teams are advised to spend about ten minutes on each vignette and to list their interventions on newsprint. The facilitator makes ten-minute announcements and calls time. (Sixty minutes.)

6. Each team is requested to post its interventions so that all can see them. (Five minutes.)

7. The total group is reassembled. Posted interventions are compared with the Team Development Intervention Sheet in the following manner: all groups' strategies for vignette 11 are compared with the sheet; all groups' strategies for vignette 12 are compared with the sheet; and so on. Team vignette 11 represents stage 1; vignette 12 represents stage 2; vignette 13 represents stage 3, and so on. The facilitator leads an ongoing discussion relating interventions to team-development concepts. (Fifteen to twenty minutes.)

8. The facilitator engages the participants in a discussion of the activity. The following processing questions may be included:

- What were your reactions as you progressed through this activity?
- How did your team members interact while you were working on this task?
- How did this reflect the team's stage of development?
- What interventions were used to move your team along?
- What have you learned about the stages of team development?
- What, specifically, did you learn in this activity about what a team leader can do to affect the group's progress?
- How can you use the information from this activity in your jobs?

(Ten to fifteen minutes.)

Variations

- Teams can work on only one, two, or three of the vignettes, thus reducing the amount of time required for the activity.
- The facilitator can demonstrate effective leader behavior using one of the vignettes.
- Each team can write its own real-life vignette and then exchange with another team to get a different perspective on it. (A real-life vignette can be role played.)
- The Team Development Summary Sheets can be distributed prior to the activity.

Submitted by Chuck Kormanski.

Chuck Kormanski, D.Ed., is a counselor for the Career Development and Placement Center at The Pennsylvania State University, Altoona Campus. Dr. Kormanski counsels college students, consults to business and industry, teaches graduate and undergraduate courses, and conducts research in group development. He has published journal articles dealing with group development, team building, and leadership and has designed and led workshops and seminars in leadership, management development, conflict management, helping relationships, group dynamics, strategic planning, and personality development.

TEAM DEVELOPMENT SUMMARY SHEET

Introduction

Like individuals, teams progress through different stages of development as they mature. Tuckman[1] identified five stages of team development: forming, storming, norming, performing, and adjourning.

In each stage, team members exhibit typical "task" and "relationship" behaviors, consistent with the basic theme of that particular stage of development. The relationship behaviors correlate with the development of the identity and functions of the group from the personal orientations of the members. The task behaviors correlate with the progress of the group in understanding and accomplishing its work. Issues and concerns must be resolved in each stage before the group can move on. The completion of each stage results in specific task outcomes as well as relationship outcomes that address member needs at that stage.

Both transactional leader skills (those that get the task completed) and transformational leader skills (those that influence and inspire people) can be used to move the team from one stage of development to the next. The leader skills listed for each stage of team development are translated into actions, or interventions, the leader can make in order to help the group to complete each stage's task.

The chart on the next page (Figure 1) summarizes the stages of group development, team building, and leadership skills.

---

[1] B.W. Tuckman & M.A.C. Jensen (December, 1977), "Stages of Small-Group Development Revisited," in *Group & Organization Studies*, 2(4), 419-427.

GROUP DEVELOPMENT

TUCKMAN STAGE	GENERAL THEME	TASK BEHAVIOR	RELATIONSHIP BEHAVIOR
1. Forming	Awareness	Orientation	Dependence
2. Storming	Conflict	Resistance	Hostility
3. Norming	Cooperation	Communication	Cohesion
4. Performing	Productivity	Problem Solving	Interdependence
5. Adjourning	Separation	Termination	Disengagement

TEAM BUILDING

TUCKMAN STAGE	TASK OUTCOME	RELATIONSHIP OUTCOME	INDIVIDUAL NEED
1. Forming	Commitment	Acceptance	Security
2. Storming	Clarification	Belonging	Social
3. Norming	Involvement	Support	Recognition
4. Performing	Achievement	Pride	Achievement
5. Adjourning	Recognition	Satisfaction	Recognition

LEADERSHIP SKILLS

TUCKMAN STAGE	TRANSACTIONAL LEADER SKILLS	TRANSFORMATIONAL LEADER SKILLS
1. Forming	Getting Acquainted, Goal Setting, Organizing	Value Clarification, Visioning, Communicating Through Myth and Metaphor
2. Storming	Active Listening, Assertiveness, Conflict Management	Flexibility, Creativity, Kaleidoscopic Thinking
3. Norming	Communication, Feedback, Affirmation	Playfulness and Humor, Entrepreneuring, Networking
4. Performing	Decision Making, Problem Solving, Rewarding	Multicultural Awareness, Mentoring, Futuring
5. Adjourning	Evaluating, Reviewing	Celebrating, Bringing Closure

Group Development, Team Building, and Leadership Skills[2]

---

[2] Based on C.L. Kormanski & A. Mozenter (1987), "A New Model of Team Building: A Technology for Today and Tomorrow," in J.W. Pfeiffer (Ed.), *The 1987 Annual: Developing Human Resources,* San Diego, CA: Pfeiffer & Company.

TEAM DEVELOPMENT INTERVENTION SHEET

Stage One: Forming. Theme: Awareness

- Allow time for members to get acquainted
- Provide essential information about content and process
- Emphasize new skills required
- Identify and relate key team values to current task
- Share stories of past accomplishments and celebrations
- Create a team vision of outcome
- Set goals to achieve outcome

Stage Two: Storming. Theme: Conflict

- Act assertively and set parameters for the team
- Listen attentively to all viewpoints
- Use mediation, negotiation, and arbitration
- Consider new perspectives and alternatives
- Suggest and solicit optional ways to view the problem

Stage Three: Norming. Theme: Cooperation

- Provide opportunity for involvement by all
- Provide opportunity for members to learn from and assist one another
- Model and encourage supportive behavior
- Open communication lines
- Provide positive and corrective task-related feedback
- Add some humor and fun to the work setting

Stage Four: Performing. Theme: Productivity

- Reward and recognize performance outcomes and positive work relationships
- Involve the team in group problem solving and futuring
- Share decision-making opportunities
- Examine how implementation will affect the team and the rest of the organization
- Use delegation to foster professional development

Stage Five: Adjourning. Theme: Separation

- Provide evaluative performance feedback
- Review task and working relationships
- Create a celebration activity with emphasis on recognition and fun
- Conduct a closure ceremony to specify the project's conclusion

---

TEAM DEVELOPMENT VIGNETTES SHEET

Instructions: Read each vignette and suggest some interventions that the team leader might make in order to improve team development.

Team Vignette #11

You are working with an old team on a new, very different, project. The task is challenging, and creative problem solving will be critical. In past efforts of the team, there were few choices and very little flexibility. Some talents that team members have but have not used recently will be needed on this project. You are concerned about increasing the motivational level of the team in addition to getting the project completed in a superior fashion.

Team Vignette #12

Team members disagree about the importance of the current project and, therefore, the time needed to complete it. One group of team members sees the task as helpful but not essential to the organization. They want to finish it adequately but quickly. A second set of team members wants to complete the task comprehensively, with the high quality characteristic of past team performance. A third group is trying to develop a compromise. A few members have not expressed opinions and are attempting to stay out of the debate. You would like to resolve the matter and get the team to reach agreement or, at least, consensus. Your personal preference is for a quality effort.

Team Vignette #13

The team has recently resolved a volatile disagreement regarding the appropriate strategy to use in the implementation of a major goal. You want to move forward as quickly as possible. The group appears somewhat hesitant and continues to look to you for direction. Members appear capable of continuing the task but are concerned about how much time will be required. Some work has been begun by individuals working independently and in pairs. Although you see some progress, you would like more of a unified effort.

Team Vignette #14

The team appears to be cohesive and unified regarding the current project. All members are competent to complete the task. The implementation and evaluation phase will be critical and will impact the total organization. Current goals are challenging but realistic. So far, quality standards have been maintained. You are eager to complete the project at this high level of performance.

Team Vignette #15

The team has just completed a major project. Although there were some difficulties getting started and some conflicts concerning the use of resources, compromises were used to move to completion. Each team member made a significant contribution, adding specific skills that were critical to the success of the project. The team views this accomplishment as a total team effort. However, all members of the team will not be needed for the next project, which is less complex. Some members will be assigned to other tasks. All assignments will be based on the skill requirements of the new projects.

Pfeiffer & Company

559. WALKING THE TALK: IDENTIFYING AND ELIMINATING ORGANIZATIONAL INCONSISTENCIES

Goals

- To acquaint participants with the concept of organizational inconsistencies.

- To help participants learn how to identify organizational inconsistencies.

- To allow participants to identify ways to correct and eliminate a variety of organizational inconsistencies.

Group Size

Four approximately equal-sized groups of three to five members each.

Time Required

Approximately one hour and fifteen minutes.

Materials

- A copy of the Walking the Talk Information Sheet and a pencil for each participant.

- A copy of the Walking the Talk Perpetual Inconsistencies Sheet for each member of one group.

- A copy of the Walking the Talk Perceptual Inconsistencies Sheet for each member of the second group.

- A copy of the Walking the Talk Timing Inconsistencies Sheet for each member of the third group.

The 1996 Annual: Volume 2, Consulting.
Copyright © 1996 by Pfeiffer & Company, San Diego, CA.

- A copy of the Walking the Talk Personalities Inconsistencies Sheet for each member of the fourth group.
- Three sheets of newsprint flip-chart paper and a felt-tipped marker for each group.
- A newsprint flip chart and felt-tipped markers for the facilitator.
- Masking tape for posting newsprint.

Physical Setting

A room in which the subgroups can work without disturbing one another, with wall space for posting newsprint.

Process

1. The facilitator welcomes the participants and states the goals of the activity. The facilitator gives each participant a copy of the Walking the Talk Information Sheet and a pencil, briefly describes the contents of the information sheet, allows time for the participants to read the sheet, and answers any questions. (Ten minutes.)

2. The facilitator informs the participants that the activity will deal with four varieties of organizational inconsistencies: perpetual, perceptual, timing, and personalities. The facilitator divides the participants into four groups of three to five members each. The facilitator gives the members of one group copies of the Walking the Talk Perpetual Inconsistencies Sheet, gives the second group copies of the Walking the Talk Perceptual Inconsistencies Sheet, gives the third group copies of the Walking the Talk Timing Inconsistencies Sheet, and gives the fourth group copies of the Walking the Talk Personalities Inconsistencies Sheet. Each group also receives three sheets of newsprint flip-chart paper and a felt-tipped marker. (Five minutes.)

3. The members of each group are instructed to read their specific sheets and then to suggest examples of the group's type of inconsistency that they have seen in organizations. Each group is then to select one example from those discussed and answer the questions from the Walking the Talk Information Sheet in relation to the group's example. The groups are told to record their answers on their newsprint sheets and to illustrate the "A" and "B" aspects of their inconsistencies. They will display their newsprint sheets when reporting back to the total group. (Twenty minutes.)

4. The facilitator calls time and reconvenes the total group. Each of the four subgroups is invited, in turn, to post its newsprint sheet(s) and to report on its organizational inconsistency, based on the questions on the information sheet. (Twenty minutes.)

5. The facilitator leads a total-group discussion of the activity. The following processing questions may be used:

   - What emotions did you experience during this activity?

   - What emotions do people experience in the workplace as a result of organizational inconsistencies?

   - What are the effects of these emotions in the workplace?

   - What is the ultimate impact of organizational inconsistencies on the organization?

   - Why do you think organizational inconsistencies continue to exist?

   - What has prevented you from calling attention to or challenging organizational inconsistencies?

   - How can you best deal with the organizational inconsistencies in your workplace? Give an example.

   (Fifteen to twenty minutes.)

Variations

- If the total group is small, it can work with each type of organizational inconsistency in turn.

- If the total group is very large, more than one group can work with each of the different types of organizational inconsistencies.

- The activity can be used to discuss and recommend solutions for a specific inconsistency that exists in the participants' organization.

Submitted by Peter R. Garber.

Peter R. Garber *is the manager of teamwork development for PPG Industries, Inc., in Pittsburgh, Pennsylvania. He has held various positions in human resources and has developed training programs in the areas of safety, quality improvement, and teamwork. He is the author of* Coaching Self-Directed Workteams *and* 30 Easy-To-Use Reengineering Activities, *and his experiential learning activity, "Adventures at Work: Experiencing Work As a Movie," appears in* The 1995 Annual: Volume 1, Training.

WALKING THE TALK INFORMATION SHEET

Organizations typically are not very good at identifying inconsistencies—differences between what the organization (top management, a manager, a department) says it does and what it actually does. Often, inconsistencies occur between the organization's (or a division's) mission statement and what actually happens in the workplace. In short, the organization does not "walk its talk."

Unfortunately, the inconsistencies that affect our work lives can be sources of great frustration. Those that have become part of an organization's culture usually are counterproductive.

The classic organizational inconsistency begins with a statement by the organization that something is a top priority when, in fact, the organization's actions are contradictory to its stated commitment. An example is a stated commitment to customer service or "quality," when the organization's policies and reward systems do not support taking the time to ensure quality or to serve customers well, and people are rewarded only for pushing more of whatever they produce through the system faster. In such a case, good customer service or "quality" is not likely to be attained.

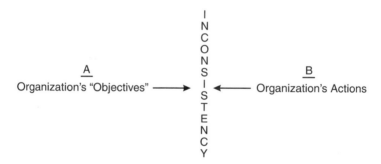

The problem is magnified when management believes that "A" equals "B" when it does not. Usually, everyone else involved realizes the discrepancy.

Organizational inconsistencies send mixed and confusing messages to employees, who often regard them as examples of the hypocrisy of management. The "do as I say, not as I do" message spreads throughout the organization and negatively influences attitudes, confidence in management, morale, and motivation.

Solving the Problems

In any communication, the closer the meaning of the message sent is to the meaning of the message received, the better. An organization must address differences in perceptions on any important subject. It must attempt to get the parties involved to understand each other's points of view. As understanding occurs, apparent discrepancies sometimes can be resolved. For example, a decision may appear to contradict the organizational mission in the short run, but may contribute to it in the long run.

Sharing information about decisions and policies (e.g., financial information, the organization's plans for the future) can be an important step. The negative effects of organizational inconsistencies are lessened when those affected are involved and understand the reasons for decisions and policies. The sooner the subject is addressed, the better, as the negative fallout from real and perceived organizational inconsistencies increases over time.

The Role of Empowerment

With the increased competition in the marketplace, the successful and respected organizations from now on will be ones that "walk their talk"—those that establish consistency regarding the values and practices that they have identified as important.

Empowerment in organizations can have a powerful effect in correcting and eliminating inconsistencies. Employees who have the most direct influence on "B" must be given the opportunities and resources to ensure that "A" does equal "B" and vice versa.

STOP READING HERE. THE FOLLOWING CONTAINS QUESTIONS THAT YOU WILL ANSWER AFTER YOUR GROUP HAS DISCUSSED ITS ASSIGNMENT.

Information About Your Group's Organizational Inconsistency

Type of inconsistency:

At what level in the organization did the inconsistency originate?

What is "A"?

How is the sponsor of "A" trying to achieve it? What resources are being committed to achieving it?

How successful has the effort been?

Pfeiffer & Company

What is "B"?

How does "B" prevent "A" from being achieved?

How can "A" and "B" be made more consistent?

What would be the benefit to the organization if it were to eliminate this inconsistency?

WALKING THE TALK PERPETUAL INCONSISTENCIES SHEET

Organizational inconsistencies tend to perpetuate themselves. The organization appears not to have learned from its experience and continues to make the same mistake over and over again. An example is conducting an annual employee survey when there is no commitment to addressing the problems identified. Employees often are aware of the inconsistency and say, "Here we go again!"

Often, there is no means for sending the feedback to management, so it remains unaware of the problem. In other cases, management has not heeded the warning, "If you keep doing the same thing, you will keep getting the same results." Sometimes, people are afraid to say anything because they think they may not know of an important reason for continuing the practice or policy. Thus, like the story of the emperor's new clothes, "A" does not equal "B," but no one risks mentioning it.

Walking the Talk Perceptual Inconsistencies Sheet

Obviously, everyone in an organization does not see things from the same perspective. One's position in the organization may affect one's perspective on a topic or issue.

When a new policy or procedure is introduced with a statement telling everyone how they should respond to the change, a perceptual inconsistency is created. A typical example is the downsizing that many organizations have experienced. Management views such changes as necessary for the survival of the business. The remaining employees experience the change as more work and more responsibilities, usually with no pay increase. Thus, "A" (management's perception of the benefits of downsizing) does not equal "B" (the employee's perceptions of the consequences). Despite any organization's or department's attempts to achieve an objective, it cannot dictate the way others feel about it.

WALKING THE TALK TIMING INCONSISTENCIES SHEET

Many organizational inconsistencies involve timing. Frequently, a message is not communicated soon enough to prevent a contrary message being spread throughout the organization.

In other cases, the timing of something is poorly planned. Even the right thing can be done at the wrong time. Those who plan things in organizations often fail to look at evidence that is contrary to what they want to believe. An example of this is an organization's desire to enter a new business or a new market. Although the decision may be a good one from one point of view, it may be at the wrong time from another point of view. Worse than not searching for negative evidence is the decision to suppress the negative evidence that is found. At least there should be a statement of why the decision was made to go ahead.

A third case is a "time warp" oxymoron. A manager may have had responsibility for a segment of a business during point "A" in time. Later, when the manager is at a higher level in the organization, he or she may continue to view the business as it was, not as it currently is. Decisions are made at point "B" from a point "A" perspective.

WALKING THE TALK PERSONALITIES INCONSISTENCIES SHEET

A personality inconsistency exists when the norms, rules, policies, etc., of an organization dictate that people behave in ways contrary to their personalities. Sometimes an "organizational personality" is created, and everyone is expected to adopt it. Often, this stems directly from the personality of the CEO or manager in charge. Just as often, there are specific personality traits expected at certain levels of the organization. For example, certain managers may be expected to wear suits and ties, work twelve-hour days, and come to work on weekends.

Personality inconsistencies can cause potentially insightful contributors to become passive or potentially cooperative people to become aggressive and competitive. When people must check their true natures at the door and play roles at work, great degrees of anxiety, mistrust, and stress are generated.

Demands for certain organizational personalities may run counter to laws regarding equal treatment. In an increasingly diverse work force, one cannot expect all people to act and react in the same manner.

560. The Flip-It Company: Exploring the Impact of Work Quotas

---

Goals

- To illustrate what happens when work quotas are assigned without consideration of the variables that affect results.

- To offer the participants an opportunity to experience typical worker reactions to work quotas.

- To give the participants a chance to generate and share ways to motivate employees and achieve organizational goals other than using work quotas.

Group Size

At least twenty participants.

Time Required

Approximately one hour and ten minutes.

Materials

- Ten pads of paper and ten pencils.

- Eleven coins (one for each of the ten production workers and one for the facilitator to use in demonstrating the procedure).

- A newsprint reproduction of Figure 1, prepared in advance.

Worker	Round 1			Round 2			Round 3			Round 4		
	Salary	HP	%	Salary	HP	%	Salary	HP	%	Salary	HP	%
1												
2												
3												
4												
5												
6												
7												
8												
9												
10												
Total												
Average												

Legend: HP = "Heads" Produced

Figure 1. Suggested Configuration for Recording Information on Newsprint

- Masking tape for posting the newsprint reproduction of Figure 1.
- A felt-tipped marker.
- A calculator.

Physical Setting

A room large enough to allow the production workers to complete the flipping procedure and hold meetings while the observers watch. An elevated stage is helpful but not essential.

Process

1. The facilitator asks for ten volunteers to be production workers for the Flip-It Company. All other participants are to observe the activity and participate in the concluding discussion. The facilitator adds that he or she will function as a manager of the company until the discussion period. (Five minutes.)

2. The ten production workers are instructed to form a row in an area where they will be easily visible to the observers. Each worker is given a coin, a pad of paper, and a pencil. Then the facilitator leads an orientation session by explaining that the Flip-It Company produces "heads" (rather than "tails") in flipping coins. The facilitator gives verbal instructions and demonstrates by flipping a coin in the air with his or her right hand, catching it in that same hand, and then putting it on the back of his or her left hand. The facilitator states that each worker is to record the results of each flip, either "heads" or "tails," on the pad of paper provided. (Five minutes.)

3. The facilitator asks the workers to practice the procedure for a couple of minutes. When all of them have mastered the procedure, the facilitator announces that the beginning pay for the job is $20,000 per year. Each production worker is instructed to complete Round 1 by flipping the coin ten times and recording the results after each flip. The facilitator posts the newsprint reproduction of Figure 1, records the names of the production workers, and lists their beginning salaries under "Round 1" in the "Salary" column. When all workers have completed the ten flips, the facilitator asks for individual results and records those results under "Round 1" in the "HP" column. In addition, the facilitator calculates the percentage of heads for each worker and records that percentage under "Round 1" in the "%" column. Average heads produced and an average percentage for the worker group are also calculated and recorded. *Note:* The boxes for Total Salary and Average Salary are not applicable. (Ten minutes.)

4. The facilitator (acting as manager) calls for a meeting of the Flip-It Company workers. During this meeting the facilitator announces that the Flip-It Company has hired the Variance Corporation (VARCO) to help streamline the work process and ensure worker motivation. After extensive study VARCO has informed Flip-It that the average worker should produce 50 percent "heads" per year. The facilitator then announces the company average for the year thus far (recorded under "Round 1" in the box for Average %) and subsequently either praises or blames the production workers, depending on whether they met or failed to meet this percentage. The facilitator delivers the praise or blame in an impassioned way, pointing with pride to the workers who met or exceeded 50 percent and stating that those who did not meet the 50-percent level did not try hard and were unwilling to pull their own weight. (Five minutes.)

5. The facilitator then announces that the company management has implemented a new incentive plan. All those who met the level of 50 percent "heads" in Round 1 will continue to be paid $20,000; those who exceeded the standard will receive $1,000 per year for each 10-percent increase over 50 percent; and those who failed to meet the standard will have their pay reduced $1,000 per year for each 10 percent under 50 percent. The facilitator records the new salaries under "Round 2," reminding the workers that this pay reflects their performance during Round 1. (Five minutes.)

6. Round 2 (another ten flips per worker) is initiated and the results recorded as in Round 1. A meeting is held with the same format as the first meeting. Salaries are adjusted as indicated in Step 5 and are recorded under "Round 3." Then the facilitator announces a bonus plan for Round 3: Those who exceed the work quota by 30 percent will earn an all-expense-paid trip to Disneyland, and those who exceed the quota by 40 percent will earn a trip to Hawaii with all expenses paid. (Ten minutes.)

7. Round 3 (another ten flips per worker) is held and the results recorded as in the previous two rounds. The facilitator presents bonus trips to the appropriate workers and then announces that the Flip-It Company has found it necessary to reduce its number of worker personnel: Any worker who did not produce 50 percent or more "heads" in Round 3 is fired. (Ten minutes.)

8. The facilitator announces the end of the role play, drops the role of manager, and asks the following questions:

   ▪ What did you experience as you worked under this system of work quotas? What worker behaviors did the observers notice? What systems or situations like this one have you experienced before?

   ▪ What are the similarities in people's reactions to this quota system? What are the differences? What can you generalize about reactions to working under a system of work quotas?

   ▪ What does the work-quota system take into account in terms of expected results? What does it not account for?

   ▪ What are the results for the organization in operating under the work-quota system?

   ▪ What are some ways to motivate employees to achieve organizational goals without using work quotas?

- What ideas can you apply in your own job or organization as a result of this activity?

(Fifteen to twenty minutes.)

Variation

- To reduce the time required, the facilitator may omit a round.

Submitted by James I. Costigan.

*The late **James I. Costigan, Ph.D.**, was a professor of communication and Chairman of the Communications Department at Fort Hays State University, Hays, Kansas. He specialized in organizational and interpersonal communication and coauthored the book* Developing Communication Skills: Influences and Alternatives. *He remained active in teaching, research, and consulting until eleven days before dying of cancer. In his teaching he sought to demonstrate that facing each day positively can prolong life.*

561. Ideal Work Place: Creating a Team Vision

Goals

- To align and energize team members through the process of visioning together.

- To encourage team members to create a collective vision of an ideal work scenario.

- To offer team members an opportunity to set in motion the actions needed to achieve that vision.

Group Size

All members of an intact work team. This activity is best used with a team that has prior team-building experience.

Time Required

Approximately two hours.

Materials

- One copy of the Ideal Work Place Vision Sheet for each team member.

- A pencil for each team member.

- A clipboard or other portable writing surface for each team member.

- An audiotape player and a tape of relaxing music for Step 2.

- A newsprint flip chart.

- A felt-tipped marker for each team member and one or more for the facilitator.

The 1996 Annual: Volume 2, Consulting.
Copyright © 1996 by Pfeiffer & Company, San Diego, CA.

- Masking tape for posting newsprint.

Physical Setting

A room large enough for the team members to work independently to create newsprint posters (see Step 7). Comfortable, movable chairs should be provided.

Process

1. The facilitator explains the goals of the activity and then introduces the process as follows:

   "You will be imagining a time when everything is perfect for you in your work place. Before we begin, we will set up an imaginary 'Later Box' outside the room where you can place any distracting thoughts, skepticism, or negativism. They'll be safe there, and you can pick them up later. In a few moments, I'll be asking you to close your eyes to eliminate any visual distractions while you are seeing the future in your 'mind's eye.' Now is the time to go ahead and deposit distracting thoughts in the 'Later Box.' If at any time during this visioning process you become uncomfortable, you may open your eyes and disengage. This vision is yours personally, you are in control of it, and you need not share anything later that is too private."

   (Five minutes.)

2. The facilitator starts the relaxing music and leads the team members through the following visioning process: [*Note to the facilitator:* The length of your pause after each question will vary, depending on the depth of the question. Pauses are never to be less than three seconds or more than forty-five seconds.]

   "Get in a comfortable position, loosen any restrictive clothing, un-cross your arms and legs, and place your feet on the floor. Allow your eyes to close easily and comfortably. Begin by paying attention to your breathing, noticing how it slows as you become more comfortable. Breathe in, clear your mind; breathe out, relax.

   "Set the scenario in the future, five to ten years from now; this will allow any limitations you see today to be gone. Imagine your work situation. Everything is perfect, the ideal situation you want for yourself. Remember that there are no rules or limits to what you can imagine.

"It's morning. One of those days when you wake up filled with eager anticipation. You're excited, just the way you might feel if you were getting on a jet bound for vacation at your ideal resort. The day feels great! Your life is great!

"You have arrived at the place where you conduct your business, which is the ideal work place you have hoped for and worked with others to create. As you walk around, you notice some things. Look around this ideal environment. What do you see? What colors surround you? What sounds do you hear? What do you smell? How does the environment feel? What else makes the environment ideal for you? Notice as many details as you can.

"You see a letter from a highly respected organization in your profession. The letter says that you are being recognized as having created the most ideal work situation in your industry. You have been asked to give a speech at the industry's national meeting. You begin to think about what to say. What will you say about your customers? Who are your customers? Where are they from? How many customers do you have? How did they find out about you? How did you discover what your customers needed? What do your customers want that your ideal organization provides? What are your products and services? What do your customers typically say about your products or services?

"Now you walk around the work areas and mingle with some of your colleagues. Who is working with you? Notice what people are doing. How do they communicate in this ideal organization?

"Picture one of your meetings. What is happening? What's your sense of how people are feeling?

"What exactly do you do in your perfect organization? What is your work? Is it full-time or part-time work? What is your level of participation? What are some areas of growth you have achieved in your 'safe' work environment?

"What gives you great joy and a deep sense of fulfillment in your life? How does your work blend with this? How do you contribute to the success of your organization?

"You see yourself strolling through your work place, feeling good. Scan the environment for any features you may have missed—sights, smells, etc.... Note them and realize how they enrich your work life, your whole life. See if you can identify the key elements that contribute to your organization's success.... It's a great organization, isn't it?

"In a moment I will ask you to return to the present. Remember what you have visualized because you will be writing about your images. Continue to hang on to the pleasant feelings you have just experienced.... Now move your fingers and feet, stretch your legs, and move your shoulders.... Now, whenever you are ready, open your eyes and come back."

(Twenty minutes.)

3. The facilitator stops the music and gives each team member a copy of the Ideal Work Place Vision Sheet, a pencil, and a clipboard or other portable writing surface. (Five minutes.)

4. The team members are asked to spend thirty minutes completing their vision sheets. The facilitator clarifies that they will not be asked to turn in their completed sheets to anyone. While the members are writing, the facilitator enforces silence to allow the creative process to unfold. (Thirty minutes.)

5. The facilitator calls time and encourages individuals to share whatever they choose from their vision sheets. Using separate sheets of newsprint, the facilitator records and posts ideas under the appropriate handout headings: Environment, Market, Products and Services, People and Functions, Individual Development, and Keys to Success. (Twenty minutes.)

6. Each individual is given a felt-tipped marker and is asked to set a priority for each idea based on how much it contributes to the "ideal work place." Newsprint ideas are to be marked "H" for "high priority," marked "L" for "low priority," or left blank to indicate "not a priority." Once all members have marked all ideas, the team may decide to weed out some ideas by using criteria such as "least effort, time, money required," "greatest return for effort," "will strengthen the team," or "will help the organization achieve its mission." At the end of the process, the members should have what they consider to be a manageable number of prioritized ideas. (Twenty minutes.)

7. The facilitator asks for volunteers to write goal statements for the six subjects that serve as handout headings, based on subjects in which they have high interest. (If no one is interested in a particular subject, that subject can be eliminated. If more than one member is interested in a single subject, those members may form a subgroup to write the statements. If the team has very few members, one or more members may take more than one subject.) Each member/subgroup is given several sheets of blank newsprint on which to write the goal statement(s) as well as the newsprint sheets with ideas for that member's/subgroup's chosen subject. The facilitator clarifies that *a goal statement must be achievable and written in specific, measurable terms.* The following examples are offered:

- *Too vague:* The team will become more knowledgeable about computer word processing.

- *Specific and measurable:* By June 1 of this year, all team members will have taken a locally offered course in WordPerfect 6.0. By September 1 of this year, all team members will have used WordPerfect 6.0 to complete at least six reports or other in-house documents for distribution.

(Twenty minutes.)

8. The facilitator asks the members to stop their work and share their goal statements with the team. (Ten minutes.)

9. The facilitator encourages the team members to take ownership of the goal statements and to take action immediately, if possible. He or she then conducts a debrief of the activity with questions such as the following:

- What parts of the activity were personally meaningful for you?

- What parts of the activity were easier or more difficult than others? How do you account for that?

- How have your perceptions of your values changed as a result of this activity?

- What have you learned about the visioning process?

- How can what you have learned help you in your pursuit of a satisfying work life? How can it help your team? Your organization?

(Ten to fifteen minutes.)

Variations

- The team members may agree to conduct this visioning process on a regular basis as on ongoing segment of team building.

- Following Step 8, the team members may be asked to determine what values the organization needs to have in order for the vision to become a reality.

Submitted by M.K. Key, Glenn Head, and Marian Head.

M.K. Key, Ph.D., is a licensed psychologist and a consultant and trainer in continuous quality improvement with the Center for Continuous Improvement of Quorum Health Resources, Inc. She works with healthcare organi-

zations in the fields of human and organization development, communication, conflict management, creativity, and leadership. Dr. Key is an adjunct assistant professor in human and organization development at Peabody College/Vanderbilt University in Nashville, Tennessee.

Glenn Head *is a member of the leadership team of Delaney, Inc., a snowboarding company offering training camps for adults in Aspen and Beaver Creek, Colorado. He also consults with clients on how to create organizations that will endure and thrive. Glenn wrote the International Award-winning book* Training Cost Analysis: A Practical Guide, *published by ASTD. He is a past president of the Association for the Development of Computer-Based Instructional Systems.*

Marian Head *is an organizational-transformation consultant. Her specialty is helping team members to envision their ideal future and then take the steps necessary to achieve that future. As manager for educational development with the U.S. Senate for nine years, she co-managed a team of thirty-four members. She also designs and facilitates meetings from the board room to international, multilingual conferences. She is coauthor of* The American Team: 7 Steps to Genuine Teamwork in the White House and Beyond.

IDEAL WORK PLACE VISION SHEET

Instructions: Record in as much detail as possible everything you experienced when you imagined your perfect organization. The following questions are organized in the same sequence as the guided imagery activity you just completed. Write down everything you can remember about each question or area that is important to you. This work sheet is for your use only; you need share only those items you choose to share.

Environment

1. When you walked into your place of business, what did it look like? What colors did you see?

2. What sounds did you hear?

3. What did you smell?

4. How did the environment feel?

5. List anything else you noticed that made the environment perfect for you.

Market

6. Who were your customers?

7. Where were they located geographically? Where were they from?

8. How many customers did you have?

9. How did new customers find out about you?

Products and Services

10. How did you discover what was really needed by your customers?

11. What did your customers need that your organization provided? What were your products and services?

12. What were some of the things customers said about your products or services?

People and Functions

13. Who was working with you?

14. What were the people in your organization like? What did they do?

15. How did people communicate in the organization? What typically happened in your meetings?

Individual Development

16. What exactly did you do in your organization? What was your work?

17. What was your level of participation in the organization?

18. What were some of the areas of growth you achieved in your work?

19. What did you envision that gave you great joy and a deep sense of fulfillment in your life?

20. How did your work blend with this?

21. How did you contribute to the success of your organization?

Keys to Success

22. What are the keys to the success of your organization?

23. Is there anything else you wish to record about this experience?

562. CALLOWAY POWER STATION: ASSESSING TEAM-LEADER EFFECTIVENESS

Goals

- To offer the participants an opportunity to analyze a case involving team-leader effectiveness.

- To provide the participants with a forum for discussing various aspects of team leadership.

- To encourage the participants to share their individual views about team leadership and how it affects team functioning.

Group Size

Three to six subgroups of four or five members each. This activity is best used as part of a leadership-development program.

Time Required

One hour.

Materials

- A copy of the Calloway Power Station Case-Study Sheet for each participant.

- A copy of the Calloway Power Station Evaluation Sheet for each participant.

- A pencil for each participant.

- A clipboard or other portable writing surface for each participant.

Physical Setting

A room with movable chairs and plenty of space so that the subgroups can work without disturbing one another.

Process

1. The facilitator introduces the goals of the activity. (Five minutes.)

2. Each participant is given a copy of the Calloway Power Station Case-Study Sheet, a copy of the Calloway Power Station Evaluation Sheet, a pencil, and a clipboard or other portable writing surface and is asked to spend twenty minutes reading the case study and completing the evaluation sheet. (Twenty minutes.)

3. After twenty minutes, subgroups of four or five members each are formed. The members of each subgroup are asked to spend twenty minutes sharing their evaluation-sheet responses and any additional observations or insights about the case, noting both similarities and differences in opinions. (Twenty minutes.)

4. The facilitator reconvenes the total group and leads a discussion by asking these questions:

   - Which areas on the evaluation sheet received high marks in your subgroup? Which received low marks?

   - What similarities among viewpoints were shared in your subgroup? What differences were shared?

   - How effective is Bob as the leader of this team? How does his effectiveness influence the team's effectiveness?

   - What have you learned about team leadership from this case study?

   - How might you use what you have learned from this case study in your own leadership approach?

   (Fifteen minutes.)

Variations

- The activity may be focused on and processed in terms of specific leadership or group-development theories, such as McGregor's Theory X-Theory Y Model (Robinson, 1972), the Tuckman Model of Group

Development (Kormanski, 1985), or Rosenthal and Jacobson's four factors of climate, feedback, input, and output (Rosenthal & Jacobson, 1968; Pfeiffer, 1991).

- The members of each subgroup may be asked to average their scores for the items on the evaluation sheet and report them. The subgroup averages may then be discussed.

- The evaluation sheet may be used as an assessment tool for the participants' own leadership abilities.

References

Kormanski, C. (1985). A Situational Leadership™ approach to groups using the Tuckman model of group development. In L.D. Goodstein & J.W. Pfeiffer (Eds.), *The 1985 annual: Developing human resources* (pp. 217-226). San Diego, CA: Pfeiffer & Company.

Pfeiffer, J.W. (1991). The four-factory theory: How leaders influence followers. In J.W. Pfeiffer (Ed.), *Theories and models in applied behavioral science* (Vol. 3) (pp. 147-149). San Diego, CA: Pfeiffer & Company.

Robinson, A.J. (1972). McGregor's Theory X-Theory Y Model. In J.W. Pfeiffer & J.E. Jones (Eds.), *The 1972 annual handbook for group facilitators* (pp. 121-123). San Diego, CA: Pfeiffer & Company.

Rosenthal, R., & Jacobson, L. (1968). *Pygmalion in the classroom.* New York: Holt, Rinehart and Winston.

Submitted by William N. Parker.

William N. Parker *is a senior training specialist in the management and professional development department at Virginia Power in Richmond, Virginia. His specialties include designing and facilitating interventions that enhance leadership, teamwork, quality, and internal customer service.*

Calloway Power Station Case-Study Sheet

Introduction and Instructions: Bob Cramer has been a maintenance supervisor for Virginia Power at its Calloway Power Station for four years. Previously he was a mechanic in the maintenance department for nine years. He leads a seven-person team whose members have experience ranging from seven to twenty years. Bob's group is one of fourteen such teams at Virginia Power that are responsible for servicing power-station equipment.

To help himself evaluate the team members, Bob has written a description of each. Read these descriptions, making notes in the margin about any information or clues about Bob's leadership effectiveness. Then complete the Calloway Power Station Evaluation Sheet. Your ultimate objective is to learn whatever you can that will increase your own effectiveness as a team leader.

TEAM-MEMBER DESCRIPTIONS

1. Andrew (Andy) Adams

Thirty-one-year-old male, married with two children. Twelve years with Virginia Power (all at Calloway). *Position:* First-Class Mechanic. Andy's father retired from Virginia Power's line department, and his brother Rick is also a First-Class Mechanic at Calloway. Andy grew up around Virginia Power.

Andy started his career as a laborer, entered the Mechanical Development Program, and completed the program with high marks all the way through. He is a very quality-oriented craftsman and loves challenging work. He is able to take on a job and complete it with little help from me. He is extremely knowledgeable about mechanical devices and likes to find out what makes new ones tick.

He has taken T/A Foreman for me this year and has performed very well. He has a strong team orientation and likes to function using teamwork principles. I keep a number of books on teamwork in my office so that the team members can read them, and Andy has read several.

Andy's attendance at work is excellent; he almost never takes sick leave or personal leave. He is always in a good mood and likes the people around him to be the same way. His hobbies are sailing, fishing, hunting, and working around the house. Andy recently joined the Jaycees so that he can contribute to his community.

---

2. Bradley (Brad) Benson

Thirty-four-year-old male, married with one child and another on the way, Air Force veteran. Ten years with Virginia Power (all at Calloway). *Position:* First-Class Mechanic. Brad came to Calloway directly from the Air Force and to this day gets upset when things are not run as efficiently as in the service.

He started in the labor gang and went through our Mechanical Development Program, completing his studies with high marks. Brad likes to do only high-quality work.

He likes working on our team and has improved in terms of his attitude toward the company. Like Andy, he has read several books on teamwork. Like me, he does not understand why more people (company managers, union representatives, and so on) do not buy into the team-work concept. As he has told me in the past, "It's a process that benefits everyone."

Brad loves to work on special projects and to find better answers and solutions as he works. He would like to break down the barrier between the union and the company so that all of us could work together harmoniously. Brad is a thinker, and at times I wonder if he is listening to me; he *is* listening, though, and he lets me know his thoughts at the proper time.

He loves to fish Ottle Creek Reservoir and to play golf. Every year he and I go off-shore fishing together.

3. Charles (Chuck) Coulter

Forty-seven-year-old male, married. Seven years with Virginia Power (first with the now-defunct System Maintenance Support group and then at Calloway). *Position:* Mechanic Trainee. Chuck is due to finish his training in two months. He is a very good employee and a very hard worker.

At this stage of his career, Chuck seems to be more of a follower than a leader. With more experience, he should be able to take charge without any problems. He likes to learn about various components and does not mind getting his hands dirty. He fits right in with the team and likes being a part of it. Even though he is older than I am, he does not seem to resent taking directions from someone younger.

Chuck always has a smile—especially for the ladies. He likes to sing in his church choir.

4. David (Dave) Dawkins

Forty-three-year-old male, married. Twenty years with Virginia Power (all at Calloway). *Position:* First-Class Mechanic. Dave is an old-timer here and has worked a lot of jobs. He has probably forgotten more than I will ever know about this power station. Dave is the person I like to consult when something on the "old side" of the plant is not working right. He does not mind sharing his knowledge with me or his teammates.

Dave is liked by almost everyone in the shop and is always ready to lend a hand. If you think your idea might be better than his, he has no problem in giving your idea a try. He likes special projects and has led several to successful completion. Dave has been a T/A Foreman for me this year as well as another time previously, and he does an excellent job in this position.

Dave is a happy man most of the time. He likes to fish, and he has a wonderful collection of antique furniture.

5. Edward (Eddie) Evans

Fifty-two-year-old male, married, Navy veteran. Seventeen years with Virginia Power (all at Calloway). *Position:* First-Class Mechanic. Eddie started with Virginia Power as a Mechanic Trainee and completed the training program with no difficulty at all. When I entered the program, Eddie was the first mechanic I worked with. We worked side by side for at least four or five months.

At that time Eddie had a reputation for shirking responsibility, but I discovered that all he wanted was to be challenged in his work. If he did not feel challenged, then he would do only what was necessary to get by. Actually, Eddie has worked some very rough jobs and has been quite successful. He led one project for me this year and did a fantastic job. I believe Eddie has worked harder for me than for others because of my emphasis on teamwork and on everyone's doing his fair share of the work.

6. Frederick (Fred) Foster

Thirty-six-year-old male, married, seventeen years with Virginia Power (all at Calloway). *Position:* First-Class Mechanic. This is the fourth year that Fred has worked for me.

Fred is a big, strong man who prefers physical work over highly technical jobs. He is faster than the others at completing rough and dirty jobs. Fred has worked on several projects for me and has completed them ahead of schedule.

He thinks he is a complainer. I think his complaints are just his way of expressing himself and his thoughts (which make sense most of the time).

Fred enjoys hunting and surf fishing.

7. Gregory (Greg) Gibson

Thirty-two-year-old male, married with three children. Thirteen years with Virginia Power (all at Calloway). *Position:* First-Class Mechanic. Greg started as a laborer and then progressed to the Mechanical Development Program, which he completed right on time, with good grades.

Greg performs each task with quality in mind. He is one of the hardest workers on the team, if for no other reason than to prove to his coworkers that one can associate with the boss outside work and still be judged strictly on merit.

Greg does not mind getting his hands dirty and is very competitive. He likes to complete tasks more quickly and with a higher degree of quality than others.

He is my best friend, and he was my competition for the job I have now. Before I was promoted, we agreed that no matter who got the job, it would be O.K. with the other.

Greg and I are both volunteers with the local Rescue Squad. He is the captain of the squad's Emergency Medical Service. Greg also has his own construction company that he runs after hours. In addition, he is on the station's Fire Brigade and First Aid Team and competes in the annual competition. He enjoys surf and gulf-stream fishing, and he has just acquired a taste for golf.

Leader's Summary

The major changes that I have observed during the year have been in Brad, Dave, and Eddie. These men were finally given the opportunity to do their assigned tasks without close supervision. I gave them ownership of their respective tasks and told them that I expected the quality work I knew they were capable of.

Our team members have pride in themselves, and that pride shows. I have told the quality-assurance people that if a job done by my team comes back for rework, I want my guys to handle it. Only one job has come back to the team this year, and, as it turned out, the problem was not caused by us initially. My guys are the best; I believe in them and what they are capable of doing.

CALLOWAY POWER STATION EVALUATION SHEET

CONCLUSIONS

On the basis of Bob Cramer's descriptions of his employees, what can you deduce about how he functions as a team leader and how the team functions as a result of his leadership? Circle the number on each continuum to indicate your choice.

1. Leader's communication of necessary information to team

Closed ⊢——┼——┼——┼——⊣ Open
      1   2   3   4   5

2. Team's ability to make decisions as a unit

Low ⊢——┼——┼——┼——⊣ High
    1   2   3   4   5

3. Team's use of member expertise

Low Degree ⊢——┼——┼——┼——⊣ High Degree
     1   2   3   4   5

4. Leader's comfort with shared leadership responsibility

Low Degree ⊢——┼——┼——┼——⊣ High Degree
     1   2   3   4   5

5. Extent to which leader has positive regard for members

Low ⊢——┼——┼——┼——⊣ High
    1   2   3   4   5

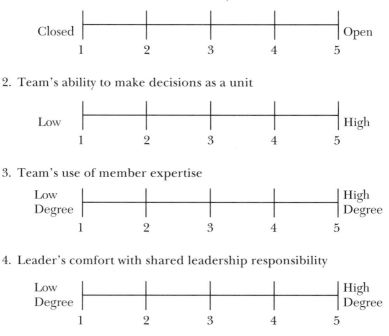

6. Degree to which leader provides any encouragement and positive feedback

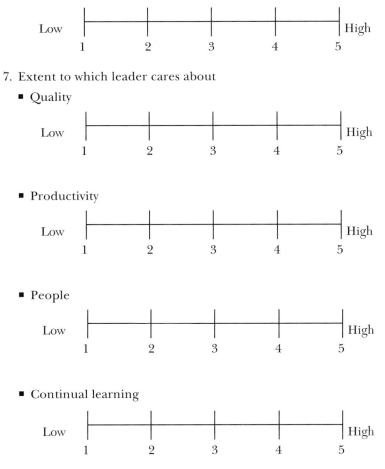

Low |——|——|——|——| High
    1   2   3   4   5

7. Extent to which leader cares about

▪ Quality

Low |——|——|——|——| High
    1   2   3   4   5

▪ Productivity

Low |——|——|——|——| High
    1   2   3   4   5

▪ People

Low |——|——|——|——| High
    1   2   3   4   5

▪ Continual learning

Low |——|——|——|——| High
    1   2   3   4   5

EVALUATION AND LEARNING

Review your ratings in the previous section and then write responses for the following items:

1. Identify two or three strengths of the team leader, Bob Cramer.

2. Identify two or three aspects of leader functioning in which Bob might want to improve.

3. Would you like to work for someone like Bob? Explain why or why not.

563: The MPM Scale: Identifying Beliefs About the Study of Organizations

Goals

- To acquaint the participants with the modern and postmodern approaches to the study of organizational behavior.
- To allow participants to identify and share their own beliefs about the study of organizational behavior.

Group Size

A maximum of five subgroups of five or six members each.

Time Required

One to two hours.

Materials

- A copy of The MPM Scale and a pencil for each participant.
- A copy of The MPM Scale: Beliefs About the Study of Organizations Sheet for each participant.
- A copy of The MPM Scale Scoring and Interpretation Sheet for each participant.
- A copy of The MPM Scale Discussion Sheet for each participant.
- A newsprint poster of The MPM Scale Interpretation Grid (prepared ahead of time) and masking tape for posting it.

The 1996 Annual: Volume 2, Consulting.
Copyright © 1996 by Pfeiffer & Company, San Diego, CA.

- A newsprint flip chart and a felt-tipped marker.

Physical Setting

A room large enough for the subgroups to work in separate areas. Chairs for the participants and tables or portable writing surfaces.

Process

1. The facilitator gives each participant a copy of The MPM Scale and a pencil, reviews the directions with the participants, and ask them to complete the scale. (Five to ten minutes.)

2. The facilitator instructs the participants to lay their completed scales aside for now. He or she reviews the goals of the activity, distributes copies of The MPM Scale: Beliefs About the Study of Organizations Sheet, and presents a brief overview of modern and postmodern approaches to the study of organizational behavior. (Five to ten minutes.)

3. The facilitator distributes copies of The MPM Scale Scoring and Interpretation Sheet and asks the participants to score their own instruments. They may talk with their neighbors and/or compare their results, if they wish. (Five to ten minutes.)

4. The participants are asked to raise their hands to determine how many found themselves in each of the nine boxes of the interpretation grid, and the facilitator records the numbers on the prepared newsprint grid. The facilitator says that the numbers indicate the diversity of beliefs within the group and that the data may be used in the general discussion of the activity, if participants so desire. (Five to ten minutes.)

5. The participants are divided into small groups of five or six members each. (These groups may be formed at random; however, the discussions may be more interesting if a variety of beliefs are represented in each group.) The facilitator gives a copy of The MPM Scale Discussion Sheet to each participant and tells the groups to begin their discussions. (Fifteen to forty-five minutes.)

6. After the discussions, the total group is reassembled. The facilitator asks the groups to share their responses to the discussion questions and to ask any further questions that their discussions may have

generated. The facilitator notes general themes on newsprint and relates them to the scores on the grid. (Ten to twenty minutes.)

7. The facilitator leads a total-group discussion based on the contributions from the small groups. The following questions may be asked:

- What have you learned about your beliefs regarding the study of organizational behavior?

- How was your participation in this activity reflective of your beliefs?

- What have you learned about others' beliefs?

- What have you learned about the study of organizations in general?

- How do your views of the study of organizational behavior affect your day-to-day behavior in your organization?

- What learnings can you apply to your organization?

(Fifteen minutes.)

Variations

- If the number of participants is small, all discussions can take place within the total group.

- As a warmup, participants can state how they study organizations in their particular job positions.

- As a follow-up, groups can be asked to design an organizational study and to explain which beliefs it is based on.

Submitted by Ernest M. Schuttenberg.

Ernest M. Schuttenberg, Ed.D., is a professor of adult education and organizational behavior in the department of counseling, administration, supervision, and adult learning at Cleveland State University. He has worked in training and organizational development at American Airlines and Honeywell. Dr. Schuttenberg has written more than thirty-five articles in the areas of educational administration, instruction, and organizational behavior, and he is the coauthor of Field Experience in Postsecondary Education: A Guidebook for Action.

THE MPM SCALE

Instructions: On the line before each item, write a number from the following scale to indicate the extent of your agreement or disagreement with the item:

> 1 = Strongly Disagree
> 2 = Disagree
> 3 = Unsure, but Tend to Disagree
> 4 = Unsure, but Tend to Agree
> 5 = Agree
> 6 = Strongly Agree

_____ 1. We should apply ways of thinking used by physical scientists in our study of organizations.

_____ 2. In the study of organizations, the assumptions, beliefs, and values shared by people are more important than the structure, goals, and flow of resources in the organization.

_____ 3. Underlying the seemingly chaotic activities of modern organizations there are discoverable patterns of logic, system, and order.

_____ 4. It is important to maintain strict objectivity in studying organizational behavior.

_____ 5. Although organizational goals are usually stated in terms of equity and equality, organizational behavior is usually acted out in terms of power and control.

_____ 6. Organizations exist only in people's minds; they have no independent physical presence.

_____ 7. Testing theories scientifically is the most reliable way of gaining valid knowledge about how organizations work.

_____ 8. There is no such thing as an "objective" study of organizations; all studies have some social or political agenda.

_____ 9. The key to improving organizations is to discover the patterns and "laws" of organizational behavior so that prediction and control are made possible.

_____ 10. In studying an organization, one starts with the whole and moves to the parts.

The 1996 Annual: Volume 2, Consulting.
Copyright © 1996 by Pfeiffer & Company, San Diego, CA.

1 = Strongly Disagree
2 = Disagree
3 = Unsure, but Tend to Disagree
4 = Unsure, but Tend to Agree
5 = Agree
6 = Strongly Agree

_____11. There can be no "true" knowledge about organizational behavior, only various "knowledges" based on different values and frames of reference.

_____12. The best way of studying organizational behavior is inductively (by observing what people actually do) rather than deductively (by testing hypotheses).

_____13. We cannot understand organizations as they really are, only as we interpret them to be.

_____14. In the study of organizations, structure, goals, and the flow of resources are more important than the assumptions, beliefs, and values shared by people.

_____15. Two investigators can come to conflicting understandings of organizational behavior, and they both can be right.

_____16. Our goal in studying organizations is to learn how they really work.

_____17. Organizational behavior should be interpreted basically as the struggle between those who have power and those who desire it.

_____18. In studying an organization, one starts with the parts and moves to the whole.

_____19. In studying organizations, we build temporary models of understanding that must be flexible and open to new information and unpredictable change.

_____20. Because of breakthroughs in technology and telecommunications, life in organizations shows promise of becoming much more satisfying and productive.

The MPM Scale: Beliefs About the Study of Organizations Sheet

The Modern Period

Until the early 1970s, the study of organizational behavior was dominated by scholars who espoused the tenets of logical positivism, a Twentieth Century philosophical movement that holds that statements, to be meaningful, must be verifiable or confirmable by observation and experimentation. Metaphysical theories and pronouncements are considered to be devoid of meaning, as they are beyond the realm of statistical or observational proof. These scholars "demanded the use of theory and scientific techniques for testing theory: techniques that were thought to be objective, detached from the people being studied, with mathematical proof the highest goal of investigation" (Owens, 1995, p. 3).

The Postmodern Period

In the 1960s and 1970s, the belief system of logical positivism came under extensive attack, not only in the field of organizational behavior but also in such areas as literature, art, and social science. The scholars who challenged the modern approaches said that there could be no single way of studying a field, that all perception was relative, and that the "truth" was subject to the interpretations of various observers. In the study of organizational behavior, the postmodernists emphasized assumptions, values, and beliefs—all of which can differ from person to person and from context to context.

Bagnall (1995) describes postmodernity as having three major characteristics:

- the interpretive nature of human perception,

- the contextualization and fragmentation of belief, meaning, and being, and

- the generalized (uncertain) nature of contemporary communication (p. 80).

Bagnall points out the disruptive nature of postmodernity. It seeks to weaken or destroy many of the cherished conclusions of modernism.

Comparison of Modernism and Postmodernism

The following list highlights the respective emphases of modernism and postmodernism:

MODERNISM	POSTMODERNISM
Objectivity	Subjectivity
Theories	Values
Control	Change
Standardization	Relativism
Logic	Intuition

With the use of The MPM Scale and accompanying materials, you will be able to examine your own beliefs about organizations and organizational behavior and discuss with others some of the implications of these beliefs.

References and Further Readings

Bagnall, R.G. (1995). Discriminative justice and responsibility in postmodernist adult education. *Adult Education Quarterly, 45*(2), 79-94.

Bergquist, W. (1993). *The postmodern organization: Mastering the art of irreversible change.* San Francisco, CA: Jossey-Bass.

Gergen, K.T. (1992). Organization theory in the postmodern era. In M. Reed & M. Hughes (Eds.), *Rethinking organization: New directions in organization theory and analysis* (pp. 207-226). London: Sage.

Hammer, M., & Champy, J. (1993). *Reengineering the corporation: A manifesto for business revolution.* New York: HarperCollins.

Hassard, J., & Parker, M. (Eds.). (1993). *Postmodernism and organizations.* Newbury Park, CA: Sage.

Heckscher, C. (1994). Defining the post-bureaucratic type. In C. Heckscher & A. Donnellon (Eds.), *The post-bureaucratic organization: New perspectives on organizational change* (pp. 14-62). Newbury Park, CA: Sage.

Lewin, A.Y., & Stephens, C.U. (1993). Designing post-industrial organizations: Combining theory and practice. In G. P. Huber & W.H. Glick (Eds.), *Organizational change and redesign: Ideas and insights for improving performance* (pp. 393-409). New York: Oxford University Press.

Owens, R.G. (1995). *Organizational behavior in education* (5th ed.). Boston, MA: Allyn and Bacon.

Peters, T. (1988). *Thriving on chaos: Handbook for a management revolution.* New York: Knopf.

THE MPM SCALE SCORING AND INTERPRETATION SHEET

Scoring

In the appropriate spaces below, write your responses to the twenty items of The MPM Scale. Then total each column.

Modern Beliefs	Postmodern Beliefs
1 _____	2 _____
3 _____	5 _____
4 _____	6 _____
7 _____	8 _____
9 _____	10 _____
12 _____	11 _____
14 _____	13 _____
16 _____	15 _____
18 _____	17 _____
20 _____	19 _____
Total: _____	Total: _____

Interpretation

You may interpret your beliefs in the modern and postmodern approaches by looking at your Total Scores in each column.

> 10-20 = Strong Disbelief
> 21-30 = Moderately Strong Disbelief
> 31-40 = Unsure Belief
> 41-50 = Moderately Strong Belief
> 51-60 = Strong Belief

THE MPM SCALE INTERPRETATION GRID

Instructions: Locate your modern beliefs total score and place an X on the horizontal axis on the grid that follows. Next, locate your postmodern beliefs total score and place an X on the vertical axis on the grid. From the Xs, draw horizontal and vertical lines so that they intersect in one of the nine boxes within the grid.

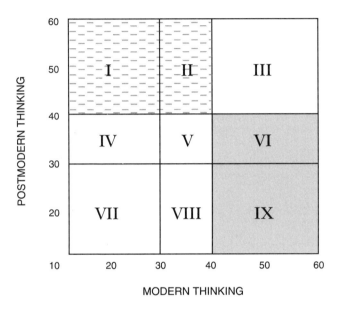

BOX   INTERPRETATION

I or II	Primarily postmodern thinker
VI or IX	Primarily modern thinker
III	Eclectic thinker (postmodern and modern)
VII	Noncommitted (neither postmodern nor modern)
IV	More postmodern than modern thinker
VIII	More modern than postmodern thinker
V	Unsure of your beliefs

THE MPM SCALE DISCUSSION SHEET

1. What do items 7, 9, 16, and 20 say about the study of organizational behavior? Why study organizational behavior?

2. Considering the meaning of truth regarding organizations, do you agree more with the statement in item 3 or the statement in item 13? Why? How does that affect your perception of behavior in your organization?

3. Judging from items 5, 8, and 17, what is the nature of organizational behavior? How closely does this correspond to your experiences in organizations? How does this affect you?

4. Consider the approaches one uses in the study of organizational behavior. Do you think that the statements in items 1, 4, and 12 or those in items 11, 15, and 19 are more valid? Why? How does this influence what you advocate in your organization?

5. Consider items 10 and 18. Which statement do you think is more valid? Why?

6. Consider items 6 and 16. Which statement is closer to your belief? Why?

7. Consider items 2 and 14. Which statement do you consider more valid? Why?

8. How is the research that you use in your job affected by modern or postmodern beliefs? How does that affect what you do?

564. Egg Drop: Using Human Resources Effectively

Goals

- To help participants to analyze the use of human resources within a group.

- To allow participants to study the relationship between managers and workers in carrying out a task.

- To demonstrate the impact of the communication process on assigning and carrying out a task.

- To allow participants to study the effects of positive and negative reinforcement.

Group Size

Twelve to twenty-four participants, divided into subgroups of six members each.

Time Required

Two hours.

Materials

- One copy of the Egg Drop Rule Sheet for each participant.

- One copy of the Egg Drop Materials Requisition for each participant.

- One copy of the Egg Drop Observation Sheet for each subgroup's observer.

- A clipboard or other portable writing surface for each observer.

- A pencil for each participant.

The 1996 Annual: Volume 2, Consulting.
Copyright © 1996 by Pfeiffer & Company, San Diego, CA.

- One egg for each subgroup.
- Twenty paper plates.
- Twenty plastic bowls.
- Fifty sheets of paper toweling.
- Twenty small Styrofoam® plates.
- Twenty Styrofoam® cups.
- Forty plastic coffee stirrers.
- Forty plastic drinking straws.
- Twenty plastic cups.
- Twenty large Styrofoam® plates.
- Forty index cards.
- Forty paper clips.
- Forty rubber bands.
- Several rolls of masking tape.
- Two boxes of facial tissues.
- A pocket calculator for the facilitator.
- A newsprint flip chart and a felt-tipped marker.
- Masking tape for posting newsprint.

Physical Setting

A room large enough for subgroups to work without disturbing one another. The room also should be equipped with a wall clock.

Process

1. The facilitator introduces the goals of the activity. The participants are told that they will assemble into subgroups to design and build a structure that will support an egg as it is dropped from a height of approximately eight feet. The facilitator states that any subgroup that completes the project within budget and without breaking its egg will be considered successful. Then the facilitator distributes copies of the Egg Drop Rule Sheet and reviews the rules with the entire group. (Ten minutes.)

2. The participants are asked to form subgroups of six members each.

3. The facilitator distributes copies of the Egg Drop Materials Requisition and pencils and then announces that each subgroup will have ten minutes to choose an observer, managers, and workers. (Ten minutes.)

4. The facilitator gives each observer a copy of the Egg Drop Observation Sheet, a pencil, and a clipboard or other portable writing surface and reviews the instructions *(but not the questions)* on the observation sheet with the entire group. (Five minutes.)

5. The facilitator gives each subgroup an egg, asks the subgroups to begin, and reminds the observers to keep track of the time. The facilitator monitors subgroup activities and assists as necessary. While the subgroups are in the construction phase, the facilitator calculates the total costs of the materials that each subgroup requisitions and records that information on newsprint. (Forty-five minutes.)

6. After forty-five minutes, the facilitator calls time and reassembles the entire group. He or she posts the newsprint listing the materials costs for each subgroup. Each observer is asked to add the amount of penalties that his or her subgroup incurred as well as the costs of the subgroup's design and construction time and to announce whether the subgroup completed its task within budget. (Ten minutes.)

7. Each subgroup's structure is tested by having one of its managers stand on a chair and drop the egg from a height of approximately eight feet. (The facilitator marks the height on newsprint so that each subgroup drops its egg from the same point.) The structure is considered successful if the egg does not break, and each successful subgroup is congratulated. (Ten minutes.)

8. The observers are asked to take turns reporting their observations. (Ten minutes.)

9. The facilitator debriefs the activity by asking the following questions:

   - How did you feel about how you acquired your role?

   - Who influenced decisions most? How was that influence exerted? How did you react to that influence?

   - How did you feel as your subgroup worked on designing and building its structure?

   - Which human resources (including yourself) were used wisely? Unwisely?

- What have you learned about the effective use of human resources? Given what you have learned, what would you do differently if you were to repeat this activity?

- If you could rewrite the rules of this activity, what would you change? How would your changes contribute to a more effective use of human resources?

- How does this experience relate to your own work process? How can you apply what you have learned to improve your own work process?

(Twenty minutes.)

Variations

- If sufficient time is available, the subgroups may be asked to repeat the activity using the rewritten rules.

- The facilitator may have the subgroups compete with one another by stipulating that the winning subgroup will be the one whose structure is successful (egg does not break) and who built its structure at the lowest cost.

Submitted by Douglas Bryant.

Douglas Bryant is an organizational development specialist for Office Depot in Delray Beach, Florida. He has developed and implemented a training program for store managers and assistant managers-in-training, and this program has been used in four hundred retail stores. Prior to assuming his position with Office Depot, he was a training specialist, an instructional designer, a team leader, an industrial engineer, and a manufacturing supervisor. Currently he is doing research in birth-order theory for the University of North Florida and designing programs for the Hugh O'Brien Youth Foundation.

EGG DROP RULE SHEET

In the upcoming activity, your subgroup's task is to design and build a structure that will support an egg as it is dropped from a height of approximately eight feet.

Your budget for completing the task is $3,000. The materials you may choose for construction purposes are listed on the Egg Drop Materials Requisition, which includes prices for these materials. In addition, as indicated below, your subgroup will be charged for the positions of observer, manager, and worker.

If the egg does not break when dropped and you stay within budget, you will have completed the task successfully.

CHOOSING OBSERVER, MANAGERS, WORKERS

You and your fellow subgroup members may choose roles in any way you wish. Note the following costs of the different positions:

Manager = $200 each
Worker = $100 each
Observer = $ 75 each
Note: Your subgroup must have one observer.

DESIGNING THE STRUCTURE

1. Managers design a construction plan.

2. Workers may not participate in the design process in any way.

3. Workers and managers may look at but not touch the resource materials.

BUILDING THE STRUCTURE

1. Once the design has been completed, your subgroup may request the materials it needs from the facilitator by completing and submitting a copy of the Egg Drop Materials Requisition. The subgroup is charged the indicated amounts for chosen materials.

---

2. All materials must be requested at one time; however, in the event that a requested item is not in stock, your subgroup may revise its requisition.

3. Your subgroup may begin the construction phase whenever it is ready.

4. Managers may offer instructions, ideas, and feedback, but they *may not touch the resource materials.* Workers are to build the structure, but they *may not use their own ideas.*

5. If either infraction in item 4 occurs, the observer will penalize the subgroup $100 for each occurrence.

> Note: The total time allotted for design and construction is
>   forty-five minutes.

EGG DROP MATERIALS REQUISITION

Budget: $3,000

Manager	# _____	@ $200.00 each
Worker	# _____	@ $100.00 each
Observer (1)	# _____	@ $ 75.00
Design Time (actual minutes)	# _____	@ $ 2.50 per minute
Construction Time (45 minutes minus Design Time)	# _____	@ $ 5.00 per minute
Paper Plate	# _____	@ $ 50.00 each
Plastic Bowl	# _____	@ $100.00 each
Paper Towel	# _____	@ $ 25.00 each
Small Styrofoam® Plate	# _____	@ $ 75.00 each
Styrofoam® Cup	# _____	@ $150.00 each
Coffee Stirrer	# _____	@ $ 5.00 each
Plastic Drinking Straw	# _____	@ $ 7.50 each
Plastic Cup	# _____	@ $175.00 each
Large Styrofoam® Plate	# _____	@ $125.00 each
Index Card	# _____	@ $ 10.00 each
Paper Clip	# _____	@ $ 1.00 each
Rubber Band	# _____	@ $ 2.00 each
Tape (inches)	# _____	@ $ 1.00 per inch
Pencil	# _____	@ $ 2.00 each
Facial Tissue	# _____	@ $ 3.00 each

EGG DROP OBSERVATION SHEET

Instructions: Your role is to observe the members of your subgroup and make notes on their behavior using the questions below as a guide. Also track the time for the design phase and for the construction phase, and note any penalties that occur. You may *not* offer input or help during design or construction.

1. How did your subgroup decide who would assume which roles? What were the key considerations?

2. How did the manager(s) approach the task? What process did the manager(s) use?

3. Did the manager(s) look at the process from the workers' point of view? How?

The 1996 Annual: Volume 2, Consulting.
Copyright © 1996 by Pfeiffer & Company, San Diego, CA.

4. What type of communication did the manager(s) engage in with the workers?

5. How was the design communicated to the workers?

6. How did the manager(s) and workers give one another positive or negative reinforcement?

7. How did the workers follow instructions? What were their reactions?

8. How effectively did the workers use their time?

9. How did the workers work as part of the team?

	Begin	End
Design Time		
Construction Time		
Penalties		

Pfeiffer & Company

565. UNDER PRESSURE:
MANAGING TIME EFFECTIVELY

Goals

- To focus attention on the HR/OD issues involved in setting priorities under pressure of deadlines.
- To increase awareness of the role of empowering others in organizations.
- To examine one's time-management skills.

Group Size

Up to thirty participants who are practicing human resource professionals or consultants.

Time Required

Two hours and ten minutes.

Materials

- One copy of the Under Pressure Background Sheet for each of the participants.
- One copy of the Under Pressure Decision/Action Form for each of the participants.
- One set of the fifteen Under Pressure Items for each of the participants.
- A pad of paper, a pencil, and fifteen paper clips for each participant.
- A newsprint poster prepared in advance with the information from the Under Pressure Decision/Action Form:

Item	Topic	Priority	Time Allotted	Who Will Handle the Item?	What Will Be Done with the Item?	Reasons?
1	Bill Bother					
2	Glades Brown					
3	Charles					
4	Outline					
5	Mike Pike					
6	Henry McDonald					
7	Dale Blake					
8	Rolf Shouve					
9	Mary					
10	Chris					
11	Batfield					
12	Robin Smith					
13	Hardy Push					
14	Ben Drake					
15	Terry Piper					

Legend: "A" priority = Handle Before the Meeting
"B" priority = Handle Today After the Meeting
"C" priority = Handle Tomorrow
"D" priority = Delegate

- One copy of the Under Pressure Suggested Response Sheet for the facilitator's use.

- A newsprint flip chart and a felt-tipped marker.

- Masking tape for posting newsprint.

Physical Setting

Tables on which participants can spread out their materials, a chair for each participant, and space to conduct small-group discussions.

Process

1. The facilitator introduces the activity and its goals. (Five minutes.)

2. Each participant is given the following materials:

   ▪ A copy of the Under Pressure Background Sheet.

   ▪ A copy of the Under Pressure Decision/Action Form.

   ▪ A set of the fifteen Under Pressure Items.

   ▪ A pad of paper, a pencil, and fifteen paper clips.

   (Five minutes.)

3. The participants are instructed to read the Under Pressure Background Sheet before beginning to work. The facilitator tells the participants that they will have one hour to complete the activity and that they probably will not have time to finish everything in their in-baskets in that amount of time; therefore, they will need to make some choices about priorities and delegation. The facilitator announces the time at which the participants will be expected to have finished setting priorities and delegating tasks. The facilitator then tells the participants to begin working, suggesting that it will save time if they clip notes to the items as they go along indicating how they plan to handle them. (Sixty-five minutes.)

4. At the end of one hour, the facilitator calls time and directs the participants to form subgroups of four or five members each. Each subgroup is instructed to discuss the following topics:

   ▪ Their thoughts and feelings as they worked through the activity.

   ▪ Their criteria for deciding priorities and the importance assigned to each item.

   ▪ How they decided which items they should attend to themselves and which should be delegated.

   (Twenty minutes.)

5. At the end of the discussion period, the facilitator reassembles the total group and posts the newsprint poster listing the in-basket items to be handled. The group uses majority rule to designate each item as "A," "B," "C," or "D" priority and to indicate whether the item should be handled personally or delegated. The facilitator explains that each item will be assigned a priority, as listed on the newsprint poster. "A" priority indicates that the item should be handled before the meeting; "B" priority indicates that the item should be handled

today after the meeting; "C" priority indicates that the item should be handled tomorrow; and "D" priority indicates that the item should be delegated. In addition, the group provides an estimate of the time required to accomplish that item. (Fifteen minutes.)

6. The facilitator leads the group in a concluding discussion based on the following questions:

   - How did your personal style of working help or hinder you during this activity? Did you handle work that was easiest for you or most essential for the company?

   - What other options are available besides do it, delegate it, or file it?

   - How can the most important factors in managing time effectively be summarized?

   - What can you now do differently in prioritizing and delegating?

   (Twenty minutes.)

Variations

- Items can be added or deleted to lengthen or shorten the activity.

- The background situation and items can be modified or rewritten to reflect the work situation of the participants.

- The facilitator may elect to establish pairs or teams, rather than having participants work alone.

- Participants can work together on actual responses to memos, phone calls, and visits.

Submitted by Glenn H. Varney.

Glenn H. Varney, Ph.D., is a professor of management, director of the Master of Organization Development program, and director of the Institute for Organizational Effectiveness (IOE) at Bowling Green State University, Bowling Green, Ohio. He also is the founder of the Self-Directed Work Team Resource Center and president of Management Advisory Associates. Dr. Varney is recognized nationally as an author, educator, and consultant in the field of organization development and change. He has published more than fifty articles and five books, including Goal-Driven Management *and* Building Productive Teams.

UNDER PRESSURE BACKGROUND SHEET

Instructions: The case you are about to study places you into a typical day in the life of an internal organization development (OD) consultant. Using your experience and knowledge of OD, you are challenged to address the various issues that face you. Fifteen situations need your attention. You are to study each situation and decide what action needs to be taken. Use the attached decision/action form to record what you decide to do. Keep in mind that you must try to satisfy your clients' needs without stepping beyond ethical boundaries.

The Rankton Company is a one-billion dollar division of a major company. The company produces auto replacement parts for international markets. The Rankton Division was acquired by the owner two years ago. At the time of the acquisition, Rankton had two new plants under construction in small-town communities. Both facilities were designed as world-class plants, using self-directed work team concepts. The new owners were attracted to Rankton because of these two innovative plants, as well as the fact that Rankton had a forward-looking management team.

The Organization Development Department was also considered a valuable asset by the new owners. The OD department is organized as follows:

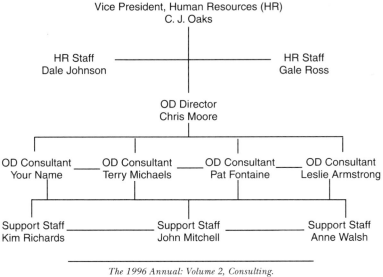

Organization Development at the Rankton Company is designed to offer organization-change consulting to twenty-one plants and a variety of staff departments. The Organization Development Department was organized six years ago with only one person; it expanded to its present size a year ago when you were hired. The culture of Rankton is considered to be unique and forward looking because of the participative style of the leadership. Many problems facing the auto-parts industry are affecting Rankton; however, Rankton has addressed these problems and is achieving considerable success in meeting competition.

You have just arrived back in your office at 10:15 a.m. on Monday, December 4th, following a meeting with your team leader, OD Director Chris Moore. The purpose of the meeting was to report the results of a weekend team-building session you conducted with nine members of the Engineering Department. You started this team-building session at 12:00 noon on Friday and ended Sunday at 4:00 p.m. In the middle of your desk is a stack of messages, correspondence, and fax messages. You have about an hour and fifteen minutes before your next meeting and you must get through the stack on your desk and still allow time to plan for your 11:30 a.m. presentation to the six maintenance supervisors in your largest plant. You want to increase their awareness of what the OD Department does. The outline for this presentation is Item 4.

You have thoroughly enjoyed your work at Rankton and have a good reputation for success. This morning, however, you feel tired and a bit frustrated because the weekend team building resulted in some harsh words being said. You feel that you may have let things get out of control during the day on Sunday.

Nevertheless, you realize you have a lot to do today, so you start through the stack on your desk. **Keep in mind you must make decisions and take action. Record what you decide to do with each item (1-15) on the Under Pressure Decision/Action Form.**

UNDER PRESSURE DECISION/ACTION FORM

Instructions: Following is a list of the items you must consider. Rank each with "A," "B," "C," or "D" priority, decide whether to handle it yourself or delegate it, and list briefly your reasons. Then estimate the time needed in order to complete each item.

Item	Topic	Priority	Time Allotted	Who Will Handle the Item?	What Will Be Done with the Item?	Reasons?
1	Bill Bother					
2	Glades Brown					
3	Charles					
4	Outline					
5	Mike Pike					
6	Henry McDonald					
7	Dale Blake					
8	Rolf Shouve					
9	Mary					
10	Chris					
11	Batfield					
12	Robin Smith					
13	Hardy Push					
14	Ben Drake					
15	Terry Piper					

Legend: "A" priority = Handle Before the Meeting
"B" priority = Handle Today After the Meeting
"C" priority = Handle Tomorrow
"D" priority = Delegate

The 1996 Annual: Volume 2, Consulting.
Copyright © 1996 by Pfeiffer & Company, San Diego, CA.

Under Pressure Item 1

```
┌─────────────────────────────────────┐
│ For    You              │ Urgent ☐  │
│                                      │
│ Date  12/1          Time  4:00 pm    │
│                                      │
│         While You Were Out           │
│ M    Bill Bother                     │
│                                      │
│ Of   Audio-Visual Dept.              │
│                                      │
│ Phone   ext. 2323                    │
│       AREA CODE   NUMBER   EXTENSION │
│  ┌────────────────────────────────┐  │
│  │ Telephoned ☐    Please Call ☒ │  │
│  │ Came To See You ☐  Will Call Again ☐ │  │
│  │ Returned Your Call ☐ Wants To See You ☐ │  │
│  └────────────────────────────────┘  │
│ Message                              │
│ You forgot to include definition     │
│ of the word "Intervention" on        │
│ the transparency you had us          │
│ prepare for you.                     │
│ Signed_____    │
└─────────────────────────────────────┘
```

Note: This refers to an overhead transparency that describes what your department can do to help clients. You need this transparency for your 11:30 a.m. meeting.

UNDER PRESSURE ITEM 2

Memorandum

TO: You
FROM: Glades Brown, *GB* Director of Financial Planning
DATE: December 3rd
RE: Team Building

I have heard that team building is a valuable way to improve the effectiveness and productivity of departments such as mine. I have decided to hold a team-building session on December 8th and wondered if you would facilitate this meeting for me?

Please let me know as soon as possible if you are available. If you are not, I know a person who has facilitated similar sessions for a group at my church who could probably help us.

/dk

I just looked over the data generated as a result of the survey we conducted last week and feel that we have really made substantial progress. This really pleased me.

Just wanted to see if you agree. I've attached the data. Let me know what you think.

Charles
Nov. 28

MEASURES

	Pre-test	Follow-up
Task	3.1	3.21
Process	3.8	3.89
Interpersonal	3.33	3.48
Leadership	2.8	3.1
Performance	3.81	3.83
Total	3.36	3.50

Scale: 1-5
1 = Very Low
5 = Very High

UNDER PRESSURE ITEM 4

OUTLINE

1) Introduction

2) What is OD?

3) Role of the OD Consultant
      Supportive
      Integrative
      Persuasive
      Analytical
      Agreeable

4) Steps in the transformation process

5) Analytical Models
      Sociotechnical
      Force Field
      Emergent Group Behavior

6) Interventions

7) Results from projects

Note: You need to put the finishing touches on the outline for your 11:30 a.m. presentation to a group of six maintenance supervisors from your largest plant. You are concerned about their level of awareness regarding what the OD department does. Look over the attached outline. Does it look OK? Is it too technical? What needs to be changed to meet the situation?

UNDER PRESSURE ITEM 5

For	You	Urgent ☐

Date 12/4   Time 8:00 am

While You Were Out

M   Mike Pike

Of   Engineering Dept.

Phone   ext. 2124
AREA CODE   NUMBER   EXTENSION

Telephoned ☐	Please Call ☐
Came To See You ☐	Will Call Again ☐
Returned Your Call ☐	Wants To See You ☒

Message

What the hell did you

say to Betty that upset

her so much?

_____

Signed_____

Note: Betty is a member of the Engineering Department staff that attended the weekend team-building session. She came to you during the session almost in tears begging you to please not ask her to participate. She said it embarrassed her to talk in front of the group. You agreed to back off. Mike Pike is an aggressive boss who "bores in" when he sees a problem and probably asked Betty what was going on.

UNDER PRESSURE ITEM 6

Memorandum

TO: Chris Moore, OD Director
FROM: Henry McDonald, C.F.O.   *Henry McDonald*
DATE: 3 December
RE: Organization Development

My purpose in writing you is to express my view of the work being performed by your department so that you will have the benefit of this information as you complete your budgeting for next year.

Quite frankly I have always viewed what your department does as a "frill" because it does not, in any way that I can see, contribute to the "bottom line." From all the reports I have heard most of what you do I would classify as "soft management."

To be more specific somehow you have aroused several of my department heads and have piqued their interest in conducting meetings they call "team building." I refer, for example, to Glades Brown who has scheduled December 8th for team building with one of your staff. She is sold on the idea and no amount of persuasion on my part seems to change her mind.

I want you to give me a report that shows me just how much this type of effort contributes to reducing costs and making us more efficient. Please have this to me by December 6th.

cc: "Your Name"
/jk

FAX TRANSMITTAL SHEET

Rankton Corporation
Forward Plant

Confidential

To: "Your Name"

From: Dale Blake, Plant Manager

Re: Pat Barnes

Please send Pat Barnes' Myers-Briggs test results to me today. We are considering Pat for a promotion and this information will help us in our decision.

Note: The Myers-Briggs test is a personality inventory that was used in a team-building meeting with a production coordinator in the Forward Plant.

UNDER PRESSURE ITEM 8

Creative Design Changes Group, Ltd.
400 Front Level Rd.
New York, NY 10001
216-888-8818

Mr./Ms. "Your Name"
OD Consultant
Rankton Company

Dear Mr./Ms. "Your Name"

We have heard great things about your company's work in QWL. We are specialists in quality-of-work-life (QWL) installation, and we have a five-step installation process that guarantees success.

An associate of mine and I will be in your area on December 5th and would like to stop by to show you what we can offer your organization.

If we don't hear from you, we'll plan to stop by at 11:30 a.m. Please let us know if this conflicts with your schedule.

Sincerely,

Rolf Shouve
Senior Partner
/st

Note: Rankton has two well-developed self-directed work sites to which these consultants probably are referring.

MESSAGE:

Francis Jones from the Local
Chapter of the M.J.S. Society
called and would like you to
address the group at the
January 7th meeting on the
subject of "Selling Staff on
System Change." Needs an
answer today.

Mary

UNDER PRESSURE ITEM 10

You promised to look over the attached survey that I want to use to measure "employee attitude" in my 200-person plant. I need your comments today.

Thanks,
Plant Manager

OPINION SURVEY

The purpose of this survey is to collect your opinions on a number of things going on around the plant. Please give us your honest opinion by checking the box that most closely represents your viewpoint. When you are finished, put this in the envelope provided and give it to your supervisor.

	I agree with the statement.	I disagree with the statement.
1) The quality of work life here is good.	☐	☐
2) My pay is good.	☐	☐
3) My benefits are fine.	☐	☐
4) I have a good supervisor.	☐	☐
5) The productivity of the plant is high.	☐	☐
6) Cooperation among my fellow workers is good.	☐	☐
7) Working conditions are good.	☐	☐
8) The plant is well managed.	☐	☐
9) I have a future here.	☐	☐
10) We make the best products in the business.	☐	☐

You may sign your name if you wish.

The 1996 Annual: Volume 2, Consulting.
Copyright © 1996 by Pfeiffer & Company, San Diego, CA.

UNDER PRESSURE ITEM 11

> Call Batfield plant manager!

Note: This is a penciled note to yourself from your morning meeting with the OD Director. The Batfield plant manager wants to talk about installing self-directed work teams as a way to eliminate one "full layer" of management. You need to call him before 11:30 a.m. The reason that self-directed work teams and other quality tools meet opposition is that they are seen as another form of downsizing. You want to explain how self-directed work teams work in the two successful plants, and perhaps offer tours of those plants. What approach will you use when you talk to him about it?

Under Pressure Item 12

Situation: It is 10:45 a.m. Robin Smith appears at your door and asks for a "minute" of your time to interpret the results of the Teamwork Survey data (attached) that you sent last week.

You explain that you have only a few minutes but will be glad to assist. Robin sits down; what do you say?

Section I—SUMMARY DATA

Overall Results

Team N = 11

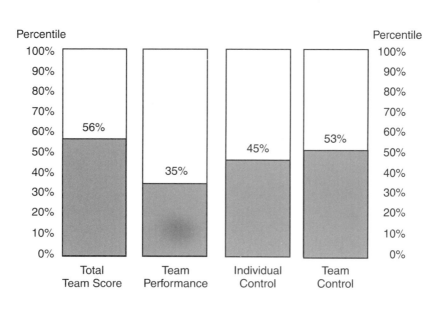

Section II—SUMMARY DATA

Effectiveness Profile

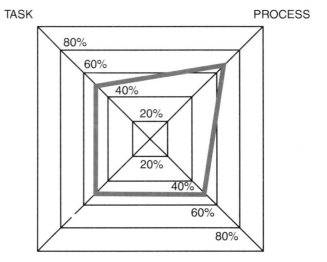

Task = 51%
Process = 63%
Interpersonal = 49%
Leadership = 49%

UNDER PRESSURE ITEM 13

For **You** Urgent ☐

Date **12/4** Time **8:30 am**

While You Were Out

M **Hardy Push**

Of **Marketing**

Phone **ext. 2262**
AREA CODE   NUMBER   EXTENSION

Telephoned ☐ Please Call ☒
Came To See You ☐ Will Call Again ☐
Returned Your Call ☐ Wants To See You ☒

Message
Could you have the conflict-
resolution plan ("model") to me
by noon today?

Signed_____

Note: Hardy Push had previously requested help in managing a conflict situation between two members of his department. You need to quickly sketch out an approach he can use to resolve the problem and get it to him before you leave at 11:30 a.m.

For	You		Urgent ☐

Date _____ Time _____

While You Were Out

M _____Ben Drake_____

Of _Drake and Drake Employment_____

Phone __1-800-800-1000_____
AREA CODE   NUMBER   EXTENSION

Telephoned ☐	Please Call ☒
Came To See You ☐	Will Call Again ☐
Returned Your Call ☐	Wants To See You ☐

Message _____

Please call a.s.a.p. Has

interesting response from

IVT Corp.

Signed_____

Note: Ben Drake called you about two months ago about a position with IVT Corporation. You expressed interest, sent your résumé, and two weeks ago spent a day interviewing for the position of Director of Organization Effectiveness. The position pays about 25% more than you are currently earning.

The 1996 Annual: Volume 2, Consulting.
Copyright © 1996 by Pfeiffer & Company, San Diego, CA.

UNDER PRESSURE ITEM 15

Situation: The phone rings while you are in your office. It's 11:00 a.m. The person on the line is the Vice President of Manufacturing, Terry Piper, who wants to know why people are so resistant to new ideas and changes being made in several of the plants. Terry asks, "Isn't there some program or training that can be used to break down this resistance?"

Under Pressure Suggested Response Sheet

Item	Topic	Priority	Time Allotted	Who Will Handle the Item?	What Will Be Done with the Item?	Reasons?
1	Bill Bother	A	5 min.	Me	Call with definition	Need for meeting; it's in my head
2	Glades Brown	B	10 min.	Me	Call after meeting	Importance of the department
3	Charles	C	5 min.	Me	Call and set up meeting to discuss	Completed—just needs reaction
4	Outline	A	10 min.	Me	Immediate action (if it needs to be retyped)	Language change
5	Mike Pike	B	10 min.	Me	Call	Already over; can call after meeting; ethically can't divulge this kind of information if trust is to be upheld
6	Henry McDonald	A	5 min.	Me and delegate	Call OD Director and get staff working on data collection	C.F.O. needs to back the OD department
7	Dale Blake	B	5 min.	Delegate	If policy is to share information, send it; if not, call and explain why	Information is needed for promotion; if it's an ethical issue, it needs to be explained
8	Rolf Shouve	B	5 min.	Delegate	Staff to call and schedule at a convenient time	Fit into my schedule without being too reactive

Item	Topic	Priority	Time Allotted	Who Will Handle the Item?	What Will Be Done with the Item?	Reasons?
9	Mary	B	5 min.	Delegate	Have staff call and give an answer	I've already talked to Mary and can call personally another time
10	Chris	B	15 min.	Me	Read after the meeting and make comments	I promised
11	Batfield	A	10 min.	Me	Call	Per OD Director, need to call before the meeting
12	Robin Smith	A	10 min.	Me	Explain what it means and set another time to talk after the meeting	The person is there!
13	Hardy Push	A	15 min.	Me and delegate	Before 11:30, sketch out and have staff deliver with note	Previous request; important for department
14	Ben Drake	B*	10 min.	Me	Call after meeting	Need to keep this job for now
15	Terry Piper	A	10 min.	Me	Give a quick answer and set up a later meeting or agree to send information	Important person to have behind us

Legend: "A" priority = Handle Before the Meeting
"B" priority = Handle Today After the Meeting
"C" priority = Handle Tomorrow
"D" priority = Delegate

* Or C, depending on how interested I am

566. PERFORMANCE UNLIMITED: SOLVING PROBLEMS AS A TEAM

Goals

- To encourage the development of group problem-solving skills.
- To encourage the development of group decision-making skills.
- To heighten participants' awareness of how group dynamics affects teamwork.

Group Size

All members of an intact work team.

Time Required

Approximately one hour.

Materials

- One copy of the Performance Unlimited Handout for each participant.
- A pencil and a portable writing surface for each participant.
- A newsprint flip chart and a felt-tipped marker for the facilitator's use.

Physical Setting

Any room in which the group can work comfortably. Movable chairs should be provided.

The 1996 Annual: Volume 2, Consulting.
Copyright © 1996 by Pfeiffer & Company, San Diego, CA.

Process

1. The facilitator explains the goals of the activity. (Five minutes.)

2. Each participant is given a copy of the Performance Unlimited Handout and is asked to read the instructions. The facilitator notes that all of the instructions are on the handout. (Five minutes.)

3. At the end of five minutes, the facilitator instructs the participants that they will have fifteen minutes to make their rankings. (Fifteen minutes.)

4. After fifteen minutes, the facilitator calls time. The spokesperson for the team reports the order in which the team decided to address the problems and provides a brief rationale for the order chosen. The facilitator records the ranking and reasons on the flip chart. (Ten minutes.)

5. The facilitator elicits discussion with questions such as the following:

   - How satisfied are you with the final ranking?

   - How do the decisions reflect the ideas and viewpoints of all members? What process did you use to arrive at the ranking and to determine which ideas to incorporate and which to exclude?

   - What elements of the process pleased you? Displeased you?

   - As you worked together, did some members' opinions conflict? If so, how were the conflicts handled?

   - What are the benefits of working together as a team to solve problems?

   - What are some drawbacks to team efforts in solving problems? How can you overcome some of these drawbacks?

   - How are these five issues handled in this team? How could they be improved?

   (Twenty minutes.)

Variations

- This activity could be used as a team-building activity or as a warm-up to solving a real work issue or problem.

- The scenario in the handout can be revised to reflect actual situations that a team is experiencing.

- The activity may be used with a heterogeneous group.

Submitted by James W. Kinneer.

James W. Kinneer, M.A., *is a support services supervisor at Indiana Hospital, Indiana, Pennsylvania. He has developed and presented numerous human resource development activities specific to the needs of the healthcare and hospitality industries. Presently he serves as chair of the Certifying Board for Dietary Managers. He frequently contributes to national publications on the topics of managing skills, quality improvement, team building, and customer service.*

Performance Unlimited Handout

Instructions: You are a member of Performance Unlimited, a team of highly skilled (and well-paid) performance consultants. Read the scenario below and decide the order in which the five work issues should be addressed by the new team leader. All of the information available is included in this handout.

Read this handout, and feel free to make notes about your ideas. Rank the issues individually. Then the group will rank the issues and provide a rationale for the ranking. Choose a member who will serve as spokesperson. You will have fifteen minutes to make your decisions.

Scenario

Pat has accepted a position as the team leader for a team of computer programmers. This is Pat's first leadership position. The team includes five other members:

- Chris is a twenty-year company veteran with a reputation for being difficult.
- Terry is a competent programmer but lacks self-confidence.
- Kim is soft spoken but impatient.
- Dale is a dynamic person with questionable technical skills.
- Kelly is a recent college graduate with many new ideas and not much follow through.

Certain issues are present with this team, and Pat must decide on the priorities for addressing these issues.

Issue: Communication

Kelly is full of good ideas but fails to communicate effectively with other members of the team. Even when Kelly does try to communicate, Chris and Kim refuse to listen and dismiss the ideas as those of a newcomer.

Issue: Power

Chris is the informal team leader. Kim and Dale always check in with Chris before following through on Pat's instructions. Kelly disrupts the team by constantly challenging Chris.

The 1996 Annual: Volume 2, Consulting.
Copyright © 1996 by Pfeiffer & Company, San Diego, CA.

Issue: Trust

Chris and Kelly do not trust each other and spend too much time trying to determine each other's motives. In conflicts, Kim and Dale defend Chris's actions while Terry supports Kelly.

Issue: Roles

The team seems to immerse itself in projects without well-defined roles. Frequently, several people work on one part of the project, leaving other parts of the project unattended. Despite this disorganization, the team always manages to deliver the finished project on time.

Issue: Equality of Effort

Often Kelly and Terry put in extra hours. Kim and Chris are willing to do their share but are not willing to work after hours. Dale often leaves early, leaving other members of the team to finish the work.

Pat should address the team's issues in this order:

Individual Ranking	Group Ranking	Rationale
1.	1.	1.
2.	2.	2.
3.	3.	3.
4.	4.	4.
5.	5.	5.

567. Taking Your Creative Pulse: Enhancing Creativity at Work

Goals

- To acquaint the participants with the six major components of creativity in the workplace.

- To offer each participant an opportunity to assess the degree of creativity with which he or she approaches work.

- To offer a forum for sharing ideas about how to become more creative at work.

- To encourage the participants to take first steps toward becoming more creative in their work.

Group Size

Eighteen to forty-two participants. Six subgroups are formed during the activity.

Time Required

Approximately two hours.

Materials

- A copy of the Taking Your Creative Pulse Quiz Sheet for each of the participants.

- A copy of the Taking Your Creative Pulse Interpretation Sheet for each of the participants.

- A copy of the Taking Your Creative Pulse Action Plan for each of the participants.

The 1996 Annual: Volume 2, Consulting.
Copyright © 1996 by Pfeiffer & Company, San Diego, CA.

- A pencil for each participant.
- A clipboard or other portable writing surface for each participant.
- A flip chart and a felt-tipped marker for each subgroup.
- A roll of masking tape for each subgroup (for posting newsprint).

Physical Setting

A room large enough to allow the six subgroups to work without disturbing one another. Movable chairs must be available, and each subgroup must have access to wall space for posting newsprint.

Process

1. The facilitator announces the goals of the activity.

2. Each participant is given a copy of the Taking Your Creative Pulse Quiz Sheet, a pencil, and a clipboard or other portable writing surface and is asked to complete the quiz according to the instructions provided. (Ten minutes.)

3. After everyone has completed the quiz, the facilitator distributes copies of the Taking Your Creative Pulse Interpretation Sheet and walks the participants through the contents of the sheet, eliciting and answering questions as necessary. (Fifteen minutes.)

4. The facilitator designates six work stations in the room, clarifying each as representing one of the six creativity components (a "Work Quality" work station, a "Future Orientation" work station, and so on). The participants are invited to form six subgroups at those work stations, each participant choosing the creativity component in which he or she would most like to improve. After participants have made their choices, the facilitator may need to ask for volunteers to leave one subgroup and join another so that each subgroup has at least three members. Once the subgroups have been formed, the facilitator gives each a flip chart, a felt-tipped marker, and a roll of masking tape. (Five to ten minutes.)

5. Each of the six subgroups is asked to spend fifteen minutes generating ways to enhance one's creativity in that particular creativity component. The facilitator stipulates that the ideas selected should be ones that can be used in a variety of professions and industries and suggests using the brief action ideas on the Interpretation Sheet as a springboard for other ideas. Each subgroup is told to list final ideas on newsprint and to choose a spokesperson to spend no more

Pfeiffer & Company

than five minutes presenting those ideas to the total group later. (Fifteen minutes.)

6. The six subgroups take turns posting and presenting their ideas. As presentations are made, the facilitator encourages clarification, discussion, and the generation of additional ideas. The facilitator also invites participants to jot down any ideas that are particularly appealing to them. (Approximately thirty minutes.)

7. The facilitator leads a total-group discussion of the activity by asking the following questions:

   - What did you learn about your own creativity? What information came as a surprise?

   - How did you use your creativity to come up with ideas for your component (Work Quality, Future Orientation, or whatever)?

   - What have you learned about workplace creativity in general?

   - In what ways does an organization benefit when its employees are creative in their work? In what ways do the employees benefit?

   - How will you use what you have learned from this activity to enhance your creativity at work?

   (Fifteen minutes.)

8. Copies of the Taking Your Creative Pulse Action Plan are distributed. Each participant is asked to decide on a first step that he or she will take to increase creativity in one of the six creativity components and to complete the portions of the plan that deal with that first step. (Ten minutes.)

9. The participants are asked to assemble into pairs, and the partners are instructed to spend ten minutes (five per person) discussing their first steps and sharing reactions as well as ideas about how to break down barriers to success, how to obtain any needed resources or help, and so on. (Ten minutes.)

10. Before dismissing the group, the facilitator recommends that the participants complete the entire plan on their own and review it from time to time to assess progress.

Variations

- This activity may be used as part of a team-building intervention with an ongoing work group. In this case the entire group works on ideas for increasing creativity in each of the six creativity components, with an emphasis on using creativity in connection with the group's specific tasks.

- If time permits, the participants may share their first steps within their subgroups or in the total group.

- The participants may be asked to suggest other components that they believe to be critical to creativity.

- The facilitator may begin the activity by asking each participant to think either of a time when he or she was creative or a person that he or she believes is creative. Subsequently, the facilitator may ask each participant to identify the creativity factors involved; then later the participants may be instructed to link these factors to the creativity components.

Submitted by Stephen R. Grossman.

Stephen R. Grossman *is the president of Double Dominance, Inc., of Maple Shade, New Jersey, a company that specializes in creative decision making and executive problem solving. He has taught, trained, and consulted in creativity, problem solving, and corporate innovation for the past decade. His fifteen years of industrial experience as a paper and fiber physicist included the directorship of new-product development for a Fortune 500 company. Mr. Grossman is the author of many papers on the relationship between creativity and technical problem solving, as well as the coauthor of* Innovation, Inc.: Unlocking Creativity in the Workplace.

TAKING YOUR CREATIVE PULSE QUIZ SHEET

Creativity in the workplace consists of six major components. Your responses to the items in the six categories below, which correspond to the six components, will help you to "take your creative pulse," revealing how creative you are in your work. Then you can consider and plan ways in which you might change your behavior so that you can realize your creative potential.

In each of categories A through F, place a check mark in the blank by the numbered statement that best describes your behavior and attitude. *Check only one numbered statement in each category.*

A. WORK QUALITY

_____ 1. I work on projects that excite me. My work is an expression of what I value in life.

_____ 2. I work hard. My work is interesting, but I don't count on it for excitement or pleasure.

_____ 3. At work I do what I have to do. I keep my job and my home life separate. I find fun and excitement during weekends, holidays, and vacations.

B. FUTURE ORIENTATION

_____ 1. I spend time dreaming about what *could be* rather than what *is.* I often fantasize about the future.

_____ 2. I sometimes dream about the future but quickly dismiss this pursuit as wishful thinking.

_____ 3. I want to get the job done. Fantasizing about what could be is a waste of valuable time.

The 1996 Annual: Volume 2, Consulting.
Copyright © 1996 by Pfeiffer & Company, San Diego, CA.

C. COMPROMISE

_____ 1. I think compromise in my work is an admission of my failure to stand up for my own ideas.

_____ 2. Of course compromise is not ideal, but it is a practical approach to living harmoniously in this world.

_____ 3. Any reasonable person looks to compromise as the basic tool for getting anything done.

D. BELIEFS

_____ 1. I believe my own conclusions are important. I listen to other opinions but rely mostly on my own research and/or instincts to make decisions.

_____ 2. I frequently shift my point of view based on negative input from people with experience.

_____ 3. I take my ideas, beliefs, and approaches from well-known authorities and experts. I see no reason to "reinvent the wheel."

E. INTERESTS

_____ 1. I read a lot. Much of what I read is unconnected to my work. I do well in games based on general knowledge or knowledge of trivia.

_____ 2. Except for newspapers and the occasional novel, most of my reading is in work-related areas.

_____ 3. I don't have time to read for pleasure. I get the news from newspapers and television.

F. KNOWLEDGE

_____ 1. I know my field well, not just the how-to but also the historical underpinnings and the beliefs of many lesser-known contributors.

_____ 2. I can't keep up with everything, but I subscribe to journals and make a point of reading relevant articles.

_____ 3. I don't have time to read all that I should in my field, but I rely on one or two key people for information.

Taking Your Creative Pulse Interpretation Sheet

A. Work Quality

There is a big difference between having an idea and making it a reality. Bringing new ideas to life calls for motivation. Motivation evokes passion and makes you persevere despite naysayers' reactions. There are lots of motivations—money, power, fear of losing your job—but the ideal creative situation is one in which the work itself provides your motivation—when you love what you do.

If you chose...	Then...
1	You are fortunate to experience such excitement in your work. Keep using that excitement to build and exercise your own creativity.
2	You might want to ask yourself how you can make your work more stimulating.
3	You might be happier in another line of work. If a job change is out of the question, consider a hobby that excites you.

B. Future Orientation

The power of fantasy is often dismissed by businesspeople, particularly crisis managers, who spend much of their time reacting to things that go wrong. Yet look at dreamers like Walt Disney, one of the most successful entrepreneurs of our age. Surely Disney has shown us that fantasy and business are not mutually exclusive. And if you cannot envision what your future will look like in your organization, it is very difficult to devise creative ways to get there.

If you chose...	Then...
1	You've seen the future; therefore, you've taken the first step toward creating that future.
2	You might want to start allowing yourself to dream; this process actually gives focus to your ideas. You might even ask your children or some of your more imaginative friends to work with you.
3	Although taking life "one day at a time" is often good advice, this approach can be limiting. Without seeing the value of what could be beyond today, it is almost impossible to create.

C. COMPROMISE

Compromise is often touted as a win-win solution. In fact, it can result in a lose-lose situation; everyone is asked to give up something for the sake of harmony. For highly creative people, compromise is unthinkable. It is precisely because innovators have been unwilling to compromise that they have created great win-win systems in which all parties involved get what they want.

If you chose...	Then...
1	This is a healthy attitude provided you meet the other criteria for creativity; knowledge, for example, is essential.
2	Compromise does not always end in harmony; sometimes people end up dissatisfied. You might want to try other approaches by asking yourself how others could get what they want without forcing you to compromise your values.
3	You might consider reexamining your point of view. Compromise can be appealing because it gets things done, but it might also keep you from promoting your ideas.

D. Beliefs

Emerson defined genius as knowing that what is true on the inside for you is true on the outside for everyone else. He said, "Speak your latent conviction and it shall be the universal sense, lest in good time a stranger come along with uncommon good sense and say what you have thought about all along and you be forced with shame to take your opinions from another." Believing your own ideas are important means not being afraid to promote them even when you are confronted by people who look at them negatively.

If you chose...	Then...
1	You believe in your own ideas and your own conclusions, and that belief is essential for creativity.
2	You might want to work on trusting your instincts more. For twenty-four hours try not to be negative about your ideas; try building up what's good about them instead. Initially try offering them only to supporters—people who will react positively to them. After twenty-four hours you can subject your ideas to potentially negative reactions. By then you will probably be able to accept and integrate negative input, thereby making your ideas even stronger.
3	You might want to allow yourself to think about things, to form your own opinions before reading what the experts say. You might be astonished to discover that your conclusions are better than anyone else's.

E. Interests

One definition of creativity is being able to find connections between things that have not been previously associated. The more you know about fields that are not related to your work, the more likely you are to make the connections that yield wonderful innovations.

If you chose...	Then...
1	You have a characteristic of every highly creative person: You are an omnivorous reader of anything that catches your eye.
2	You might want to broaden your interest base. You could expand your reading to unaccustomed fields, anything that is different and seems interesting. Do not worry about relevance; your mind will make the necessary connections.
3	It might be worth your while to try obtaining your information from a variety of sources. You might also want to set aside a little time to read for pleasure.

F. Knowledge

Creative breakthroughs generally come from people who know a lot about their respective fields. You've probably heard the story of Land's invention of the Polaroid camera. His little daughter suggested that he put the darkroom in the camera so he would have more time to spend with her. Land's daughter is cited as the inspiration for the Polaroid—and she was—but it's important to note that she was not the inventor. Her father took his cue from her and used his knowledge of photography to turn her vision into reality.

A solid knowledge of a field is basic to thinking creatively within that realm. Many businesses promote "creativity by musical chairs"—transferring personnel from one department to another in hopes that such changes in venue will make them more creative. This approach rarely works, because people are asked to operate without a base of accumulated knowledge. They can come up with ideas—the necessary inspiration—but it takes someone with a strong background in the field to act on that inspiration.

If you chose...	Then...
1	You have the knowledge base that allows you to work creatively.
2	You might want to delve deeper into your field and strive to understand the concepts as well as the day-to-day details. Consider a speed-reading course so that you can accelerate your learning.
3	You might want to rethink the extent to which you are executing other people's ideas. Even if these people are experts in the field, you might be able to add to their ideas by making time to read.

TAKING YOUR CREATIVE PULSE ACTION PLAN

Creativity Component I Want to Work on	First Step I Will Take	By When	Whose Help I Will Need
Work Quality			
Future Orientation			
Compromise			
Beliefs			
Interests			
Knowledge			

568. PBJ CORPORATION: USING IDEA-GENERATING TOOLS

Goals

- To acquaint participants with two idea-generating tools often used by groups during problem solving: brainstorming and the nominal group technique.
- To offer the participants an opportunity to practice using these tools by applying them to a case-study problem.

Group Size

Two to five subgroups of four to seven members each.

Time Required

One hour and thirty minutes to one hour and forty minutes.

Materials

- A copy of the PBJ Corporation Information and Task Sheet for each participant.
- Blank paper and a pencil for each participant.
- A newsprint flip chart and a felt-tipped marker for each subgroup.
- A roll of masking tape for each subgroup (for posting newsprint).

Physical Setting

A room large enough so that the subgroups can work without disturbing one another. (The subgroups should be placed as far apart as possible.) Each subgroup should have a table, movable chairs, and access to plenty of wall space for posting newsprint.

Process

1. The facilitator explains that the activity will concentrate on two ways of generating ideas during the process of group problem solving. Each participant is given a copy of the PBJ Corporation Information and Task Sheet and is instructed to read the handout. (Five to ten minutes.)

2. The facilitator elicits and answers questions about the task, ensuring that the participants understand how to use brainstorming and the nominal group technique. (Ten minutes.)

3. The participants are asked to form approximately equal-sized subgroups. Each subgroup is assigned to its own table and is given a newsprint flip chart, a felt-tipped marker, and a roll of masking tape. In addition, each participant is given blank paper and a pencil. (Five minutes.)

4. The facilitator tells the subgroups that they have forty minutes to complete the task, suggests that they spend approximately ten minutes on each factor (Methods, Personnel, Materials, and Machinery), and asks them to begin. The facilitator remains available while the subgroups work to provide any needed clarification or assistance. Also, the facilitator reminds the subgroups of the remaining time at ten-minute intervals. (Forty minutes.)

5. After forty minutes the facilitator calls time and asks the members of each subgroup to spend ten minutes identifying the idea they like best in each category (Methods, Personnel, Materials, and Machinery) and selecting a spokesperson to share those four ideas with the total group. (Ten minutes.)

6. The facilitator reassembles the total group and asks the spokespersons to take turns reporting ideas. (Five minutes.)

7. The facilitator leads a concluding discussion by asking the following questions:

- What were your reactions to the two tools, brainstorming and the nominal group technique?

- What were the advantages and disadvantages of brainstorming? What were the advantages and disadvantages of the nominal group technique? Which tool did you prefer and why?

- How would the task have been different if you had not been given the four categories of Methods, Personnel, Materials, and Machinery? What can you learn from that?

- What have you learned about the tools of brainstorming and the nominal group technique as an aid to problem solving?

- How might you use these tools in your own work group? What benefits might your group derive from them?

(Fifteen to twenty minutes.)

Variations

- The time for using brainstorming and the nominal group technique may be cut from forty to twenty minutes, five minutes per category (Methods, Personnel, Materials, Machinery).

- The facilitator may give the four categories (Methods, Personnel, Materials, Machinery) to only half of the subgroups. Then the processing may include a question about the differences in the task for those who were given the categories and those who were not.

- If the activity is used with ongoing teams, after the last step each team may be asked to generate its own case using the same four categories (Methods, Personnel, Materials, and Machinery) and applying the tools of brainstorming and the nominal group technique.

Submitted by Phil Ventresca and Tom Flynn.

Phil Ventresca is president and founder of Advanced Management Services, Inc., a management consultancy in Stoughton, Massachusetts. The firm specializes in total quality, process improvement, customer service, and organizational development. Mr. Ventresca is the coauthor of High-Performance Quality, People and Process: Tools for Continuous

Improvement, *and is the publisher of a quarterly newsletter,* Transformations™. *In addition, he developed a model for continuous improvement called* High-Performance Quality™, *which combines management development, process control, and scientific quality methods. He serves as an adjunct faculty member for Boston University Metropolitan College Corporate Education Center.*

Tom Flynn *is president and founder of T.A. Flynn & Associates and is a project consultant at Advanced Management Services, Inc. Mr. Flynn delivers leadership, motivation, and change training for national and international organizations. He consults in Japanese/United States business negotiations, serving as the United States Branch Chief and General Secretary for the Kyokushin organization. Coauthor of* High-Performance Quality, People and Process: Tools for Continuous Improvement, *he also serves as an adjunct faculty member at Boston University Metropolitan College Corporate Education Center.*

PBJ Corporation Information and Task Sheet

The Situation

You are part of a management team for the PBJ Corporation, which produces peanut butter and jelly sandwiches. One of PBJ's largest customers is MegaSnack, a company that supplies hundreds of vending machines across the city.

A number of businesses that rent MegaSnack's machines have reported that customers are dissatisfied with "too little peanut butter" on the sandwiches. Consequently, MegaSnack is unhappy with PBJ's current performance and has announced that it will look for another supplier if PBJ cannot rectify the situation.

You and your fellow managers have been tasked with determining possible reasons *why so many sandwiches have less peanut butter than Mega-Snack has specified they should.* Later a task force will investigate these possible reasons and recommend actions to solve the problem.

MegaSnack's Specifications

Here are the specifications that MegaSnack has given PBJ to use for each sandwich:

- White bread, two 1.0-ounce slices per sandwich;
- Grape jelly, 1.0 ounce per sandwich;
- Smooth peanut butter, 1.0 ounce per sandwich; and
- Total sandwich weight 4.0 ounces, +/-0.25-ounce variance.

PBJ's Process for Making Sandwiches

The white bread is purchased from a vendor that slices to exact weight specifications of 1.0 ounce per slice. The weight of the bread is checked randomly at delivery; so far weight variance has been extremely rare and virtually insignificant.

The bread is set up on the assembly line so that sandwiches can be made. A tube dispenser system applies jelly in a 1.0-ounce amount to every other slice of bread on the assembly line (one slice has jelly, the next one does not, and so on). Each application is weighed electronically by computer and automatically ejected. The dispenser system is checked for calibration hourly and tuned daily.

After the application of jelly, the bread continues down the assembly line. Numerous on-site checks have shown that each sandwich meets MegaSnack's weight specifications up to the point at which peanut butter is added. Peanut butter in the amount of 1.0 ounce is applied and spread manually to each slice of bread that has not had jelly added. (A number of automatic machine tubes have been tried for dispensing and spreading the peanut butter, but all have had a tendency to clog and have been abandoned.)

Due to equipment restrictions, the weight of the peanut butter is not checked until after the peanut butter has been applied to the bread. The 1.0-ounce spoons used to measure the peanut butter are made to PBJ's specifications by a number of suppliers. With each application each spoon is first leveled with a knife and then scraped clean.

After the peanut butter has been spread, the slices of bread with jelly and the slices with peanut butter are put together manually to form sandwiches. Then each completed sandwich is weighed. MegaSnack has allowed for a total sandwich weight variance of 0.25 ounce, but PBJ's sandwiches are frequently 0.20 ounce underweight, with all of the variance attributable to peanut butter.

Organizing for the Task

You and your fellow managers are to come up with four newsprint lists of ideas, each list covering one of the major factors affecting this process problem: *Methods, Personnel, Materials,* and *Machinery.* If you think other factors might be affecting the process in addition to these four, create lists for them as well.

To create your lists for the factors of *Methods* and *Personnel,* use the idea-generating tool known as "brainstorming." To create your lists for *Materials* and *Machinery,* use a different idea-generating tool known as the "nominal group technique." Descriptions of these techniques follow.

Brainstorming generates a large number of ideas quickly by encouraging people to build on one another's thoughts:

- Clarify the objective.
- Call out ideas in turn around the group (one idea per person per turn).
- Record each idea on a flip chart.
- Build on and expand the ideas of others.

- Pass when an idea does not come quickly to mind.
- Resist stopping when ideas slow down.
- After all ideas have been exhausted, clarify each idea and eliminate exact duplicates.
- Categorize similar ideas.

Nominal Group Technique *generates a large number of ideas by encouraging people to create lists independently and then share list contents:*

- Clarify the objective.
- Have each person list as many ideas as possible.
- Take turns sharing the contents of individual lists, one idea at a time. If someone has already mentioned an idea, the person reading skips that idea and goes to the next.
- Record each idea on a flip chart.
- When a person's list is exhausted, he or she passes or contributes a new idea.
- After all ideas have been listed, clarify each idea and eliminate exact duplicates.
- Categorize similar ideas.

Introduction

to the Inventories, Questionnaires, and Surveys Section

Inventories, questionnaires, and surveys are feedback tools that help respondents to understand how a particular theory applies to their own lives. Understanding the theories involved in the dynamics of their own group situations increases respondents' involvement. Instruments allow the facilitator of a small group to focus the energies and time of the respondents on the most appropriate material and also to direct, to some extent, the matters that are dealt with in a session. In this way, the facilitator can ensure that the issues worked on are crucial, existing ones, rather than the less important ones that the members may introduce to avoid grappling with the more uncomfortable issues.

The contents of the Inventories, Questionnaires, and Surveys section are provided for training and development purposes. These instruments are not intended for in-depth personal growth, psychodiagnostic, or therapeutic work. Instead, they are intended for use in training groups; for demonstration purposes; to generate data for training or organization development sessions; and for other group applications in which the trainer, consultant, or facilitator helps respondents to use the data generated by an instrument for achieving some form of progress.

Each instrument includes the theory necessary for understanding, presenting, and using it. All interpretive information, scales or inventory forms, and scoring sheets are also provided for each instrument. In addition, Pfeiffer & Company publishes all of the reliability and validity data contributed by the authors of instruments; if readers want additional information on reliability and validity, they are encouraged to contact instrument authors directly. (Authors' addresses and telephone numbers appear in the Contributors list that follows the Presentation and Discussion Resources section.)

Other assessment tools that address certain goals (and experiential learning activities and presentation/discussion resources to accompany them) can be located by using our comprehensive *Reference Guide to Handbooks and Annuals*. This book, which is updated regularly, indexes all of the *Annuals* and all of the *Handbooks of Structured Experiences* that we have published to date. With each revision, the *Reference Guide* becomes a complete, up-to-date, and easy-to-use resource for selecting appropriate materials from *all* of the *Annuals* and Handbooks.

The 1996 Annual: Volume 2, Consulting includes three assessment tools in the following categories:

Groups and Teams

U.S. Style Teams (USST) Inventory, by Gaylord Reagan (page 141)

Consulting and Facilitating

Working with Resistance to Change: The Support for Change Questionnaire, by Rick Maurer (page 161)

The High-Performance Factors Inventory: Assessing Work-Group Management and Practices, by Robert P. Crosby (page 175)

U.S. STYLE TEAMS (USST) INVENTORY

Gaylord Reagan

Abstract: Research has shown that the use of organizational teams, which works well in the Japanese culture, often does not work well in organizations in the United States. The characteristics of the predominant U.S. culture do not support—and, in fact, may work against—effective team functioning. For particular reasons, quality-circle teams, management teams, and cross-functional teams tend not to be as effective as expected.

The shamrock team, with a small core membership and others who join and leave as the need arises, is more suited to the needs of U.S. organizations. However, three team norms—that work with, rather than against, U.S. culture—must be adopted before even this type of team can be effective. The U.S. Style Teams Inventory measures the extent to which the respondent's organization supports and implements the three critical norms.

Despite years of caution from experts (Dean & Bowen, 1995; Floyd & Woolridge, 1994; Krishnan, Shani, Grant, & Baer, 1993; Lawler, 1994; Miner, 1974; Muczyk & Reimann, 1987; Reger, Gustafson, Demarie, & Mullane, 1995; Sitkin, Sutcliffe, & Schroeder, 1995; Szwergold, 1992), management gurus and organizations in the United States demonstrate an unquestioned faith in the ability of teams to produce competitive advantages while adding value for customers. Although they have much to offer in organizations, teams may have been oversold, particularly when they are utilized in reengineered, reinvented, and restructured organizations. After reviewing the results of a survey of 4,500 teams in fifty U.S. organizations, Nahavandi and Aranda (1994) report that:

> Despite the many success stories on the use of teams..., success has been uneven. Recently, there has been much frustration on the part of managers and employees...that teams might not be the panacea everyone hoped for, especially at senior management levels. As a result, many employees feel that teams are a waste of time. The time spent on developing trust and agreement does not translate easily into high creativity and performance.... Overall, teams have not done consistently for the U.S. what they did and are continuing to do for Japan. Dramatic improvements rarely emerge with increased use of teams. There is little evidence that employees are more creative or more motivated when they work in teams. (p. 59)

CHARACTERISTICS OF U.S. CULTURE

Nahavandi and Aranda (1994, pp. 60-61) contend that unhappy results with teams often can be attributed to characteristics of U.S. culture. They identify seven cultural features that appear to diminish the payoffs derived from using teams in reengineered organizations. The seven features are as follows:

1. A long-held belief that performance improvements are attained through individual ingenuity and creativity. Visions of individuals tinkering in their workshops dominate U.S. thinking in regard to the sources of new products. Ingenuity is depicted as two young men in a garage cobbling together the first Apple computer. Similarly, great leaders are relied on to come to the aid of troubled corporations.

2. *An emphasis on individual rights and nonconformity rather than on conformity and group harmony.* The Europeans who came to North America centuries ago often did so because they did not fit in their own cultures. Their nonconforming religious practices, rebelliousness toward traditional social and economic restrictions, desire to be judged by what they could do instead of by their family names, need to escape famines and wars, responses to punishments for various misdeeds, and belief in individual rights led them to establish societies that stressed their values. In many ways, these values are still reflected in contemporary U.S. organizations. Those values do not encourage conformity, group harmony, and team work.

> *Seven cultural features appear to diminish the payoffs derived from using teams in reengineered organizations.*

3. *A high level of tolerance for conflict and competition at the expense of cooperation and unity.* U.S. organizations vigorously recruit the aggressive, results-oriented, competitive, independent, take-charge, bottom-line oriented, overachievers who eat problems for lunch and are then perplexed when their team-building efforts produce few positive results. When one raises and rewards wolves, one cannot expect to have cooperative house pets.

4. *An almost ingrained distrust of power, hierarchical structures, and management.* Disputes between labor and management are part of U.S. history. Much of the U.S. labor force believes some of the following: You cannot trust management; power corrupts; listen, but verify; divide and conquer; it's all politics; they're only looking out for themselves; nobody asks for my opinion!

5. *An emphasis on attaining quick results, while ignoring both the past and the future.* Given the nature of the U.S. economic system, it is logical for organizations to continually ask their personnel and suppliers, "What have you done for me today?" Unfortunately, loyalty has become something of an outdated concept. Investment-portfolio managers demand strong quarterly returns. If those are not forthcoming, takeovers threaten organizations. Quick, current results are what counts.

6. *A preference for dynamic action, instead of slow, steady, incremental progress.* "This organization must be turned around in thirty days, or else!" Those who display a willingness to make the dirt fly are rewarded. The vision is short term rather than long term.

7. *The presence of high levels of demographic diversity and heterogeneity in society and the work place.* Studies have shown that in the short-to-moderate

term, reaching agreement is simpler in homogeneous groups (Watson, Kumar, & Michaelsen, 1993). Heterogeneity slows things down: different values, genders, cultures, religions, ethnic traditions, customs, behavioral patterns, communication styles, expectations, and norms confront individuals with complex packages of information to decode and act on. In contrast, in more homogeneous cultures—such as Japan's—where central values are shared, reaching agreement is considerably simpler (Nahavandi & Aranda, 1994).

The combined impact of these seven cultural features often thwarts efforts to install Japanese-style teams in U.S. organizations. Significant resources are invested in teaching personnel that they "need to become cohesive...more cooperative, and patient with process and slow change" (Nahavandi & Aranda, 1994, p. 61). Organizations encourage team problem-identification and resolution; they urge employees to rise above cultural diversity and demographic heterogeneity in a quest for higher levels of teamwork; and then they wonder why their implementation efforts produce so little return on investment. In search of an explanation, they wonder if they have used the wrong training materials, purchased the wrong videotape, or should have selected another consultant, should have relied less (or more) on the internal training staff, or should have read a different book or research study. Alas, none of these explanations offers much help.

A TYPOLOGY FOR TEAMS

Nahavandi and Aranda (1994) also present a useful, although somewhat broad, typology for gaining insights into why team efforts do not work as planned. Their model describes four types of teams, three of which are currently in use and a final one designed to take advantage of U.S. cultural characteristics.

1. Quality-Circle Teams

Quality-circle (QC) teams first appeared in the U.S. in the mid to late 1970s. Their fluidity of membership is very low, and members are first-level operating personnel. The complexity of tasks they focus on is also low and consists mainly of internal issues. Members report to management. The major need of this type of team is for training. Given its stable membership and its focus on simple issues, the QC team is not suited to dealing with the broad, complex problems that confront contemporary organizations. The model commonly is found in organizations that are relatively new to the use of teams.

2. Management Teams

The fluidity of membership of teams of mid-level and higher managers is low. The complexity of tasks they deal with is high; they identify, sell, and implement potential solutions. Team members focus on external issues (issues outside the team). The major need of this type of team is for empowerment. Although these teams deal with complex issues, their stability of membership renders them largely unsuited for dealing with the strategic problems that face organizations. Management teams commonly are found in organizations that have adopted more complex structures and face more complex problems.

3. Cross-Functional Teams

Much favored in organizational/process reengineering, cross-functional teams have fluid membership and focus on comparatively simple, internal problems. The major need of such teams is for organizational structures that will help their multidisciplinary members function together. Although such teams enjoy fluid membership, their focus on simple issues tends to make them unsuited for dealing with strategic problems. Unfortunately, this model commonly is found in organizations that have adopted more complex structures and face more complex problems.

4. Shamrock Teams (U.S. Style)

This team model, first proposed as an organizational model by Charles Handy (1989), is named for the Irish clover with three leaves to each stem because a shamrock team has three staffing components:

- A stable core of three to five members who see the task through to completion;
- Specialized resource people who join and leave the team as needed; and
- Temporary or part-time members who are called on for brief periods of time when the team needs additional labor or expertise.

The highly fluid membership of this team concentrates on resolving complex, strategic, internal and external issues. The major needs of this type of team are understanding and capitalizing on its diversity, involving "outsiders" (such as customers) in its activities, and being creative. The shamrock model is best suited for use by organizations that face radical changes within a highly complex environment—as do most large organizations today.

	Quality-Circle Teams	Management Teams	Cross-Functional Teams	Shamrock Teams
Fluidity of Membership	low	low	high	high
Membership Components	first-level operators	middle to top management	multidisciplinary	multidisciplinary
Complexity of Tasks	low	high	low	high
Locus of Issues	internal	external	internal	internal and external
Members Report to	management	board members or executive managers	matrix	(varies)
Major Team Need(s)	training	empowerment	supportive organizational structures	understanding and capitalizing on diversity, involving outsiders, being creative
Not Suited for	broad, complex problems	strategic/ complex problems	strategic/ complex problems	simple, narrowly defined problems

IMPORTANT NEW NORMS FOR U.S. TEAMS

Adopting the shamrock-team model requires that managers and employees in the U.S. first work together to reconceptualize the paradigms within which they think about what teams do and how they do those things. Then the managers and employees need to work together to adopt three behavioral norms that will help their teams to take advantage of U.S. cultural patterns (Nahavandi & Aranda, 1994). These norms are as follows.

Value and Endorse Dissent Among Team Members

Given the emphasis in the United States on individualism, conflict, competition, quick results, success, and action within a highly diverse and heterogeneous society, Japanese-style harmony may not be a realistic goal. Contentious entrepreneurship has long been a strength in the U.S., so disagreement and differences should be valued as key parts of a creative process instead of being targeted for elimination through the efforts of trainers and videotapes. Instead of pursuing harmony and agreement, recent studies suggest that teams should pursue creative tension (Pascale, 1990).

Instead of identifying and promulgating the company way of thinking, a more productive approach is to teach teams to manage (not eliminate or resolve) conflict, fight by agreed-on rules, innovate, draw out different points of view, and utilize productive disagreement (not consensus decision making). Tom Peters (1994) refers to this approach to business as getting "weird, flat, and horizontal." If everyone is in agreement, the idea probably is not weird enough.

Strongly Encourage Fluidity of Membership Within Teams

"It is not clear that stability of team membership is in the best interests of either teams or organizations. In fact, we have long been aware of the detrimental effects of too much stability and cohesion" (Nahavandi & Aranda, 1994, p. 63). Current thinking suggests building a core of three to five project-long team members, supplemented by temporary or part-time members and longer-term specialized resource personnel. Nahavandi and Aranda have found that this "movement of members in and out of teams, together with the presence of the core members, prevents the development of too much cohesion and complacency, allows for the dynamic renewal of teams and their members, and leads to better use of our diverse population" (p. 64).

Empower Teams to Address Key Results Areas and to Implement Their Decisions

Teams frequently are prohibited from addressing certain fundamental issues in the organization (which are reserved for senior management's attention) and usually are required to obtain permission from higher levels prior to implementing their decisions. "In order to gain permission to implement their ideas, teams are forced to suggest easily acceptable and non-controversial solutions to problems" (Nahavandi & Aranda, 1994, p. 64).

Not surprisingly, these restrictions can easily disempower and marginalize teams. This eliminates solutions that are innovative, entrepreneurial, paradigm shifting, frame breaking, boat rocking, or simply weird—the very features that attract customers in a highly competitive marketplace. These restrictions also work against those features of U.S. culture that have long conveyed competitive advantage: a willingness to take risks, an openness to seeing things differently, and an inclination to experiment and ask "What if?"

Building team-implementation efforts around the three norms specified above will encourage participants to take advantage of their culture's strengths (individualism, competitiveness, and speed) instead of producing frustration by trying to avoid using those strengths.

THE U.S. STYLE TEAMS (USST) INVENTORY

Purposes

The USST Inventory is designed to accomplish the following objectives:

1. To familiarize organizations with the need to utilize team strategies that are culture sensitive.

2. To offer a constructive critique of popular team models being implemented in U.S. organizations.

3. To identify the seven cultural features that need to be considered when implementing team models in U.S. organizations.

4. To identify strategies that will help U.S. organizations to reap a greater return on investment from their team-implementation efforts.

5. To offer U.S. organizations a format to use as they assess their readiness to implement teams.

Validity

The U.S. Style Teams (USST) Inventory is designed for use as an action-research tool rather than as a data-gathering instrument. Applied in this manner, the inventory has demonstrated a high level of face validity when used with audiences ranging from executive managers to nonmanagement personnel.

Administration

The following suggestions will help facilitators to administer the USST Inventory.

Completion of the Inventory

Distribute copies of the USST Inventory and read the instructions aloud. After reading each of the thirty-three statements, respondents should make check marks next to the statements that accurately characterize team norms in their organization. Resolve any questions about how to take the inventory. Urge respondents to avoid overanalyzing their choices. Ask respondents to wait to score their inventories until they are directed to do so.

Theory Input

When respondents have completed the inventory, discuss the shortcomings of traditional team models, the seven critical features of U.S. culture, the team typology, and the three norms for new teams. Answer any questions pertaining to these bodies of information.

Prediction

Ask the participants to predict whether their organizations will score "high," "medium," or "low" in terms of support for U.S. norms in utilizing teams.

Scoring

Distribute copies of the USST Inventory Scoring Sheet to the respondents. The same process is used to score each of the three norms. First, in the upper grid, respondents should circle indicated numbers that correspond to the statements they checked on their inventories. Then, in the lower grid, they should circle indicated numbers that they did not circle on their inventories. The "reverse scored" statements in the lower grid indicate norms that run counter to the norms described in positively scored statements. This wording hinders attempts to complete the inventory in an unreflective manner.

The number of circled items in each column should be determined and the result written in the space designated "Total." Each total should be multiplied by three and the result written in the space designated "Score."

Scores for all three norms should be added together and the result written in the space designated "Grand Total." This result will vary from a low of zero to a high of ninety-nine.

Interpretation and Discussion

Distribute copies of the USST Inventory Interpretation and Discussion Sheet to the respondents. Respondents should check the score interpretation box that corresponds to their "Grand Total" figures. Some groups find it helpful to record individual scores on a collective chart with appropriate boundaries.

After scoring their inventories and discussing the resulting scores, respondents should read and discuss the four brief guidelines for implementing U.S. style teams (item 4 on the USST Inventory Interpretation and Discussion Sheet).

Finally, respondents should prepare and discuss answers to the discussion questions. These answers can serve as the basis for action planning.

References

Dean, J., & Bowen, D. (1995). Management theory and total quality: Improving research and practice through theory development. *Academy of Management Review, 19*(1).

Floyd, S., & Woolridge, B. (1994). Dinosaurs or dynamos? Recognizing middle management's strategic role. *Academy of Management Executive, 8*(4).

Handy, C. (1989). *The age of unreason.* London: Random Century.

Krishnan, R., Shani, A., Grant, R., & Baer, R. (1994). In search of quality improvement: Problems of design and implementation. *Academy of Management Executive, 8*(4).

Lawler, E., III. (1994). Total quality management and employee involvement: Are they compatible? *Academy of Management Executive, 8*(1).

Miner, J. (1974). *The human constraint: The coming shortage of management talent.* Washington, DC: BNA Books.

Muczyk, J., & Reimann, B. (1987). The case for directive leadership. *Academy of Management Executive, 1*(3).

Nahavandi, A., & Aranda, E. (1994). Restructuring teams for the re-engineered organization. *Academy of Management Executive, 8*(4).

Pascale, R.T. (1990). *Managing on the edge: How the smartest companies use conflict to stay ahead.* New York: Simon & Schuster.

Peters, T. (1994). *The Tom Peters seminar: Crazy times call for crazy organizations.* New York: Vintage Books/Random House.

Reger, R., Gustafson, L., Demarie, S., & Mullane, J. (1995). Reframing the organization: Why implementing total quality is easier said than done. *Academy of Management Review, 19*(1).

Sitkin, S., Sutcliffe, K., & Schroeder, R. (1995). Distinguishing control from learning in total quality management: A contingency perspective. *Academy of Management Review, 19*(1).

Szwergold, J. (1992, August). Why most quality efforts fail. *American Management Association Management Review.*

Watson, W., Kumar, K., & Michaelsen, L. (1993). Cultural diversity's impact on interaction process and performance: Comparing homogeneous and diverse task groups. *Academy of Management Journal, 36*(3).

Gaylord Reagan, Ph.D., *is an independent consultant specializing in management training, organization development, and high-performance management systems. In addition to serving as an adjunct instructor at six colleges or universities, he has been a director of training and management development, manager of employee education and development, human resource manager, and internal consultant for organizational development. His professional memberships include the Academy of Management, the American Management Association, and the Society for Human Resource Management.*

U.S. STYLE TEAMS (USST) INVENTORY

Gaylord Reagan

Instructions: Read the following list of thirty-three questions. Make a check mark in the box preceding each question that accurately describes team norms in your organization. Avoid "overthinking" your responses. Your initial choices often come closer to your true perceptions.

☐ 1. The organization places a strong, positive value on achieving harmony.

☐ 2. The organization values high levels of cohesion among team members.

☐ 3. Teams are trusted to make major decisions.

☐ 4. People in the organization hold diverse cultural values.

☐ 5. Teams welcome new ideas and perspectives from resource people with special skills.

☐ 6. A team's tasks are clearly tied to the organization's strategic plans and initiatives.

☐ 7. The assumption is that the organization's way is the right way.

☐ 8. Members are encouraged to play different roles within the teams on which they serve.

☐ 9. Teams are usually required to seek permission before they can implement any of their recommendations.

☐ 10. Disagreement is viewed as being the basis for creativity.

☐ 11. The organization uses flexible employment relationships with its personnel.

☐ 12. A team's ideas must be easily acceptable and noncontroversial to be implemented.

☐ 13. The organization stresses incremental improvement rather than innovation.

The 1996 Annual: Volume 2, Consulting.
Copyright © 1996 by Pfeiffer & Company, San Diego, CA.

☐ 14. People believe that teams need high levels of stability in order to be productive.

☐ 15. Teams are encouraged to define their own goals and their areas of impact.

☐ 16. People productively manage dissent and controversy.

☐ 17. People tend to have more or less permanent memberships on certain teams.

☐ 18. Teams are well-anchored in organizational realities.

☐ 19. My coworkers draw out and value different points of view.

☐ 20. People can enter and exit teams as their skills and knowledge are needed.

☐ 21. People realize that teams must look outside themselves for ideas and feedback.

☐ 22. The organization provides training in attacking problems and creating innovative ideas.

☐ 23. Temporary and part-time personnel play active roles in the organization's teams.

☐ 24. Teams accept the fact that other people's perspectives can be more valuable than those of the team members.

☐ 25. The organization values individualism and independence.

☐ 26. Culturally diverse populations are actively involved in the organization's teams.

☐ 27. Team members realize that cooperation and coalition building form the basis for team success.

☐ 28. Competitiveness is valued at most levels of the organization.

☐ 29. Teams welcome new ideas and perspectives from customers.

☐ 30. Coalition building is emphasized by the organization's teams.

☐ 31. Team members know how to be creative.

☐ 32. Teams have a stable core of no more than three to five long-term members.

☐ 33. Teams are encouraged to empower themselves.

USST Inventory Scoring Sheet

Instructions: Using the scoring grid below:

1. In the top part of the grid, circle the numbers of the indicated statements that you did check on the USST Inventory. In the lower part of the grid, circle the numbers of the indicated statements that you did not check on the inventory. The numbers in the lower part of the grid represent statements for which a reverse scoring process is used: If you did not select these statements, their scores count.

2. Total the number of statements in the columns for each norm and enter the totals in the boxes provided. Then multiply each norm total by three and enter the sums in the boxes provided. The three resulting scores reflect your perception of the comparative levels of support that your organization offers to the suggested team norms.

3. Add together the three norm scores to produce a grand total. This number indicates your perception of the overall level of support your organization offers for U.S. style teams.

	Norm #1	Norm #2	Norm #3
	1	5	3
	4	8	6
	10	11	15
Upper Grid	16	14	18
	19	20	21
	22	23	24
	25	26	27
	28	29	30
	31	32	33
Lower Grid	7	2	9
	13	17	12
	Norm #1 Total _____	Norm #2 Total _____	Norm #3 Total _____
	Norm #1 Score_____ (Norm #1 Total x 3)	Norm #2 Score_____ (Norm #2 Total x 3)	Norm #3 Score_____ (Norm #3 Total x 3)
	Grand Total _____ **(Norm #1 Score + Norm #2 Score + Norm #3 Score)**		

USST Inventory Interpretation and Discussion Sheet

1. Check the box whose range includes your "Grand Total" score.

☐ 99 - 85 You perceive strong organizational support for all three norms underlying U.S. style teams. If you also support these norms, your main task is to identify ways to ensure their continued existence within your work group and the overall organization. If you do not support these norms, you might feel a bit uncomfortable with the direction in which you perceive your organization to be heading.

☐ 84 - 75 You perceive moderate organizational support for U.S. style teams. Many aspects of the three norms are present and being rewarded. If you support these norms, your main task is to identify ways you can demonstrate their value to your work group and, eventually, to the overall organization. The next time you lead a team, you might suggest that members try out these norms.

☐ 74 - 65 You perceive some organizational support for U.S. style teams. The norms are mentioned from time to time, but little practical or consistent use is made of them. If you support these norms, you might inject them into training programs or demonstrate their use in a low-key way within your own work group or in a task team.

☐ 64 - 0 You perceive erratic, inconsistent organizational support for U.S. style teams. Some people and some teams occasionally utilize aspects of one or more of the three norms. Some individuals are vaguely aware of one or more of the norms, but the norms are not reinforced. Your organization may have a strong preference for another style of teamwork or may prefer not to use teams.

2. Which of the three norms received the highest score? How does your perception compare to those of other people from your work group—how are your scores alike and different? This score represents your organization's strength. How can your organization retain and build on this score? What is your action plan for helping this to happen?

3. Which of the three norms received the lowest score? How does your perception compare to those of other people from your work group—how are your scores alike and different? This score represents your organization's greatest opportunity for improvement. How will you strengthen this score? What is your action plan for doing so?

4. Researchers who have studied U.S. style teams offer a deceptively brief set of guidelines for their implementation.[1]

   a. Begin with less-complex team models (quality-circle teams, top management teams, cross-functional teams) and gradually move into U.S. style teams. If your organization currently does not utilize teams, you may find that it is easier to adopt the new model because you will not have to overcome existing norms regarding the operation of teams.

   How and where could you begin to implement this model?

   b. Start any changes in team operation in small doses; avoid beginning with organization-wide changes. Use a "pull strategy" (attract converts with the good results your model is achieving) instead of a "push strategy" (ordering everyone to implement a change and punishing those who cannot or will not do so).

   What would be a good starting point for you to begin to implement this change in team norms?

[1] A. Nahavandi & E. Aranda (1994), "Restructuring Teams for the Re-engineered Organization," *Academy of Management Executive, 8*(4), 66.

c. Provide team members with lots of "cafeteria style" training (user choice with respect to type and quantity) in productive controversy, constructive thinking, creativity, and political behaviors. Avoid training in consensus decision making and reaching agreement.

How can you help to bring about this type of training?

d. Managers need to demonstrate the productive use of U.S. style teams in their own work areas. Help personnel around you (and on teams to which you belong) to have positive experiences with constructive dissent, fluid team membership, and empowerment.

How can you help people around you in the organization to have this kind of experience?

5. How can you implement these four guidelines in your organization? What problems can you foresee, and how would you overcome them?

WORKING WITH RESISTANCE TO CHANGE: THE SUPPORT FOR CHANGE QUESTIONNAIRE[1]

Rick Maurer

Abstract: Resistance to change is a natural human response. Attempting to overcome it only intensifies it. Therefore, it is important that change agents (clients and consultants) know how to work with resistance. One key element is to identify the level of resistance and recognize its source.

The three levels of resistance each represent several issues that could make it difficult if not impossible to implement organizational change. The Support for Change Questionnaire allows change agents to survey a cross-section of organizational members in order to identify levels and categories of potential resistance. A program for using the questionnaire in the process of implementing change also is presented.

[1] Article and questionnaire adapted from *Beyond the Wall of Resistance: Unconventional Strategies that Build Support for Change* (Austin, TX: Bard & Stephen, 1996). By permission of the author. Copyright © 1996 by Rick Maurer.

$\mathbf{W}$ith the unrelenting change that is occurring in organizations, knowing how to work with resistance is a critical skill for consultants and clients. Resistance and change go together: it is virtually impossible to have significant change without resistance. People naturally resist anything that seems unfamiliar or potentially harmful from their points of view.

Unfortunately, resistance usually is viewed as bad and as something to be overcome. Many books and articles use the phrase "overcoming resistance to change." This is dead wrong. Fighting, ignoring, or attempting to manipulate resistance intensifies the differences between those who want the change and those who resist it.

When we attempt to overcome, we enter into a win-lose contest. Winning is fine in sports, but inside an organization it is deadly. When we need people's support, winning at another's expense can be devastating. In 279 A.D., the army of the emperor Pyrrhus won at Asculum, but at a considerable cost of life. He is reputed to have said, "One more such victory and we are lost." Many organizations have not learned this lesson and continue to win Pyrrhic victories.

THE INTENSITY OF RESISTANCE

An important step in dealing effectively with resistance is understanding its intensity. Categorizing resistance on one of three levels, from least intense to most intense, may be somewhat arbitrary but can help consultants and clients begin a conversation about the subject.

Level 1: The Idea Itself

Level 1 is resistance to the change itself. People simply oppose, question, or are confused by the change. For example, management wants to paint the office pea green. Others resist. Their objection is simple: they hate the color pea green. There is no hidden agenda. Consider this low-grade resistance.

In Level 1, people resist change for the following reasons:

- They do not understand exactly what management is trying to accomplish;
- They do not know why it is important;

- They like the status quo;
- They do not know what impact the change will have on them;
- They do not think management realizes what the change will cost in time or money;
- They have their own ideas about what the organization should do;
- They like the idea but think the timing is wrong.

Most articles and books on the subject deal with resistance at this level. These publications usually suggest informing people about the change and getting them involved to some degree. Unfortunately, most resistance is deeper than Level 1, so a broader range of strategies is needed. Using the Support for Change Questionnaire is one strategy that can help a client and consultant identify and begin working with deeper levels of resistance.

Level 2: Deeper Issues

Level-2 resistance is always deeper than the particular change at hand. It indicates that there are other forces at work. For example, this level of resistance over the color that the office is to be painted has little to do with the actual color and a lot to do with other—often unspoken—issues. Conversations focused on the topic of color will not reveal the true nature of the resistance.

Most organizational resistance falls in Level 2, deeper than just the change itself. This resistance appears in a number of ways, as the sections that follow explain.

Distrust

Distrust arises when people believe they have been hurt in the past by someone or some group. Typically, people believe that management (or a consultant) has pushed through changes without regard for the human toll. They may believe that management (or a consultant) has made promises that were not kept. They resolve not to trust this person or group again. They question motives; read between the lines; and extract hidden meanings from every word, nuance, or perceived slight.

Because trust is low, anything can disrupt change at this level. People are likely to remain suspicious throughout the process, wondering if management is up to something. Rumors of a layoff, a contentious grievance settlement—almost anything—can drive the resistance even deeper.

Bureaucratic Culture

In traditional organizations with many layers of reporting, people often feel powerless—and well they should. People survive in bureaucracy by lying low and keeping things predictable. Success is sometimes measured by amassing whatever power one can get. For example, controlling critical information may make a worker seem indispensable. Change upsets the precarious balance.

Punishments and Rewards

If what is rewarded gets done, it is also true that what is punished is avoided. People will resist change that runs counter to the rewards and punishments inside the organization. For example, a company wanted to change how it handled billing because a typical bill moved through many departments on its way to the customer and the process was slow and prone to error. The vice president asked each department to assign a representative to a task force to do something about the problem. The project had difficulty making any progress because people's "real work" kept piling up when they attended meetings. Soon, they began to send substitutes to meetings, and the process disintegrated.

> *Level-2 resistance is always deeper than the particular change at hand.*

Need for Respect and Status

People need to save face. Change often threatens that strong human need. People are afraid that change may result in loss of respect, status, power, or control.

When one company tried to implement quality improvement, a manager asked if everything they had been doing to that point had been worthless. From his vantage point, this change was a repudiation of his life's work. He was not resisting quality, he was resisting the strong personal blow to his self-esteem.

Fear of Loss

The need to be part of something is strong for most people. When they believe that they will be cast out as a result of a change, they resist it. The need to be included is so deep that we may not be aware that it is guiding our actions. Although resistance may come out in a variety of ways (e.g., face-to-face criticism, silence, malicious compliance), it might not reveal that the concern is really about not belonging any more. Unless the consultant and client can find ways to hear this concern, they run the risk of solving the wrong problem.

Pfeiffer & Company

Events in the World

The world does not begin and end at the edge of the organization. People read articles about downsizing, outsourcing, and mergers, some of which relate to changes their organization is trying to implement. People are afraid that a change is really the start of something bigger and deeper. The events of the world have an impact on the change agent's ability to get things done.

Lack of Resilience

The pace of change in many organizations is so rapid that people may be worn out. They do not necessarily resist a particular change, they just cannot imagine taking on something else (Conner, 1993). When resilience is low, resistance takes the form of chronic fatigue.

Level 3: Deeply Embedded

This is the deepest, most entrenched level of resistance. The problems are big and may seem overwhelming. In the example of painting the office, resistance at this level has nothing to do with the color of paint and a lot to do with negative perceptions of those who want to make the change. People resent or do not trust the management and may regard it as the enemy.

Major reasons for Level-3 resistance include the following:

Historic Animosity

Distrust is deeply entrenched. Often the hurt goes back a number of years, perhaps even generations. Some management-labor relationships have not improved since the growth of the labor movement in the early 1900s. When Frank Borman, former chairman of the ill-fated Eastern Airlines, was asked what he thought of employee involvement, he replied, "There is no way I'm going to have the monkeys running the zoo" (Gibney, 1986). Such an attitude makes cooperation extraordinarily difficult, if not impossible.

Conflicting Values and Visions

What management wants and what the people who have to live with the change want may be far apart. The two sets of goals may appear to be in direct opposition. Moreover, when historic animosity and conflicting values and visions meet, Level-3 resistance is extremely difficult to deal with.

Combination of Level-2 Factors

Some of the issues identified for Level 2, if particularly severe, become Level-3 concerns. In particular, distrust, punishments and rewards, need for respect and status, and fear of loss often appear in combination when resistance is deeply embedded.

USING THE SUPPORT FOR CHANGE QUESTIONNAIRE TO INITIATE CONVERSATION

The Support for Change Questionnaire provides consultants and clients a means to assess the intensity of resistance to change. Responses to the questionnaire act as a springboard for conversation about change and resistance.

The quality of the scores is determined by who takes part. If the survey is used only with the senior management team, the result probably will be a skewed view of reality. It is better to obtain data from a cross-section of the organization in order to create a more complete picture.

The actual scores are less interesting than the reasons that people responded the way they did. Conversations with clients should focus on the stories that accompany the scores. For example, if the CEO rates everything seven (high), middle managers' scores range from three to five, and the nonmanagement staff rates everything low, you have the makings of a very intriguing conversation.

The purpose of the conversation is to get opinions and feelings out in the open. Obviously, the consultant's skill at facilitating dialogue is critical.

Using the Questionnaire

The following is a recommended format for working with the Support for Change Questionnaire.

Prework

Explain to the client the importance of working with, rather than against, resistance. Suggest that a cross-section of the organization complete the questionnaire. This need not be a large group as long as the scores reflect the range of opinions about whatever change is being considered. Make certain not to overlook individuals or groups who may be critical to implementing the change.

Inform the people who will be completing the questionnaire of its purpose; why they have been selected to respond to it; the date, time, and place of its administration; and any other pertinent details.

Administration

Thank the selected participants for coming and state the purpose of administering the questionnaire and the value of their spending their time on it. Distribute copies of the questionnaire and pencils to the participants, read the instructions aloud, and answer any questions. Before they leave, tell the participants when they will receive feedback on the results and thank them for their efforts.

Scoring

Score the responses. (A scoring sheet is provided after the questionnaire for your convenience, or you may prefer to develop one appropriate to the organization's particular needs.) Provide anonymity for individuals, but break out the scores by stakeholder groups. For example, use one color to indicate scores of senior management, another color for those of middle managers, and so forth.

Reporting to the Client

Meet privately with the client to go over the scores prior to providing feedback to all others concerned.

Reporting to Respondents and Others

Prior to the meeting, review the "Interpretation" section that appears after the questionnaire. Use this information to help form questions to ask during the meeting. No matter what the scores are, the following questions probably will be of value:

- What interests you about the scores?
- Where do you see patterns?
- Where are the greatest points of agreement?
- Where are the greatest points of disagreement?

Convene a meeting of all interested parties.

1. Present the three levels of resistance.

2. Display the scores on large sheets of flip chart paper, slides, or overhead transparencies. Preserve anonymity for individual respondents, but display the scores by stakeholder groups, e.g., different colors for senior management, middle management, etc.

3. Encourage people to explain why they scored the way they did. Do not force anyone to speak involuntarily. When people do speak, keep the atmosphere "safe" so that people can describe the reasons for their scores. (This is especially important if most scores are on one end of the scale.) Do not allow people to try to convert their colleagues.

4. Once you have explored the reasons behind the scores, consider asking the following questions:

   - What are the implications of these scores for this change?

   - If we proceed with the change, what must we do to build support for it?

   - How can we get people actively involved in the change process?

   - How can all individuals and groups be treated with dignity and respect during the planning and implementation of the change?

References

Conner, D. (1993) *Managing at the speed of change: Guidelines for resilience in turbulent times.* New York: Random House.

Gibney, A. (1986, June). Paradise tossed. *The Washington Monthly, pp. 24-34.*

Rick Maurer is a consultant who specializes in helping clients find ways to build support for change. Through his company, Maurer & Associates, Arlington, Virginia, he works with a variety of public and private sector clients. He is the author of Caught in the Middle, Feedback Toolkit, *and* Beyond the Wall of Resistance: Unconventional Strategies that Build Support for Change.

SUPPORT FOR CHANGE QUESTIONNAIRE

Rick Maurer

Instructions: This article and questionnaire[2] are designed to help people understand the inherent level of support or opposition to change within the organization. Please respond to each item according to how true you think it is in your organization. Circle the appropriate number on the scale that follows the item.

Not True	Usually Not True	Somewhat Untrue	Neutral	Somewhat True	Usually True	True
1	2	3	4	5	6	7

Values and Visions

1. Do people throughout the organization share values or visions?

History of Change

2. Does the organization have a good track record in implementing change smoothly?

Cooperation and Trust

3. Is there a lot of **cooperation** and trust throughout the organization (as opposed to animosity)?

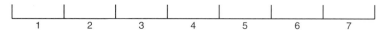

---

[2] Adapted from *Beyond the Wall of Resistance: Unconventional Strategies that Build Support for Change* (Austin, TX: Bard & Stephen, 1996). By permission of the author. Copyright © 1996 by Rick Maurer.

Not True	Usually Not True	Somewhat Untrue	Neutral	Somewhat True	Usually True	True
1	2	3	4	5	6	7

Culture

4. Does the organization's culture support risk taking (as opposed to being highly bureaucratic and rule bound)?

Resilience

5. Are people able to handle change (as opposed to being worn out from recent, unsettling changes)?

Punishments and Rewards

6. Does the organization reward people who take part in change efforts (as opposed to subtly punishing those who take the time off other work to get involved)?

Respect and Status

7. Will people be able to maintain respect and status when the change is implemented (as opposed to losing these as a result of the change)?

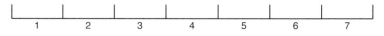

Status Quo

8. Will the change be mild (and not cause a major disruption of the status quo)?

SUPPORT FOR CHANGE QUESTIONNAIRE
SCORING SHEET

	Overall Total	Average	Group 1	Group 2	Group 3	Group 4
1. Values and Visions						
2. History of Change						
3. Cooperation and Trust						
4. Culture						
5. Resilience						
6. Punishments and Rewards						
7. Respect and Status						
8. Status Quo						

The 1996 Annual: Volume 2, Consulting.
Copyright © 1996 by Pfeiffer & Company, San Diego, CA.

Support for Change Questionnaire
Interpretation Sheet

Consider the following elements when interpreting the results of the questionnaire.

Numbers Need to Be Explained

Even though 1, 2, and 3 should be considered low scores; 4 and 5, mid-range scores; and 6 and 7, high scores; these are just numbers. One person's "5" is another person's "3." The value lies in understanding the meanings people give to their scores.

Generally, low to mid-range scores should be cause for concern. Lower scores indicate fertile soil for the growth of resistance.

Look for Patterns

Are scores similar or clustered on particular items? If so, this probably indicates agreement among most people regarding the relative support for change on that scale.

Are scores split on particular items? This may indicate that one respondent group (e.g., nonmanagement staff) consistently rates things low, while another group (e.g., supervisors) rates things high.

A pattern of high scores may indicate that the resistance will be Level 1. The organization's culture and history are such that people probably feel free to speak their minds. Therefore, conversations about change should be relatively easy to facilitate. However, it should be remembered that anything can drive resistance into Level 2. For example, a rumor or a newspaper report about downsizing in the industry could increase people's fears.

A pattern of low scores indicates deep (probably Level-3) concerns. Clients and change agents must take these concerns seriously. They will need to take a long-range view of change. It is imperative that they get people involved and begin building bridges.

Any low or mid-range scores indicate resistance waiting to happen. Mid-range scores also may indicate that there are concerns deeper than the change itself (Level 2). It is important to get these issues out into the open for discussion.

There are no right or wrong answers. Scores merely reflect people's perceptions.

ITEM ANALYSIS

Examine each item on the questionnaire. Use the following explanations to form questions to ask during the meeting.

Values and Visions

Low scores may indicate Level-3 concerns. Values may be in conflict, and individuals and groups may not see any common ground. This is serious. It almost guarantees that any major change will be resisted unless people learn how to build a shared set of values. On the other hand, low scores may indicate a communication problem. In some organizations, values and visions remain secret. People do not know where the organization is going. This communication problem needs to be solved but may not indicate deeper potential resistance.

History of Change

Low scores indicate a strong likelihood that a change will be resisted with great force. Those who want the change will need to demonstrate repeatedly that they are serious this time. People are likely to be very skeptical, so persistence will be critically important.

Cooperation and Trust

Low scores probably indicate Level-3 concerns. This should be taken seriously. It is difficult, if not impossible, to build support for any major change without some degree of trust. The opposite of trust is fear, so a low score indicates not just the absence of trust but the presence of fear.

Culture

Mid-range to low scores indicate that it may be difficult for people to carry out changes even if they support them. They are saying that the systems and procedures in the organization hinder change. The change agents must be willing to examine these deeper systemic issues.

Resilience

Low scores probably indicate that people are burned out. Even though they may see the need for change, they may have little strength to give to it. Two important questions should be asked:

- Is this change really necessary at this time?
- If it is, how can the organization support people so that the change causes minimal disruption?

Punishments and Rewards

Low scores indicate strong potential resistance. Who in their right minds would support something that they knew would harm them? If the respondents' perceptions are accurate, the change agents must find a way to move forward with the change *and find ways to make it rewarding for others.* If the low scores indicate a misperception, the change agents must let people know why they are misinformed. It is likely that this message will need to be communicated repeatedly (especially if trust is low as well).

Respect and Status

Low scores indicate potential Level-2 concerns. The change agents must find ways to make this a situation in which all can win.

Status Quo

Low scores indicate that people regard the potential change as very disruptive and stressful. The more involved people are in the change process, the less resistance they are likely to experience. Most often, people resist change when they feel out of control.

THE HIGH-PERFORMANCE FACTORS INVENTORY: ASSESSING WORK-GROUP MANAGEMENT AND PRACTICES[1]

Robert P. Crosby

Abstract: Twenty-five factors have been identified that are necessary for the creation of an empowered and high-performing organization. The High-Performance Factors Inventory can be used to assess a group and/or its manager in terms of these factors and to identify areas in which further development is needed. Research has shown that when these factors are attended to, productivity, quality, and employee satisfaction are high.

In this article, the twenty-five factors are explained, and a four-step plan is presented for working through the inventory and planning action steps based on the results.

[1] Adapted from the book, *Walking the Empowerment Tightrope* by Robert P. Crosby, © 1992, published by Organization Design and Development, Inc., King of Prussia, PA. Copies of the book may be ordered from the *HRD Quarterly,* 2002 Renaissance Boulevard, Suite 100, King of Prussia, PA 19406.

$\mathbf{E}$mpowerment in organizations is a balance of management authority and employee influence. It is also helping people to channel the power they already have toward qualitative and productive ends. Unfortunately, many managers flip from being too authoritarian to being too permissive and back again. Finding the appropriate balance is difficult.

The creation of an empowered and high-performing organization is dependent on many factors; twenty-five that impact performance have been identified through the use of data resulting from the author's instrument, the *People Performance Profile*. When these factors are attended to, productivity and quality are high, absenteeism is low, accidents are reduced, and employees are more likely both to enjoy and be motivated in their work environment.

The twenty-five high-performance factors are influenced by the manager of the work team or leader of the group. In teams without any management or leadership, the use of consensus is overly time consuming and often is controlled by the most rigid or resistant group members. Authoritarian management often is associated with pinpointing what is wrong and blaming. Permissive management often is associated with avoidance of responsibility and chaos. The balanced management approach is focused on "making it work."

The leader must have enough authority to create a participative culture and a loyalty that motivates followers. The opportunity to do productive work in a humane organization, with clarity of direction, is the most powerful motivating and esteem-enhancing force known. It also leads to bottom-line results.

HIGH-PERFORMANCE FACTORS

The twenty-five high-performance factors are as follows.

1. Sponsorship

The most critical factor in the success or failure of a plan or change project is the presence or absence of clear sponsorship from all managers and supervisors whose employees are involved in or affected by the plan or change. Sponsorship must be cascaded so that all are aligned. When such alignment is missing, employees receive conflicting messages. Lack of clarity about sponsorship is a primary cause of mistrust and dysfunction. Clarity reduces ambiguity and increases the possibility of success. This includes clarity about both direction and implementation. The fundamental principle is that one can only sponsor direct reports. Therefore, alignment down and across the organization is critical.

2. Openness

When autocratic managers refer to "troublemakers," they often are referring to people who bring up problems, ask questions, or make suggestions. Effective managers create an open climate in which information flows overtly rather than covertly. This involves "practicing what you preach," welcoming open—rather than underground—resistance, and listening actively so that people know that their messages have been heard and they have a chance to clarify any misperceptions. When the manager and group members have been trained in communication, arguments and blaming are reduced, and productivity increases.

> *Empowerment is a balance of management authority and employee influence.*

3. Influence

Everyone should understand that the manager's or group leader's role is necessary. Likewise, the group members have roles. The manager makes certain decisions and puts certain systems in place. Group members must ensure that they have clarity about their jobs, about who decides what, and about how they are doing. All need to have the ability to get commitments from others, information they need to do their jobs, and materials or other resources they need to do their jobs. All need to have the ability to impact productivity and quality issues and to influence decisions that affect them, such as work space and environmental factors, procedures and processes, equipment, measurements of work, schedules, compensation, and openness about what is and what is not working.

4. Distinguish Between Decision Making and Influence

The group leader and the group members must understand the different decision-making and influence styles and know which ones they employ. Lack of clarity about decision making and influence is a dominant cause of mistrust and low productivity. It is also important to know who makes which decisions. In different circumstances, the leader may make a unilateral decision, describe the problem and ask for recommendations from group members before deciding, accept a majority decision from the group, ask for a consensus decision, or delegate the decision. What the leader should not do is make a decision and then pretend to solicit input. In each case, the type of decision should be made clear.

5. Decisions Are Made

Taking too much time to make a decision is as bad as not taking enough time or not making a decision at all. A person with a high need for accuracy often postpones decisions, always seeking more information. A person with a high relationship orientation may postpone decisions while striving for agreement or consensus. On the other hand, a hard-charging person could make a decision without understanding its impact. It is important to understand one's decision-making style and *manage* it productively. Group members also can help one another and their manager by "calling" one another on decision-making problems when needed.

6. Implementation

Many organizations and managers announce plans or changes and then act as if a magic wand had been waved and the plans or changes were immediately in effect. In fact, implementation is the most critical step. If the people affected by the plan or change are to buy into it, they must be involved in the planning of both the plan or change and the implementation strategy. As with other factors, clarity is essential in all aspects of the implementation.

7. Input Needs

Input is what is received into the unit. Throughput is what happens to that material, information, order, etc., as it moves through the unit—the work flow and processes. Output is what goes to the internal or external customer. Building relationships with suppliers can improve the quality and timeliness of input. More timely notification of needs and better adherence to procedures about paperwork can help the suppliers achieve this.

8. Throughput

Continuous improvement of throughput processes is essential. Initially, survey feedback is a useful tool if there is a lot of data to be gathered regarding manager/employee relations, role clarity, accountability, intergroup issues, and other dimensions related to group effectiveness. Often, other groups and the relationships with them need to be considered, and the groups' processes may need to be aligned. Creating models of each process, developing flow charts, and clarifying individual tasks and perceptions are useful in the development of efficient throughput. Measurement of results is critical. Then continual review of processes with the goals of updating and improving helps to keep things productive, keep quality up, and ensure safety.

9. Output

Obtaining feedback on output is the best way to track quality and customer satisfaction. Developing a feedback form may be problematic if the persons involved have different perceptions of their jobs, so creating clarity and alignment again is essential. The feedback form can contain yes/no questions, multiple choice questions, scaled responses, and/or open-ended questions (these are more difficult to score, but a wider range of information can be obtained). If the feedback reveals problems, the manager and group engage in identifying the actual problem, identifying possible solutions, analyzing solutions and possible results, and developing a plan for action.

10. Meetings

Most meetings can be improved. Deciding on the purpose of each meeting; asking whether the purpose can be served better by means of telephone calls, memos, or electronic mail; and determining who actually needs to attend and who does not can help to keep meetings from becoming time wasters. An agenda should be developed for each meeting, with estimated times, and all key agenda items should be addressed. Discussions that can be conducted with smaller groups should be assigned to another time. All commitments and action items should be recorded, with the "who," "what," and "by when" specified. All members should feel empowered to comment on process, such as when the meeting strays from the topic. Finally, each meeting should be reviewed briefly with the aim of continually improving the process.

11. Creativity

A climate for creativity is built when people are thanked for contributing ideas, whether one agrees with them or not. Brainstorming is a good way to introduce the creative process. Looking for the kernel in wild ideas often yields productive applications. If the group members are assured of the manager's support, they will learn to keep contributing, even when some of their ideas are not accepted or implemented.

12. Job Clarity

Confusion about priorities is a common cause of lack of job clarity. Confusion between the understood job assignment and what one is asked to do and assignments or requests from multiple sources are other causes. If other people are unclear about a person's role, they may ask that person to do things outside of the person's understood role. The manager should clarify his or her expectations of each member's role, and members should clarify their expectations of one another. Duplication of effort can be eliminated, and gaps can be filled.

13. Person-Task Fit

Organizations function best when their members can do what they do well and enjoy doing. Of course, some routine, uninspiring tasks need to be done, but it is often possible to adjust tasks in order to achieve a better person-task fit. The manager and group members can discuss the possibilities for shifting work around or doing it differently. Team planning also can lead to trading of tasks and cross-training so that people can support one another better.

14. Authority

A recurring problem in organizations is that people have responsibility for tasks but not the authority to carry them out. Authority may mean being able to enlist help or attain resources. This is experienced by managers as well as others. If this problem can be solved without bringing it to the attention of higher levels, so much the better. If not, it is important to identify the sponsors of the tasks and enlist their aid.

15. Resource Availability

Resources include people, information, time, materials, equipment, and repairs. Availability of resources is a system issue and demands a system response. To tackle this issue, both workers and decision makers must be involved. It may require an ad hoc team effort, with membership from all parts of the organization and a skilled facilitator. Dialogue must be kept open between key decision makers and the problem solvers, and the effort may take some time. Nevertheless, the effort is required, as lack of resources cannot be solved at the work-group level although it greatly impairs productivity at that level.

16. Team Measurements

Many aspects of input, throughput, and output are measurable. The idea of continuous improvement is based on measurement to chart progress. Choosing what is to be measured is a shared activity, and it must be remembered that measurement is aimed at improvement, not at assigning blame. If measurement devices are kept simple, they will not impede the usual work flow.

Productivity measurements may include increases in numbers of items produced or processed, profit, accuracy, new clients, etc. They also may include reductions in time, absenteeism, costs, returns, incorrect shipments, and so on.

17. Big-Picture Perspective

Most people work better when they understand the "big picture" related to a task and their role in it. When group members understand the manager's and the group's goals, risks, and market opportunities, they are better able to participate in creating success. It is important that the group leader answer questions and realize that different people may want different information. Keeping group members informed of changes in the marketplace, the organization, and the competition helps them to understand why they are doing what they are doing.

18. Training

"Just in time" training is based on the idea that training loses its effectiveness if it does not immediately precede application. For example, computer training at an outside facility is largely forgotten if the workers do not immediately begin to use what they have learned on computers in the workplace. Implementing continuous improvement and measurement practices will help to pinpoint training needs, which should be met as soon as possible so that inefficient practices do not become part of work habits.

19. Priorities

Lack of clear priorities is a common complaint in organizations, although it may be expressed as "I have too much work" or "I have too many bosses." Many people find it difficult to say no or to draw boundaries. Thus, they feel stressed and victimized. It is important that the manager take responsibility for setting priorities or determining exactly how they are set. Clear job descriptions and task expectations help. Often, a lead member of the team may be assigned responsibility for keeping track of priorities. Task priorities should be related to each member of the team at least once each week.

20. By-Whens

When people leave a meeting, it should be clear who will do what and by when it will be done. "I'll get around to it" is not a commitment. Each meeting should begin with a review of the commitments made at the previous meeting. The right to ask for a "by-when" must go up and down and laterally across the organization. Whoever has responsibility for a task must be empowered to remind others of their commitments when breakdowns occur.

21. Follow Through

Making a good decision is not the same as taking action. Too often, assumed action does not take place. People do things to which they are committed. If someone says, "I'll try...," it is an indication of low commitment, whereas "I will..." is an indication of dedication to achieving results. In addition to obtaining "by-whens," it is important to obtain acceptance of responsibility for .achievement. When people give their word, others need to be able to count on it so that actions can happen in a predictable way. People also need to know that if they have overcommitted, they can go to the manager or the group and rectify the situation. When a group norm of following through on commitments has been established, schedules are met, budgets are accurate, and a new energy flow is created.

22. Single-Point Accountability

It is important that someone be accountable for the satisfactory completion of each task. This person can keep track of schedules, resources, and people, and spot small problems or delays before they become major ones. This person is a catalyst of the task. Accountability is a particular problem in a matrixed organization. Matrices create holes through which fingers can be pointed and people can escape from accountability. When two or more groups share a task, it is important that managers agree among themselves about where accountability for each segment will lie. Each manager then communicates this to his or her employees.[2]

23. Reinforcement

A fundamental principle of psychology is that people repeat behaviors that they are rewarded for. Too often, people in organizations only hear about what they have done wrong. Managers can reward employees by giving them a chance to work with people, projects, or equipment they are interested in; by sponsoring their attendance at training events and conferences; by providing relief from repetitive tasks; and by saying "thank you" privately and publicly in a timely manner. Organizations can introduce motivational profit-sharing programs and can celebrate achievement by inviting employees to dinners and cake breaks and by handing out free passes to movies or other events. Timely recognition that states specifically what performance is being recognized will reinforce that achievement.

24. Reprimands

If managers' expectations are made clear, and employees have clarity about their roles and responsibilities, reprimands are not needed as often and are not as much of a surprise when they occur. When reprimands are stated in general and judgmental ways, they are destructive. In order for them to be constructive, certain preconditions must be met: job assignments and expectations must be clear, positive reinforcement must occur when things are done right, and there must be a climate of openness in the organization. Then reprimands must be given privately, not publicly; they must be specific about which behaviors are unacceptable; and the timing of the reprimand must be close to the event that

---

[2]Crosby's book, *Solving the Cross-Work Puzzle* (Seattle, WA: LIOS Publishing, 1994) is about these issues.

required it. After making a reprimand, the manager should make it clear what behaviors should replace the undesirable ones and should assure the employee of his or her value to the group.

25. Work Relationships

Most conflict at work is not interpersonal but is caused by poor sponsorship, unclear roles and priorities, and confused authority and decision making. However, people often assign blame for these things to others and complain about the person rather than attempting to solve the problem. In this triangle, the person being complained about has no chance to defend himself or herself or to solve the problem. A norm of speaking directly to the person involved can help to nip many work-group problems in the bud. If the issue is severe, a third party or skilled facilitator may be asked to moderate the conversation. If work-group members are focused on problem solving rather than on blaming, interpersonal issues are resolved more easily.

Many of the factors discussed here are organizational system problems rather than individual problems. It is important to remember the formula used by Kurt Lewin: Behavior is a function of the person and the environment.

USES OF THE INSTRUMENT

The High-Performance Factors Inventory can be used by members of a group or team to assess the group's functioning. It also can be used by the manager of a team or by a team leader to assess his or her management influence. The respondent(s) then should follow the steps outlined below to generate an improvement plan and follow through for the group.

ADMINISTRATION OF THE INSTRUMENT

Step One: Appraising the Group

The facilitator can begin by stating the purpose of the instrument without divulging its content to the point that respondents attempt to give the "right" answers. Each respondent is given a pencil and a copy of the High-Performance Factors Inventory and reviews the instructions on the inventory.

Step Two: Reviewing the Results

When the respondents have completed the inventory, copies of the High-Performance Factors Scoring and Interpretation Sheet are distributed to them. They add up the scores they gave the items on the inventory and read the feedback for their totals.

Step Three: Developing an Improvement Plan

The respondents are asked to review the items for which their scores were lower than they would wish and to think about some specific ways to improve them. The facilitator then posts the list of the twenty-five High-Performance Factors and explains each factor, in turn. Respondents may be asked to reveal their ideas for improving their scores for that factor, while the facilitator records all suggestions on newsprint.

The facilitator suggests that the respondents list actions that they would want from others and also list what they intend to do to improve those factors rated low. The principle is as follows:

> You are your words and your actions. If your words are "probably," "I hope," "if I can," "I'll try," "I don't know when," "it wasn't my fault," and "nobody told me," you will create a pattern of not achieving, of blaming, and of finding excuses. If your words are "here's what I expect," "how can I support you?," "when do you need this?," "I'll complete it by (when)," and "here's when I need this from you," you will create a pattern of achieving. You must not only meet your commitments, you must provide others with the resources and support they need to make their commitments. You can begin to recast accountability and support in your organization. You create by initiating your own behavior.

The respondents and supervisor agree on specific actions and record who will do what and by when.

Step Four: Involving Work-Group Members in Follow Through

The next step, which should be taken within approximately a month, is to meet again and review the agreements. Members and managers can score each agreement on a "1" to "10" scale ("1" is low and "10" is high) and discuss their results. Some will score high, and some will score low. There will be successes and breakdowns. Celebrate the successes and fix the breakdowns.

Robert P. Crosby founded the Leadership Institute of Seattle (LIOS) in 1969. Currently he is a senior faculty member at the Bastyr University/LIOS Graduate Program for Applied Behavioral Science. Crosby is principal consultant in LIOS Consulting Corporation. In addition to Walking the Empowerment Tightrope: Balancing Management Authority and Employee Influence, *he has written* Solving the Cross-Work Puzzle: Suceeding in the Modern Organization *(Seattle, WA: LIOS Publishing), and* Living with Purpose When the Gods Are Gone *(Ojai, CA: Times Change Press).*

High Performance Factors Inventory[1]

Robert P. Crosby

Instructions: For each item that follows, circle the number on the continuum that best represents your work group.

1. Sponsorship

The supervisor firmly supports his/her direct reports, providing direction, resources, clarity, and enthusiasm to guarantee success.

Almost Always   Almost Never

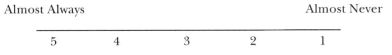

5	4	3	2	1

2. Openness

Data flows accurately so that problems are identified. Disagreements are viewed as opportunities for dialogue and are dealt with directly.

Almost Always   Almost Never

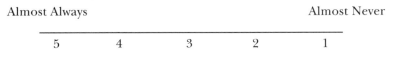

5	4	3	2	1

3. Influence

Employees have input and influence on factors that impact their work life, i.e., suggesting solutions, often seeing suggestions being acted on, and getting feedback when suggestions are rejected.

Almost Always   Almost Never

5	4	3	2	1

---

[1] Reprinted from the book, *Walking the Empowerment Tightrope* by Robert P. Crosby, © 1992, published by Organization Design and Development, Inc., King of Prussia, PA.

4. Distinguish Between Decision Making and Influence

Managers are clear about the distinction between "who is deciding" versus "who is influencing" and communicate that.

Almost Always   Almost Never

5	4	3	2	1

5. Decisions Are Made

Decisions are made in an expedient amount of time; it does not take forever to get a decision made.

Almost Always   Almost Never

5	4	3	2	1

6. Implementation

Once decisions are made, they are effectively implemented in a timely way.

Almost Always   Almost Never

5	4	3	2	1

7. Input Needs

We get on time and with quality what we need from outside or inside suppliers, such as materials, maintenance support, information, equipment, and/or commitments to service.

Almost Always   Almost Never

5	4	3	2	1

Pfeiffer & Company

8. Throughput

Once input is received, we are organized in the best possible way to produce quality output in a timely manner with clear and efficient processes. Our equipment is up-to-date and effectively used.

Almost Always   Almost Never

5	4	3	2	1

9. Output

We give to others what they need and provide excellent service, on time and with quality. This includes internal customers (within the organization) and external customers.

Almost Always   Almost Never

5	4	3	2	1

10. Meetings

Our meetings are effective. Time is not wasted. Appropriate people attend. Participation is shared. When needed, we solve issues, and decisions are made.

Almost Always   Almost Never

5	4	3	2	1

11. Creativity

New ideas for improving work processes, communication, product development, etc., are encouraged. It is easy in our climate to suggest or try something new.

Almost Always   Almost Never

5	4	3	2	1

12. Job Clarity

I know exactly what I am to do. My boss' expectations are clear. My job does not unnecessarily duplicate someone else's job.

Almost Always   Almost Never

5	4	3	2	1

13. Person-Task Fit

The right people are doing the right tasks. My skills and the skills of others are being used effectively here.

Almost Always   Almost Never

5	4	3	2	1

14. Authority

People have the authority to do what they are expected to do. They typically do not have to be persuaded or manipulated to act in the absence of higher authority.

Almost Always   Almost Never

5	4	3	2	1

15. Resource Availability

We are able to get the resources we need to do our jobs well. These include information, equipment, materials, and maintenance.

Almost Always   Almost Never

5	4	3	2	1

Pfeiffer & Company

16. Team Measurements

We have measurements that help us regularly track key factors related to our input, throughput, and output so that we can monitor and quickly solve identified problems and issues.

Almost Always   Almost Never

5	4	3	2	1

17. Big-Picture Perspective

We know the larger picture, i.e., where our organization is headed, how world and national economic and competitive factors affect us, and how we are doing. On everyday tasks we know why we are doing what we are doing.

Almost Always   Almost Never

5	4	3	2	1

18. Training

Members of our work team are well-trained technically as well as in teamwork and communication skills.

Almost Always   Almost Never

5	4	3	2	1

19. Priorities

No time is wasted wondering which task is more important. Priorities are consistently clear.

Almost Always   Almost Never

5	4	3	2	1

20. By-Whens

Whenever a decision is made, someone clarifies who will do what and by when. Also, by-whens are not only *given* to bosses but *received* from them as well.

Almost Always   Almost Never

5	4	3	2	1

21. Follow Through

Commitments are effectively tracked, i.e., reviewed at subsequent meetings or tracked by computer. Missed commitments are discussed and recommitted or are reassigned to someone else.

Almost Always   Almost Never

5	4	3	2	1

22. Single-Point Accountability

There is one person accountable for each task. Even on a matrixed group across departments, one person holds the single-point accountability rather than the group.

Almost Always   Almost Never

5	4	3	2	1

23. Reinforcement

People are appreciated for work well done. Expressions of thanks are clear enough so that the receivers know precisely what they did that was liked.

Almost Always   Almost Never

5	4	3	2	1

24. Reprimands

When our supervisor is unhappy with our work, he/she tells us as soon as possible, privately. The reprimand is clear and very specific about the unappreciated work or action but not accusatory, judgmental, or vindictive.

Almost Always   Almost Never

5	4	3	2	1

25. Work Relationships

Work relationships are maintained. When two or more people disagree, the issue is dealt with directly and effectively rather than avoided or escalated.

Almost Always   Almost Never

5	4	3	2	1

HIGH PERFORMANCE FACTORS SCORING AND INTERPRETATION SHEET[2]

Instructions: Total the numbers that you circled for each of the items on the High-Performance Factors Inventory and write the total here:

107 and Over: Outstanding

Congratulations, your group is among the rare, high-performing groups. The chances are that your leader and group members are open, nondefensive, and problem-solving people who balance caring with clarity about expectations.

95 to 106: Excellent

Your group is in the top tenth of those studied. You are doing very well and could easily reach a higher goal.

77 to 94: Good

Many groups score in this range. Applying the insights from your discussions about group performance can boost your scores. Achieving a higher level of performance is within reach.

76 and Below: Needs Improvement

The majority of groups score in this range. Opportunities abound. To make improvements, your group may need some coaching. The lower your score, the greater the need to seek skilled, outside help from someone who can see the high-performance factors either happening or not happening. A skilled consultant also notices when intentions do not

---

[2]Reprinted from the book, *Walking the Empowerment Tightrope* by Robert P. Crosby © 1992, published by Organization Design and Development, Inc., King of Prussia, PA.

---

match behaviors within the group and can help the members to learn more effective ways of interacting and working.

Conclusions

In addition, you may want to consult with two or three other groups that have scores for the twenty-five factors. Share your scores and support one another by making suggestions in areas where you have high scores and others have lower scores. If you are the group's manager or leader, you may want to consult with other managers or leaders whose groups have completed the inventory.

Answering the following questions can help you to prepare for looking at how to improve your group's functioning:

- What is the mission of the group? If it is part of a larger organization, what is the organization's stated mission? What is the group's "piece of the pie"?
- What values are important to the group members? To the group collectively? Are these in line with the organization's stated values? Do the organization's values impact its day-to-day activities or are they simply slogans?
- What are the group's business objectives? What do the members want to achieve in the next twelve months?
- Who supports and has ownership of the objectives? The group leader or manager? The members? A higher manager?
- Are the mission, values, and business objectives known and integrated in the daily work life? Do group members know what they can do to impact these? Do they know their "piece of the pie"?
- Are organizational progress reports regularly made available to all group members?
- Are you (as the group's leader or manager) able to state the group's specific business objectives and values? Can you state what is expected from group members to achieve these?

Introduction
to the Presentation and Discussion Resources Section

Every facilitator needs to develop a repertoire of theory and background that he or she can use in a variety of situations. Learning based on direct experience is not the only kind of learning appropriate to human-interaction training. A practical combination of theory and research with experiential learning generally enriches training and may be essential in many types of cognitive and skill development. Affective and cognitive data support, alter, validate, extend, and complement each other.

The 1996 Annual: Volume 2, Consulting includes eight articles, in the following categories:

197

Leadership: Theories and Models

The Eight-Systems Model for Implementing Total Quality Management, by Homer H. Johnson (page 275)

Leadership: Strategies and Techniques

The Changing Face of Power: How Can Consultants Prepare to Help Managers Through the Power Shift?, by Linne Bourget (page 199)

Leadership: Top-Management Issues and Concerns

Putting the Management in Total Quality Management: Creating a Strategic Framework, by Donald T. Simpson (page 217)

As with previous *Annuals*, this volume covers a variety of topics; not every article will appeal to every reader. Yet the range of articles presented should encourage a good deal of thought-provoking, serious discussion about the present and the future of HRD. Other articles on specific subjects can be located by using our comprehensive *Reference Guide to Handbooks and Annuals*. This book, which is updated regularly, indexes all of the *Annuals* and all of the *Handbooks of Structured Experiences* that we have published to date. With each revision, the *Reference Guide* becomes a complete, up-to-date, and easy-to-use resource for selecting appropriate materials from *all* of the *Annuals* and *Handbooks*.

THE CHANGING FACE OF POWER: HOW CAN CONSULTANTS PREPARE TO HELP MANAGERS THROUGH THE POWER SHIFT?

Linne Bourget

Abstract: The power structure in today's organizations is beginning to shift from the "old" control style to a more collaborative style. Many leaders and managers are experiencing difficulty with this shift, and it is up to consultants to help them through this change.

This article explores some of the myths related to power and how these myths are inhibiting the power shift. The concept of role clarity is introduced as central to a consultant's ability to assist a client during such a power shift.

T he exciting shift from authoritarian, top-down power structures to more collaborative, team-related forms of power has raised perplexing issues and questions for leaders and consultants. This article examines myths and realities about power and the significance of role clarity for managers and internal and external consultants. It also offers perspectives and raises questions that consultants and managers need to explore as they work together to make this shift successfully.

MYTHS AND REALITIES

One myth bedeviling the shift of power in organizations is that power is bad. Although people are beginning to believe otherwise, role models of people who have a high degree of power and exhibit a high level of caring are still rare.

Power is simply applied energy; it is constructive or destructive depending on how it is used. Constructive power is the energy to get things done. Clearly leaders, employees, and consultants must use constructive power to accomplish major changes in organizations. There is a great need for leaders and consultants who are comfortable with power, who use it wisely, and who do not abdicate their responsibilities.

Power used wisely provides others with reassurance and steadiness and frees up energy for making key changes. The shifting of roles and power structures does not justify abdicating power. The failure to use power is perceived as a lack of leadership skills, and it causes great anxiety during change. I have seen as much needless suffering in organizations from the underuse of power as I have from its overuse.

A second myth is that leaders lose power when they give up the control style. Actually, leaders who rely solely on authoritarianism are rapidly losing the power to make effective change. It is more accurate to say that leaders are changing forms of power, rather than losing power itself. Because of the increasing demand for collaborative power, more power is available in making this shift than in not doing so.

A third myth is that directive power (clear delegation of tasks without the fear-based authoritarian trappings) is no longer welcome because it is too much like the "old school." Not true. In a transition, people hunger for leaders who can be directive and decisive while also empowering others to act.

THE NEW HYBRIDS

The transition process from authoritarian to collaborative power is a new phenomenon and thus can make for awkward situations. Sometimes hybrids of the two kinds of power appear. These hybrids are to be expected in a major transition without precedent, yet they can be upsetting to those involved. For example, a senior executive set up a team to solve a problem, rejected the team's solutions, and then used her own ideas. This outcome was upsetting and disempowering to team members and weakened the executive's credibility.

A more positive example of hybrid power stems from my first quality-improvement project with a client manager in a computer company. This manager had requested a quality-circle approach to making some much-needed changes in his financial operation. About fifteen minutes into our first meeting, I smiled and said, "I understand your management style; you are rigidly participative." He beamed and said, "Good, you do understand me. We'll work well together."

> *Power is simply applied energy; it is constructive or destructive depending on how it is used.*

He insisted that his staff become more participative, take more responsibility, and make more decisions. He was also willing to let go of some of his power, even though doing so was a challenge for him.

Although insisting on participation seems paradoxical, the project was a great success. The manager knew what was necessary for success, and he was very straightforward about his own role and the difficulties involved in the power shift. He knew that in giving up one form of power and control, he would end up with a different form of power that would unleash his staff's potential and free him for other things. The team members faced some tough moments but were proud and pleased with their success—and rightly so.

Even with the increasing use of consulting services, change leaders and managers may not know how to use consulting skills most effectively. Consultants need to coach leaders and managers on how to best use consulting services. Aspects of consulting that will be most helpful for the client's situation can be highlighted. This coaching is even more important when clients are working through the power shift and are uncertain, confused, and stressed.

Changes in the leadership role because of the power shift necessitate changes in the consultants' roles. For example, consultants must be more up-front about their own power and roles, rather than expecting clients to know which consulting services they should use. Consultants must not only explain their roles in detail before projects start but also remind clients of these roles periodically during projects.

ROLE CLARITY AND CONSULTANTS' POWER

When working with clients who are making the shift from authoritarian to collaborative forms of power, the consultant will find that role clarity is a key source of power. To achieve such clarity, a consultant must first be clear about his or her personal mission, vision, and purpose. This clarity gives a consultant the power of self-awareness and thus the ability to model more effectively for client managers.

Role modeling the use of power based on inner clarity is a core skill for consultants and is essential in helping clients make it through this challenging shift. Client managers need to be shown how to let go of control, and both managers and nonmanagerial personnel need to be shown how to take responsibility for their choices.

To be clear on the consulting role means being at peace with operating as a consultant. This is a decision I have made and reconfirmed several times. As an external, independent consultant, I have survived temptations and challenges to my decision and have still held my ground. Like many of you, I have been offered other options, chances to pursue an executive career, to be an internal consultant, to be a senior partner in a consulting firm, or to grow my own firm into a larger operation.

In all cases, though, I decided to retain the role I had originally adopted. Because I am at peace with how my external consulting role expresses constructive power, I know that I can reach more people—and enjoy myself more—by operating independently and bringing in colleagues when needed as project associates.

To be helpful to clients in times of changing power, a consultant must first be at peace with his or her choice of roles; otherwise part of the consultant's awareness and energy will be tied up in internal conflict. It is best to honor oneself by choosing the role that feels right, that makes one feel most "at home."

Each consultant role expresses different types of power, for example, decision making, recommending, creating options, collaborating, delegating, and so on. To be able to model serenity for clients during a time of change is an enormous contribution. If a consultant reveals inner conflict, that feeling will ripple through the client's organization, causing more anxiety. The job of the consultant is to lower anxiety, not to raise it.

POWER AND ROLE CLARITY: QUESTIONS FOR REFLECTION

The following questions may help consultants and client managers clarify their approaches to power and roles:

1. How comfortable are you with your own power? What issues do you need to clear up in order to be clear and comfortable?

2. Who are your role models for the constructive use of power?

3. What did/do these role models give you that is helpful? What do you see that is not helpful?

4. For what aspects of power do you have no role models? What habits have you adopted in their absence? How well do these habits work for you?

5. What would it look like if you used your power with confidence and were comfortable with that power?

6. What fulfilling avenues for expressing power does your current role allow?

7. What fulfilling aspects of power are not included in your current role? How important are they to you?

8. What is your ideal role and use of constructive power? What are the issues to be resolved on the way to living your ideal?

These are challenging questions, and answering them requires a great deal of reflection. The power shift discussed in this paper is a global issue deserving significant consideration, and the answers are different for each person. Before using these questions with clients, a consultant should be sure to answer them for himself or herself in order to be able to speak to the issues that arise in the process. Careful, continual two-way clarification of expectations is essential between clients and consultants and between managers and their employees. The more personal clarity a consultant brings to the process, the more he or she can help; the less clarity a consultant brings, the more he or she hinders.

AN INDEPENDENT PERSPECTIVE

Consultants can and should "roll up their sleeves" and truly participate in the implementation of a power shift, for the issues involved require frequent intervention. Yet consultants need to maintain objectivity in order to provide a larger perspective. For internal consultants, it is important to work outside of the immediate reporting structure at least part of the time, to keep from being co-opted by the culture there. Norms and cultures are powerful—they can shift a person's thinking before he or she realizes it. When possible, swapping assignments with other internal consultants and debriefing afterward may be helpful.

It is a consultant's responsibility to provide an expert viewpoint that is independent of the organizational culture. Keeping this aspect of the role clear strengthens a consultant's power as a role model and reassures the client of the consultant's objectivity.

ROLE CLARITY AND ADVOCACY CONSULTING

The power of combining role clarity with advocacy consulting represents a key skill-set to model for clients. The power that comes from role clarity about living out an organization's vision lies at the heart of successful transformation from authoritarian to collaborative power. Advocacy consulting means that I stand for certain things. Not all behavior is acceptable. I set limits and encourage clients to do so. People need norms and guidelines to create change processes that do not damage or destroy. I have found that norms and guidelines are needed more when the environment is characterized by high levels of confusion and uncertainty. Assume, for example, that an organization's senior executives know that verbal attacks and put-downs are not permitted. Establishing this norm not only helps them to build trust throughout the organization but also encourages them to adopt the norm themselves.

ADVOCATING AND LETTING GO: A BALANCE OF POWER

With power issues, I use frequent process observation and feedback, letting the client organization see how it is using "old" or "new" power and its various hybrid forms. I recommend how to proceed, explaining the reasons behind my advice. Then I let go and trust that the client will make the appropriate decision. Consequences of alternative decisions are explored. If an issue is not raised, I raise it. I am clear that I can ask for decisions to be made and can influence those decisions, but I do not make them.

This clarity frees me to make my interventions more powerful. As clients know I will not intrude on their decision making, I can recommend a course of action without worrying about taking over their process. When I serve as an advocate in a client's business decision, I make recommendations, sometimes strong ones, in addition to consulting and facilitating. Rarely have executives tried to get me to make their decisions, but when they have, I have maintained role clarity, restated my recommendation, and reiterated that the decision is theirs. In a few cases when clients have been reluctant to move forward on decisions, I have honored their concerns while helping them arrive at and communicate decisions.

An issue closely related to the power shift is learning when to let go and when to intervene to make things happen. Consultants can advocate, yet they always need to be willing to let go of their own ideas and be open to better ones. A consultant's ideas may add value by catalyzing others' ideas as well as by providing final solutions. In one client meeting I withdrew my idea after I heard a better one from a team member, explaining that I thought her idea was superior. To my surprise, a shocked silence pervaded the room. When I asked why, team members said that they couldn't believe I had relinquished my idea so easily. I said that my top priority was the best solution for them, regardless of the source.

It turned out that their habit was to fight doggedly for their own ideas simply because those ideas were theirs. This misuse of power can keep people from generating the best solutions and create unnecessary suffering. The cost of this struggle is very high at a time when competitive advantage derives from diverse input into solutions. Constructive power involves getting satisfaction from the best solution, not just from one's own contributions.

Leaders embracing the new power recognize that they are not just giving up the old power; they are developing new forms of power that are better than the old forms because times have changed. Each type of power has costs and benefits; as culture changes over time, those costs and benefits shift in importance and value. For example, the original benefit of authoritarian power—keeping people in line—is now regarded negatively.

A key indicator of the power shift is the acknowledgment that the function of supporting and sparking others' ideas is as important as generating one's own ideas.

SKILLS

Several skills are required to use collaborative power effectively:

1. *Positive listening:* Listening for the good news, not just for the problems;

2. *Managing by strengths:* Focusing on the strengths each employee uses, not just on weaknesses;

3. *Specific positive feedback:* Developing employees to their highest performance potential by emphasizing their specific positive characteristics;

4. *Connecting:* Responding and providing feedback to others' input so that they perceive you as connecting with them quickly. This level of dialogue goes far beyond "You share your news, and I'll share mine";

5. *Specific negative feedback:* Providing negative feedback based on employees' specific behaviors, not based on their general weaknesses; and

6. *Enjoying diversity:* Expressing genuine interest in others different from oneself.

SUMMARY

The planet-wide shift from authoritarian to collaborative power is a complex issue facing nearly every change leader and consultant. A consultant must be clear about his or her role, choose a role that fits, and be at peace with his or her own power and role before being able to help leaders, managers, and employees make this power shift in a healthy way. Combining advocacy consulting with letting go and trusting clients to make the right choice are additional keys to facilitating this shift.

Linne Bourget, M.B.A., Ph.D., *is the director of the Institute for Transformation Leaders and Consultants (ITLC), providing consulting services for leaders, consultants, and organizations in transformation. For over twenty years, Dr. Bourget has been a pioneer in positive collaborative approaches to organizational transformation. She specializes in vision-based strategic planning, leadership communications strategy, organizational healing, and partnership/team cultures for change and quality. Dr. Bourget has taught at several universities, authored three books and numerous articles, appeared on television and radio, and belongs to several professional organizations.*

LEARNING FROM THE INTERVENTION ITSELF: FROM STRATEGY TO EXECUTION

Milan Moravec

Abstract: Consultants and clients need to continually assess all aspects of organizational change in order to learn from it. A large-scale change initiative at British Petroleum Exploration generated fifteen lessons for the organization and twelve lessons for the consultant. All these insights are applicable to any reengineering, organizational change, and/or any consultant-client relationship.

$\mathbf{I}$n a true learning organization, managers and human resource development (HRD) people pay attention not only to what the enterprise is doing but also to how it is doing it. Assessment of both is critical to success. Identifying the processes that work as the organization evolves through various changes is the key to continuous improvement and learning. Continuous learning is essential to competing effectively in today's dynamic, global economy.

It is also important to keep track of what works in an intervention facilitated by a consultant. It is important not only for the organization but for the consultant, too. The consultant as well as the client ought to be a "learning organization."

A CASE EXAMPLE

After a massive transformation effort in British Petroleum Exploration, the internal program manager for the change process and the consultant reflected together on what they had learned about the consulting process itself. Some of the learnings were confirmations or enhancements of assumptions they had made previously; others emerged as they proceeded through the intervention. Before these learnings are summarized, a little background will be provided.

The Problems

British Petroleum Exploration (BPX), the arm of British Petroleum that finds and develops oil and gas reserves, was—like many other multinational corporations—confronting explosive changes in technologies and markets. The company was all too aware of the need to become flexible and innovative in order to respond to customer priorities. It was aware, as well, that BPX currently fell far short of this goal.

In short, BPX was hobbled by bureaucracy. A staff survey revealed that people were stifled by paperwork, unable to get things done. Because they believed that they had no real influence, they were reluctant to assume responsibility or take initiative, and management was highly averse to risk. Cynicism, alienation, and frustration were rampant.

It soon became clear that system-wide reengineering, not only of the organizational infrastructure but also of mind-sets, was needed.

The Change Initiative

The major changes initiated by the program manager and the consultant included the following:

1. *Dual career paths.* At BPX, career success had come to be equated with a management title. To move up the hierarchy, individual contributors eventually were forced to become managers, regardless of desire or aptitude. The new dual-track system provided one career path for would-be managers and another, comparable in terms of influence and rewards, for individual contributors. Thus, development of creativity and technical skills received as much encouragement as development of managerial skills. The two paths stayed parallel all the way to the top, and people could switch from one path to another as their accomplishments, qualifications, and customer requirements evolved.

To develop these dual paths, work teams from various levels, functions, and worldwide locations in the company worked to replace the old job descriptions with skill matrices and lists of competencies that reflected the roles in the matrices.

2. *Upward feedback.* To open up communication and improve the ways in which managers and employees worked together, BPX launched a program in which employees assessed their managers on the ways they managed people. System design and training ensured that those who participated felt minimum pain and optimum gain and that new awareness was translated into specific changes in behavior and unit action plans.

The proposal for the program received such an overwhelming endorsement from both managers and staff—who were obviously hungry for honest communication—that its development was accelerated.

3. *Personal-development planning.* This process, self-guided but supported by training, was designed to assist employees in identifying their skills, interests, and values, and in marketing themselves within the company. It enabled employees to take charge of their own careers and it could be used for life planning in general.

Personal-development planning was related specifically to the skills matrices developed for the dual career paths and was also related to the upward-feedback program. Performance appraisal, training, and compensation systems were redesigned to dovetail with these programs.

4. *Attitude surveys.* Attitude surveys were administered to promote interaction, decision making, and action. Survey results were used as the basis for action planning, in which employees at all levels participated.

Discussions of survey results were incorporated into the upward-feedback program.

In summary, the change initiative at BPX focused on weaving customers' priorities, organizational culture, processes, technology, structure, and people into a seamless business strategy.

LESSONS FOR THE ORGANIZATION

Following are the lessons that BPX learned, from this comprehensive intervention, about creating large-scale organizational change:

1. *The focus of the change must be on competitive needs—what will benefit customers.* If there is no clear connection between new processes and what the customer is demanding, one needs to ask, "Why do this?" In the case of BPX, satisfying the customer required initiative, faster decision making, and all the innovation and creativity the company could muster in the face of increased competition. As a multinational corporation with worldwide operations, it also needed a culture in which people and ideas could move freely in response to changing requirements.

2. *Organizations need to decide whether competitive ability is better served by incremental change (more of the same only more efficient and better) or by paradigm shift.* If they need the latter, as BPX did, gradual changes in structure and policies won't work. Change must occur on so many fronts simultaneously that everyone—managers and employees alike—finds it impossible to continue behaving in the old ways.

3. *The business (internal and external environments, roles/processes, and technology) and the organization (structure and people) need to be managed as a whole system.* Change in one part of the system affects other parts, and each part influences, and is influenced by, the whole.

4. *Senior management must consider, very carefully, how involved it should become in decision making.* Although leaders must have a vision of excellence (as well as courage and a keen knowledge of their industry and the competition) before undertaking a major transition, the road to transformation is paved by those who act on new procedures and processes.

If senior management is trying to empower people, it must let go and have the people make some of the key decisions about how to change. Otherwise, the people will keep expecting top management to "fix things," and the bureaucracy will never be dismantled. It may be necessary to keep reinforcing this concept. It is very difficult to withdraw from the command-and-control habits of a lifetime.

5. *A blueprint for change is helpful but it is only a beginning and it oversimplifies what can be done.* A blueprint—the formal announcement of change—does not reflect the chaos that needs to be managed or the challenges of implementing new ideas. Transformation does not begin until people have finished talking about it.

6. *The line organization must lead the change.* If HRD or organization development (OD) people do it, employees do not see the business evidence of management's commitment to change. Line managers are not above the process; they need to "walk the talk" and go through transitions themselves in order to establish credibility. They need to model the desired new behaviors.

7. *At some point, it will appear that nothing is happening.* Employees will be waiting and testing management, thinking, "Maybe we won't have to change." This is a good time for management to walk the boards, create task forces, provide resources to get the new work done, and actively demonstrate its commitment.

A good way to reestablish momentum is to pick the low-hanging fruit: find projects where change can be brought about quickly and where people can witness positive results. Such projects must be central to competitiveness. (It may help to get customers and suppliers involved in task forces.) When change begins to percolate, the process is on track again.

> *Use disequilibrium as a means to unleash creativity.*

8. *It is important to maintain urgency by linking what is being done to some compelling competitive priority.* The goal must connect the organization to its environment. Establishing a theme of "We have to attract new customers" or "We need to reduce errors by 70 percent" is more effective than saying, "We're going to improve ourselves." Additionally, do not waste time fixing what does not need to be done in the first place.

9. *Inertia needs to be managed.* Inertia is a more powerful force than many people realize. State at the beginning that employees and managers are equally responsible for change; it is not a top-down activity. When one group loses steam, the other may have to take a larger or more active role for awhile. If some managers keep resisting change, they may have to be moved out of influential roles.

10. *New behaviors and practices will be at odds with the old system at first.* You cannot have change without disequilibrium, so you might as well use disequilibrium to unleash creativity. Cut the chains of command and

encourage people to try new approaches without having to get approval for every step.

11. *You cannot let nature take its course; you need to lead endings, new beginnings, and periods in between.* Watch out for the Tarzan effect: swinging from endings to new beginnings without paying attention to the neutral zone (where people can absorb and try out different ideas), and then swinging back as soon as you meet resistance. Also avoid the Marathon effect, in which management is so keyed up about the process and runs so far ahead that others in the organization begin to lose sight of them.

12. *Change involves emotions.* Do not be surprised by periods of low trust and morale: "Whose idea was this, anyway?"; "We never had to go through this before and we were successful." People may be stressed, angry, and distracted at times. Even those who are energized may not always agree on how things should be done.

13. *You must maintain the vision.* Some interventions are lost, some are won, and some are rained out, to be played again. The vision, along with the organization's stated values, provides the forward pull that creates positive change and learning. It is also what holds the organization in alignment during periods of disequilibrium.

14. *You cannot demand loyalty.* "Loyalty" is a relic of the old, clumsy, hierarchical system. A loyal individual goes along to get along. A more valuable contributor speaks up about better ways to do things. Commitment can no longer be demanded; if you try, you'll only get compliance, at best.

15. *The change process is never finished.* Always be ready to start again. Ideally, you should not just be encouraging change; you should be creating an organization that thrives on it. Keeping change going and learning from each cycle require the personal attention and guidance of leaders—both managers and individual contributors.

LESSONS FOR THE CONSULTANT

A large-scale change process also generates certain lessons for the consultant involved:

1. *You cannot succeed as a one-person show.* Do not expect to be followed or listened to just because you are an expert. You need to build alliances, networks, and credibility in order to orchestrate a coordinated group effort. Develop internal change agents. At BPX, the external

consultants began to train HRD people in consulting and leadership skills, as their help was needed to turn the organization around.

2. *Do not expect the existing culture to welcome change.* The organizational culture will fight you to maintain its equilibrium—to survive. Culture *is* resistance to change. It is your job to instill a compelling desire to try the unfamiliar and the new.

3. *You must empower yourself.* Do not expect senior management to run interference for you, even if the HRD people ask top management to "require" line management to behave in certain ways. Do not wait for total commitment from top management; that comes with results. Proceed as if you have all the authorization that is needed.

Organizations will not accept a consultant they do not believe in, and they will not believe in you unless you believe in yourself and in your mission. However, do not be overly controlling; show care and respect for others; solicit their perspectives and opinions; listen; and be a team player. Do take action promptly and decisively. Inspire confidence by making things happen.

> *Organizations will not believe in you unless you believe in yourself and in your mission.*

4. *Be intolerant of inaction and inertia.* People who are using new power will make some mistakes, but after these mistakes are admitted, you need to move on quickly. Recognize those who hustle and nip at those who seem to be dragging their feet. If some people refuse to go along with the change process at all, respect their decision and leave them alone. You may have to inform senior management of any bottlenecks, but first discuss the situation with the bottlenecks themselves.

5. *You cannot reconcile all differences or achieve full consensus during the transformation process.* Once you have agreement on where you are going, rely on your own expertise regarding how to get there. Some people will not get on board until they see examples that work. Remember, the organization's customers cannot wait for consensus. Acknowledge differences and emphasize the need to go forward despite these differences. Do not try to force agreement or pretend that agreement exists.

6. *You are a role model.* Leaders and employees will watch you intently. Demonstrate your involvement with what the organization is trying to accomplish. Set an example: put in extra effort, working evenings and weekends when necessary; rock the boat; be a conveyer of

urgency; and demonstrate commitment to milestones and schedules. Display insight, passion, energy, and drive.

7. *You will need to deal with volatile emotions.* During large-scale change, people feel vulnerable, threatened, and uneasy. You need to be seen and available. Stop, listen, and talk at the emotional level. Solicit opinions and suggestions, even negative opinions. Continually ask, "How do you feel about that?" Offer understanding (not sympathy) as well as words of encouragement and nods of appreciation. Appropriate physical contact (handshakes, pats on the back) is a powerful reinforcement of verbal thanks. Celebrate small victories.

8. *Be honest; do not promise what you cannot deliver.* If you lack the power or resources to control a decision, it is better to say so rather than to promise to have something completed by tomorrow and then having to go back and admit you need more time.

9. *Be a partner, not a doctor.* This means being involved, being yourself, and learning along with the client. Friendship is not necessary and can even complicate matters, but it also can make the work more pleasant for both you and the client. Do not be afraid to spend a coffee break or lunchtime with people in the organization.

10. *As clients trust you more, they risk more.* Resistance about size, costs, and timing of projects indicates unwillingness to take risks. Accomplishment builds trust but, at the same time, raises the stakes. Do not expect others to take risks that you yourself would not take. Remember that the client is responsible for unpredicted results.

11. *Clients pay more attention to what works than to any other element of their relationship with you.* If you do not actually accomplish something together, the relationship is in trouble. When you debrief about a project or a meeting, point out how you contributed to each accomplishment and identify ways in which you can contribute to future success.

12. *Bring who you are to what you do.* There is no one right way. Although you want to behave in a manner consistent with the client's values, you need to stay true to your own. Express your personality—people need to see that you are human. If they know that you are authentic, they will allow you some leeway even if they do not completely agree with you.

In today's complex business environment, both the organization and the consultant need to slice through the theoretical hype, popular misconceptions, and wishful thinking about change and transition. Both need to keep learning. In a solid relationship, both can admit to each other that they are not all-knowing but are continuing to learn and improve.

In order to learn from experience, it is crucial to evaluate what you do together. It is also essential to look continually for opportunities to reinvent processes and infrastructures. Doing more of what made you successful in the past is a sure route to failure in the future.

Milan Moravec, of Moravec and Associates, Walnut Creek, California, is an organization, management, change, and reengineering consultant with a special focus in implementation. He has consulted internationally with such clients as Corning, Tektronix, Cummins, Bechtel, Exxon, and Sanwa Bank. His approach is to align business and organization strategy with processes, technology, and human resources; he has successfully provided change management and reengineering training, facilitation, leadership, and support for many large and small companies. Mr. Moravec has coauthored From Downsizing to Recovery: Strategic Transition Options for Organizations and Individuals *(CPP Books, 1994).*

PUTTING THE MANAGEMENT IN TOTAL QUALITY MANAGEMENT: CREATING A STRATEGIC FRAMEWORK

Donald T. Simpson

Abstract: The leadership of top management is one of the most important elements in identifying and implementing improvement projects in organizations.

The strategic-framework process begins with identification of the organization's mission and vision, based on customer requirements. Key results areas (KRAs) are identified. Quantitative, data-based key results measures (KRMs) are used to assess how the organization is performing in each KRA, against industry standards and benchmarked goals. Gaps become major improvement opportunities (MIOs). Management assesses MIOs and sets priorities; it then develops improvement strategies. These lead to improvement projects at all levels of the organization. Within each project are action plans with improvement activities, all of which are linked back to the KRAs and the organization's mission and vision. The management team must monitor the strategic framework over time, continually evaluating the results of improvement activities against goals and shifting priorities. The process is cyclical.

Total quality management (TQM) is a long-term trend in all types of American organizations. The concepts of total quality have caught on, in spite of cynics, inappropriate applications, and unrealistic expectations.

There is one thing total quality is not. It is not an excuse for poor management. In TQM, management is more important than ever. Without management's bold and visible leadership, an organization-wide TQM effort is headed for trouble. Worse, it can be frustrating for employees and dysfunctional for future improvement efforts.

Management leadership is important because activities throughout the organization must be aligned (Figure 1). That is, what anyone and everyone in the organization does must be done toward common goals. If parts of the organization are oriented in different directions, the result will be inefficiency of the system as a whole. The organization itself will become dysfunctional.

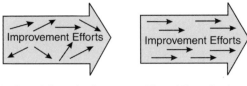

Unaligned Organization   Aligned Organization

Figure 1. Alignment

It is the responsibility of executive management to set direction, to envision and plan the future of the organization. Of course, managers are no better at predicting the future than anyone else, but through sound planning and forecasting, and with a clear mission and shared vision, what people in the organization do today influences the future.

THE STRATEGIC-FRAMEWORK PROCESS

Creating a strategic framework begins with developing or reviewing the mission and the vision of the organization. Within the scope of the mission and the vision, the management team identifies specific areas in which success is critical to the success of the overall organization (Figure 2).

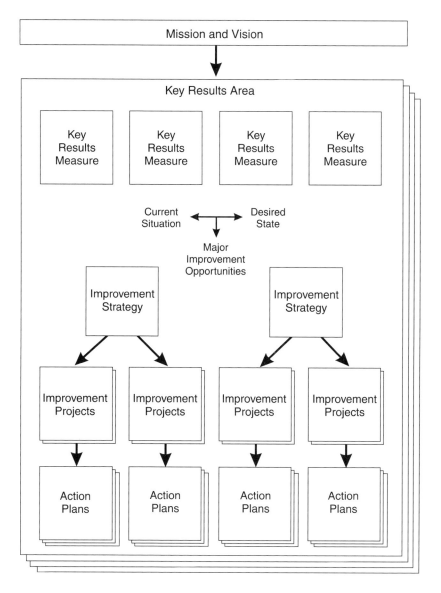

Figure 2. Creating the Strategic Framework

Measurement in each of these key areas tells the team how the organization is doing in each area, compared to a goal, standard, or expectation. From this analysis, the team can identify major improvement opportunities and, then, specific improvement strategies. The strategies, in turn, lead to improvement projects.

Finally, activities of people throughout the organization bring the projects to fruition. Thus, improvement activities are linked to key results areas.

Mission and Vision

The process starts with the organization's customers—the end users of the organization's products or services. Before developing the strategic framework, the management team must consider its customers' requirements. The team determines the key outputs of the organization.

Most managers and consultants are familiar with mission and vision statements.

Mission. The mission statement defines the nature of the organization—what business the organization is in—and articulates the organization's purpose—its reason for being. It identifies, in a sentence or two, who, what, why, and for whom the organization exists.

Vision. The vision statement, in a few short paragraphs, describes the organization's direction—its desired future state. The vision statement becomes a star to steer by, a force pulling the organization as it undertakes its developmental journey.

The mission and vision must come from the organization's executive leadership. Although input from the ranks is desirable and, in most cases, necessary, top management bears the responsibility for developing the mission and vision (Figure 3).

It is important to note that the mission statement is not the same as a clear sense of mission, nor is the vision statement the same as a commonly held vision. Mission and vision are intangibles; the statements are outward reflections of them.

Key Results Areas

Key results areas (KRAs) are the parts of the organization's work in which success is critical to the organization's overall success. The management team must ask, "In order to perform the mission and move toward the vision, in what areas must we be a success?" It is important that the

Information Office Mission		Information Office Vision
Who We Are	*The City Information Office*	*The Information Office is the first place that comes to mind when a citizen, area business, or visitor wants to know what's happening in the City. The departmental hotlines carry up-to-date information about events and activities. The courteous and knowledgeable staff can direct inquiries quickly to the most appropriate City office. County and State government employees also enjoy rapid access to City offices through the Information Office.*
What We Are	*is an agency of the municipal government*	
What We Do	*that provides access to events information on a daily basis*	
For Whom	*for residents, businesses, and visitors, and for City, County, and State government personnel*	
Why We Do It	*to facilitate contact and information dissemination*	*The well-trained Information Office staff uses a computerized database for accessing City offices. The information is always current and accurate.*

Figure 3. Example of Mission and Vision Statements

management team identify results areas, not measures of activities. When the results areas are measured and the results are compared to earlier measurements and a goal, the organization can evaluate its progress and improvement efforts.

Key results areas are logical extensions of the organization's mission and vision. These KRAs originate from considering the outputs of the organization, its customers' requirements, and regulatory concerns. Some typical areas for identifying KRAs include:

- customer satisfaction
- output quality (products and/or services)
- financial viability
- employee development and satisfaction
- safety and environmental concerns
- regulatory compliance
- cycle time
- delivery of products and/or services

- technological development and/or application
- technical expertise
- administration
- community service
- sales and marketing
- productivity
- human resources utilization

The management team lists areas of endeavor, then sets priorities to ensure that it has identified the key areas. In each case, the team makes sure that the area actually is key—that it is linked directly to the mission and vision. Usually the team identifies four to six KRAs (Figure 4).

Key Results Areas	Description	Why Important to the Organization
Information Accuracy	Information disseminated by the hotline or Information Office staff is timely and accurate. Events are described accurately and completely. Names, offices, telephone numbers, and other data are correct and current.	One key reason that the Information Office exists is to disseminate information to the public and to government offices.
Proper Routing	Calls are routed to appropriate office to deal with caller's needs. For multiple referrals, the most urgent (in caller's mind) is routed first.	Callers want to be connected with the appropriate person/ office to handle their needs. Properly directed calls avoid frustration of the caller, receiver, and this office.
Timely Routing	Calls are referred and routed while the caller waits. If the intended receiver is unavailable, the next person in line in that office is called.	Avoid caller frustration while forwarding a call. Also avoid tying up Information Office lines.
Data-Based Management	Names, telephones, addresses, etc., of appropriate people in City offices are current and correct. The database is updated regularly.	The database is the source for all our information, hotlines, and referrals.

Figure 4. Example of Key Results Areas

Key Results Measures

Key results measures (KRMs) permit the management team to measure the organization's performance in each KRA. Within each KRA there are a number of measures (often in terms of ratios, such as sales revenues to cost of production or patient morbidity to total patients). The team selects measures within each KRA that are indicators of performance in that area. The number of KRMs for any KRA varies. Progress in one KRA may be adequately described by a single measure. Another KRA may require two or three KRMs. Normally, six KRMs is a practical limit for any one KRA.

The team employs KRMs in order to determine a base line—how the organization is performing—in each KRA. The team may use subsequent measures to assess improvement efforts or it may compare current performance to a goal or standard.

In identifying or developing KRMs, the management team might consider the following:

What to measure: Time, cost, quantity, number of people served, productivity, etc.

How to measure: Availability of data, cost of measuring, suitability for dissemination or display, etc.

When to measure: Timeliness of data, timeliness of summarized data, etc.

In identifying or developing key results measures, the management team might consider criteria such as the following:

- Is it an accurate measure of performance in the KRA?
- Is it important to the organization?
- What is the availability of data?
- Is data collection under the control of the team?
- Is the measurement repeatable?
- Is it timely?
- Are the benefits of the measurement worth the cost of making it?
- Is there a balanced set of measures in each KRA?
- Is there a combination of leading, current, and lagging measures?
- Is it meaningful to the people in the organization?

Ideally, measures should be quantitative and data based. Quantitative measures allow ease in collecting and displaying data and aid in interpreting the data. They are less subject to varied interpretation and disagreement. The measures should be timely, too. A customer satisfaction survey taken annually may be too infrequent for a good KRM. Measures usually include leading measures that predict performance in the KRA, current measures, and lagging measures that summarize performance over a given period of time (Figure 5).

Key Results Areas	Key Results Measures	Unit of Measure	Frequency	Goal/Standard vs. Actual
Information Accuracy	Misdirected calls	Number of calls	Qtr*	0 calls misdirected vs. 14 calls per quarter now
	Inaccurate hotline information	Number of messages	Qtr*	0 inaccurate messages vs. 4 or 5 per quarter now
	Outdated hotline information	Number of messages	Wk	0 outdated messages vs. 2 or 3 per week now
Proper Routing	Misdirected calls or referrals	Number of calls	Qtr*	Fewer than 5 calls misdirected per quarter vs. 14 per quarter now
Timely Routing	Callbacks	Number of calls	Qtr*	Minimize number of callbacks (data not yet available)
		Number of callbacks	Qtr*	Average referral within 2 minutes vs. 4 minutes now
Data-Based Management	Update rate	Period for update	6 Mo.	Database updated weekly vs. semiannually now
				*Data collected daily, summarized quarterly

Figure 5. Example of Key Results Measures

Improvement Strategies, Projects, and Action Plans

Key results measures, when applied in the corresponding key results area, tell the management team how the organization is doing. The question is, "Compared to what?" KRM can indicate progress or lack thereof, but only by having a particular goal will the team be able to effectively assess organizational improvement. The comparison can be made against a recognized industry standard, a team-developed target, or some benchmarked goal. Well-understood KRAs and KRMs are ideal tools for determining what should be benchmarked.

The comparison identifies a gap between the present state and the desired state. That gap is the major improvement opportunity (MIO). The management team compares MIOs and sets priorities. It then develops overall strategies for closing the gaps (Figure 6).

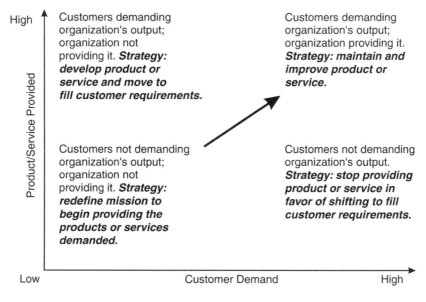

Figure 6. MIO/Strategy Guidelines

The improvement strategies naturally result in improvement projects. Within each improvement project are action plans with improvement activities, all linked back to the key results areas and, in turn, to the mission and vision (Figure 7).

After developing improvement strategies, the management team begins to cascade the strategic-framework process into the organization. Department managers and their staffs become involved in identifying improvement projects in their areas of responsibility. Often this process extends to the lowest levels of the organization. Those closest to the work are important sources of ideas for improvement projects.

Key Results Area	Key Results Measures	Empowerment
Proper Routing	Number of misdirected calls or referrals	Sponsor: Manager, City Information Office. Improvement team has complete authority to alter procedures for determining caller's needs and identifying appropriate City office to handle the call. Estimate 2-4 hr/wk for 8 wks. Must coordinate with improvement teams in other areas through Manager, City Information Office. Status reports weekly.

Strategy

Analyze reasons for misdirected calls. Review procedures. Develop checklist/guidelines for determining caller's needs and identifying appropriate office.

Project Description	Initial Team Composition

Team Outputs:
 ❑ *Guidelines for assessing caller's need*
 ❑ *Descriptions of City offices functions*
 ❑ *Solution strategy creative, innovative, breakthrough*
 ❑ *Implementation plan with cost/benefit analysis*
 ❑ *Appropriate contingency plans and risk analysis*
 	
 Solution Requirements:
 ❑ *No significant increase in office space or equipment*
 ❑ *No increase in staff*
 ❑ *Target: Less than 5 inappropriate routings/quarter*
 ❑ *Implement by third quarter this year*
 ❑ *Stay within budget*
	Info Office—
	    Kay Serra (Team Leader)
	 Mayor's Office—
	    Dusty Rhodes
	 MIS—
	    Tally M. Upp
	 City Engineer's Office—
	    Carrie A. Slipstick
	 Special Projects—
	    Maggie May (Facilitator)

Figure 7. Example of Project Description

Improvement projects consist of various activities. These activities are arranged in sequence, and responsibilities are assigned, resources are identified, and schedules are developed. The sum of these is an action plan. Within the action plan, the actual improvement work is accomplished (Figure 8).

MONITORING THE FRAMEWORK

The intent of a strategic framework is to ensure that quality-improvement efforts are linked to the organizational mission and vision. It is not

| Goal: Minimize misdirected calls coming into City Information Office | | | Schedule | | | | | | | | | | | | |
| | | | July | | | | | August | | | | September | | | |
Activities	Responsibility	Output	1	8	15	22	29	5	12	19	26	2	16	23	30
1. Review call logs	Kay Serra	Misrouted calls identified, listed	▓												
2. Interview selected office managers	Kay Serra	Interviews completed and summarized		▓											
3. Conduct focus group of residents/ businesses	Tally Upp	Focus groups completed and summarized			▓										
4. Conduct problem-solving sessions	Kay Serra	Causes for misrouted calls identified						▓							
5. Develop and draft new guidelines	Dusty Rhodes	Draft guidelines written										▓			

Figure 8. Example of Action Plan

enough to develop a good strategic framework; the management team must monitor it, continually reviewing and evaluating the results of improvement projects against the goals in each KRA. In time, priorities shift as improvements take hold and are institutionalized. The process is cyclic. Goals are revised, the mission and vision change, the environment changes, and organizational priorities change. Only a systemic, real-time process can provide the tracking and linkages necessary for effective management of improvement.

Top management holds review meetings periodically (e.g., quarterly), during which the strategic framework and status of projects are reviewed. Reviews of action plans take place at lower levels at critical points in the plan.

Strategic-Framework Document

The strategic-framework document summarizes the work of the management team and enables the team to monitor the activities of the various project teams. The document is made available to the project teams in order to ensure that they can link their activities with the strategic intent. Typically, the strategic-framework document includes:

- The organization's mission and vision statements,
- A list of key customers and their requirements,
- Key results areas (often with a statement of their importance to the organization),
- The key results measures for each KRA,
- An assessment against identified targets (often benchmarked) or expectations,
- A description of major improvement opportunities resulting from the assessment,
- Improvement projects, identified with department managers,
- Action-team assignments and charters.

And, as the projects are undertaken:

- Status reports and updates on action teams' work, and
- Provisions for reassessing the organization and updating the strategic framework.

Conclusion

The strategic-framework process ensures that activities in the organization are linked to strategic intent. The direction and vision must come from the organizational leadership—the management team. Management, as it models the process and its commitment to continuous improvement, disperses its influence throughout the organization.

Donald T. Simpson, Ed.D., is a management and organization development consultant and trainer based in Rochester, New York. He works with business, social service, health care, government, academic, and financial institutions, providing training and consulting in supervision, communications, team building, and total quality management. Dr. Simpson has a master's degree in mechanical engineering and in adult education and a doctorate in human and organization development from the Fielding Institute. His published work appears in recognized journals and handbooks.

IMPLEMENTING ORGANIZATIONAL CHANGE: SIX STEPS AND A CASE STUDY

Paul Jansen and Rendel de Jong

Abstract: True cultural changes in organizations, that is, changes in behavior, do not happen as a result of management edicts or mission statements. This article presents a six-step process for introducing real change in organizations and presents a case study of changes at KPN and PTT Telecom in The Netherlands.

The steps are a formulation of shared values, behavioral concretization of the values, commitment to change, learning to manage interfaces, embedding the values in structures and systems, and making behavior clearly visible and quantifiable. The general scheme of the project, phases in the implementation, roadblocks, and successes are discussed.

The 1996 Annual: Volume 2, Consulting.
Copyright © 1996 by Pfeiffer & Company, San Diego, CA.

As a result of research conducted in over 200 U.S. companies, Kotter and Heskett (1992) identified "culture" as the key variable in performance. They distinguish "superficial culture" (visible behavioral patterns or "how we do things here") and "depth culture" (shared values and standards). Depth culture is difficult to change because it is omnipresent. Moreover, depth culture is maintained by being embedded in superficial cultural systems and procedures.

Many of the cultural edicts made by top managers prove to be very superficial when one examines who gets promoted in their organizations. For example, many companies encourage behavior A (e.g., empowerment, taking risks, responding to the customer) but, in fact, reward behavior B (e.g., conformity, rigid management, responding to internal needs first).

A revised reward system can be a strong anchor for a new organizational structure. In their treatise on internal entrepreneurship, Kuratko, Hornsby, Naffziger, and Montagno (1993) conclude that "employees are willing to work on new projects and challenging teams if the rewards are apparent." They add that steps in this direction do not need to be confined to simple pay rises. "It should be mentioned that the exact rewards for corporate entrepreneuring are not yet agreed upon by most researchers."

CULTURAL CHANGE IN ORGANIZATIONS

Cultural changes appear to come from above. They stand or fall with power, in the sense that somebody has to start "pushing," albeit subtly. According to Beer, Eisenstat, and Spector (1992), local behavior will not change automatically because the head office announces change programs, training courses, quality programs, and so on; only the formal organization changes. A different stacking of the building blocks of the organization is no guarantee that the behavioral patterns of the employees in those blocks will change. On the contrary, keeping the old working methods in place perpetuates the old organization. It is wrong to assume that the formal organization (structure) and the informal organization (work and behavior) are separate systems.

Beer et al. (1992) discovered during a four-year study in six large companies that real change takes place in a way "demarcated by situations." The managers of local business units concentrated on "real work" rather than "abstractions such as 'participation' or 'culture.'"

Changing means learning, and the only way this can occur meaningfully is in concrete situations. Change does not result from general attitudes or knowledge but from the way people behave at work. Because behavior depends on where a person is embedded in the organization (i.e., his or her role), any attempt to change behavior must start by placing the person in a new organizational setting, creating a new environment with different requirements, or assigning a new collection of competencies conducive to effective operation.

A Six-Step Plan for Changing Organizations

The following is a six-step plan for changing organizations proposed by Beer et al. (1992):

1. Mobilize involvement in the process of change by means of a joint (workers and management) diagnosis of the issues facing the organization. Let people explain what they think is wrong and what needs to be done.

2. Develop a joint vision of organizational and managerial requirements that will lead to a strong competitive position. This diagnosis is, in effect, task-oriented medication.

3. Ensure that there is consensus on the new vision; make sure its implementation is understood by all; and ensure that there is cohesion so as to guarantee continuity. This requires three things:

   ▪ Strong leadership from local management,

   ▪ Sufficient support from training programs and other areas, and

   ▪ The resolve to replace people who cannot or will not change, after they have been given an opportunity to prove themselves.

4. Expand the change to all departments without exerting pressure from above. Allow each department to "reinvent the wheel" if necessary.

5. Institutionalize the change in the form of formal policies, systems, and structures.

6. Evaluate strategies and adjust them to solve problems in the change process.

Schein (1993) arrived at a similar approach, from a strong orientation to the psychology of the individual. In simple terms, he proposes that fear of change should be overcome "paradoxically" by creating an even greater fear. The key word is "destabilization." Schein contends that information entirely out of keeping with the existing working methods should be imparted boldly and credibly. Moreover, he believes that a direct relationship should be forged between what the environment (usually customers) wants and everyday working behaviors. Misfittings should be pointed out. Everyone must take responsibility. If the primary fear of changing makes way for a greater concern (created on genuine grounds) about how things are done now, the result will be a fear of not changing, thus, the laying of foundations for change. The third step is the cultivation of a sense of security by sketching solutions in practical terms, by outlining ways in which people might alter their behavior and giving them a chance to practice. This shows employees that the road to a different organizational culture is not littered with obstacles.

> A direct relationship between customers and workers needs to be established.

Based on the step-plan presented by Beer et al. (1992), and on similar schemes proposed by other authors (e.g., see the voluminous work by Glaser, Abelson, and Garrison [1983]), the present authors have designed the following general six-step plan for the change of work behavior and the introduction of a learning organization. This is summarized as follows:

1. Demonstrate clearly what effective behavior is (show clearly what the objectives are and how they can be achieved). Also describe the benefits of achieving goals (what does the employee get out of it?). Reinforce with behavior by senior management in accordance with the new culture.

2. On a behavioral level, constantly confront the ineffectiveness of methods being used (it does not work that way anymore). It is essential to have reliable information. Keep policies simple, but devote a lot of attention to the actual work (instead of complex policies and a simplistic approach to work).

3. Give people the opportunity to decide whether they want to change their behaviors. Commitment is the key, wanting to change the way one works. People can no longer avoid making the choice. They will automatically feel the repercussions if they persist in working inefficiently. The aim is to have people enjoy working in a different way.

4. Provide necessary assistance, coaching, and feedback. Knowledge and ability must be organized properly. Ensure that signals from colleagues and managers are consistent, which means establishing a strong social construction.

5. Obstacles to doing things differently must be removed; the budget must allow for this and for training and rewards. Make people aware of adverse circumstances. Manage cultural changes.

6. Maintain a consistent focus on evidence of desired behavior by means of assessments and rewards (not just money). To enable this, make behavior clearly visible and quantifiable. Make sure that people do not start feeling cynical about the changes.

THE CASE OF KPN AND TELECOM: INTRODUCING PERSPECTIVE

The Postal and Telecommunications Services of The Netherlands was privatized in 1989, becoming the Koninklijke PTT Nederland NV (KPN). KPN is the largest private-sector employer in the Netherlands, with a work force of around 100,000. In order to be the best provider of information transport, KPN had to change its internal working methods and adopt an entrepreneurial approach.

PTT Telecom is one of the major operating companies of KPN. It employs around 30,000 people who work in several business units, including National Networks, Business Communications, Residential Market, and International Telecommunications. A number of corporate-policy and corporate-service units operate from the head office. The business units bear responsibility for business areas. A business area is composed of a business unit, which directs operations at the central level, and those parts of the thirteen Telecom districts that are concerned with the specific field covered by the business area. A business unit may set regulations and control activities. Through a system of "integration management," the districts are ultimately the people who carry out the company's mission and pursue its objectives at operational levels.

PTT Telecom decided to invest in total quality management and to simplify and inject uniformity into its business processes in order to be ready for growing international competition and a rapidly changing marketplace. "Perspective" was the name given to a major reorganization program that began in 1990 and will affect virtually all the company's employees. Table 1 provides an indication of the direction in which the company is moving with Perspective.

Table 1. Major Cultural Changes Within PTT Telecom

From	To
public sector	private sector
monopoly	competition
production	service
subscriber	customer
technical by nature	customer satisfaction
costs	profit
rules/procedures	results
powers	responsibilities
functional control	integral control of operations
knowing	doing
giant tanker	fleet of maneuverable ships
security	risks
managing	entrepreneuring

The president of PTT Telecom visited all departments of the company to sell the program to the employees and to assure them that Perspective would be implemented without any loss of jobs. As a change agent, the intermediary staff—the "management of change"—was established at headquarters to cooperate closely with managers in creating customer-driven employees, formulas, and organizations.

Essentially, the general aim of Perspective is to reengineer work in such a way that it is no longer cut into separate bits. By means of Perspective, Telecom management intends to simplify the organization and to make Telecom more transparent, both for customers and for employees. When work is reorganized in business processes that are oriented toward customers, management becomes equivalent to process management, to management of the employee who manages the process. The manager coaches employees to help them serve the customers in optimal ways.

In order to give the company a face that was immediately recognizable by customers, it was decided to set up thirty-two Telecom regions with far-reaching competencies. This approach allowed an alert and effective response to customers' requirements. Each region has a work force of 200 to 300 and is responsible for 200,000 to 300,000 customers in its own area. Each region is responsible for all activities performed for a customer according to the principle of one-stop-shopping. It deals with everything from consulting to sales, from installation to service, and from invoicing to collection. The advantage is that customers perceive that one part of the Telecom organization is handling all their business in a simple and clear fashion. The new approach also has made things simpler and clearer for employees.

The other parts of PTT Telecom's internal organization (the business units and head office) are going to be reorganized to create shorter lines of communication with the operational branches (the regions), with recognizable structures and tools for getting goods, services, and systems to customers in the marketplace. As a consequence, almost 24,000 members of the work force of 31,000 will be affected by the reorganization into Telecom regions (8,000 employees), customized project units (1,800 employees), and engineering and maintenance (14,000 employees).

All positions in the first and second management layers of all these new or revamped organizations are being filled through the internal advertising of vacancies throughout KPN nationwide. An innovation is that employees in grades that make them eligible for an advertised management position are expected to submit an application, which may be turned down. It is not easy to manage and solve the social problems that arise out of this approach. A separate follow-up program has been established to devote attention to this matter. By the time Perspective is completed, more than 500 management positions will have new incumbents.

Making Perspective Happen

In PTT Telecom, it had been observed that many new organizational missions tended to become bogged down in mere rhetoric. Consequently, they have no effect on the culture, basic values, and standards of the organization. It appeared that modifying organizational structures was no guarantee of a transformation in actual work behavior. Several reasons were identified for work behaviors lagging behind transformational messages. Each of these correlates directly to one of the steps in changing work behavior from the six-step plan presented here.

1. Lack of clarity about the new behavior, e.g., what is meant by "intrapreneurship" or "taking the initiative" or "having a commercial attitude?"

2. Lack of feelings of necessity; conditions are not experienced as serious or alarming.

3. Lack of commitment to the new behavior.

4. Lack of knowledge and ability.

5. External obstacles frustrate employees in their efforts to demonstrate new behaviors.

6. Old, traditional work behaviors are still being reinforced (for instance, by the organization's promotion or salary systems).

In accordance with this, it was concluded that a change of work behavior would come about only when it had been made abundantly clear that the way things had been done in the past was no longer effective. In accordance with the second step, people had to be confronted with this sobering fact. It was necessary to show people why changes were essential, using hard facts rather than theories. This made it necessary to outline alternatives, to formulate new ways of doing things. It was imperative to describe the new culture in terms of a set of commonly agreed on and recognized Telecom shared values. In accordance with step 1 of Glaser et al. (1983), a concrete behavioral depiction of these work norms was mandatory. In addition, feedback had to be given on the new values (step 6). Thus, learning and experimenting with a new way of doing things had to be supported (step 4). Finally, the new behaviors had to be embedded in structures, with contractually agreed arrangements, bonuses and targets, performance appraisals, a system of management development, and so on (step 5).

Step 1. Formulation of Telecom Shared Values

The KPN management style was set down in a manual—a yardstick for a new, results-oriented performance-appraisal system. The manual was circulated among all managers (over 7,000) at KPN and was discussed with them at great length in "management-to-management talks." The emphasis was on the way the general principles of the management style needed to be expressed in everyday management (e.g., in appraising the performance of employees).

KPN's general management principles were compressed into seven shared values for PTT Telecom, and these have become the *modus operandi* for managers and employees alike. These PTT Telecom values and standards (see Figure 1) were formulated after lengthy discussions within PTT Telecom. The president of PTT Telecom led the rally in a way that made the values explicit and showed everybody what needed to be done. The values and standards consist of a mixture of "controlled management" (completion of high-quality work on time, according to the customer's needs, and cost consciously) and "strategic entrepreneurship" (exhibiting enthusiasm, commitment, and audacity with a sharp eye for the market).

1. Thinking and Acting T-Wide
Breaking through limitations; adopting various approaches; having vision, a broad outlook, and market consciousness; cohesion; creating added value; not placing people and things in boxes
2. Commitment
Doing what you say and saying what you do; avoiding ambiguous messages; showing pride in the organization; not exhibiting cynicism; having feelings of ownership; working for consensus; team work; loyalty in word and deed; taking responsibility; getting involved
3. Belief in Action
Focusing on results; expecting and appreciating hard work; displaying initiative; having a sense of purpose and drive; being decisive; being active mentally and physically; taking a gutsy approach
4. Goal-Directed and Consistent Management
Giving clear guidance; making roles/tasks distinct; clarifying responsibilities; motivating by setting goals; managing people instead of projects; pointing out and celebrating successes; being systematic; creating incentives
5. Openness and Honesty
Having an open attitude; being available; being willing to participate; talking less and listening more; showing respect for and interest in people's advice; sharing credit; encouraging ideas; accepting mistakes
6. Practical management
Maintaining close involvement in day-to-day activities; being clearly present; having a direct approach toward getting things done; being noticeable; coping with matters immediately and working them through; being "hands on"

Figure 1. The Shared Values of PTT Telecom

At the root of the values and standards is the realization that the Telecom intrapreneurs must combine management and successful entrepreneuring in the best possible way. Management is a question of doing things properly, i.e., on time, tailored to needs, alert to what the customer wants, and efficiently/effectively. To some extent, this can be achieved by rearranging work processes, e.g., by standardizing business formulas. This standardization touches on the company's desire to present a single "face" to the customer.

Step 2. Making the Values Behaviorally Concrete

To make the values more concrete and to confront the existing work force with concrete behavioral guidelines, it was decided to interview people at several layers of Telecom (top-level managers, general managers of telecom regions, and mechanics) about the relationships between their work and the Telecom values. Summarized with respect to the values deemed most critical, the findings were as follows:

Thinking and Acting Telecom-Wide was considered the most important value. It requires a helicopter view: being able to ascend and descend, as a general overview of the organization and its environment is not obtained by desk research but by setting out to explore. It was stressed that employees are responsible for acquiring this broad outlook. It implies that one has to get used to variations in levels of abstraction in work: thinking and doing, "flying in the sky," and "drudging in the mud" are parts of the same job. This means that this shared value is not to be isolated from practical management.

Commitment at Telecom was assessed as low at the time of the interviews. Although people seemed to work hard and do as they were told, in practice, organizational units went their own ways. Commitment, as demonstrated in actual behavior, was limited to the work group or to the district organization at the most. Saying "yes" but doing "no" seemed to be a tradition, because employees had the feeling that it was not all right to say "no" openly. This was especially true of the relationships between managers and their employees. The cause of the behavior was a lack of openness and honesty. Especially when one has to cooperate with other departments, and initial personal contacts or feelings of belonging to the same district are absent, commitment is low. Therefore, it was necessary for managers to keep in close contact with employees and to organize on a human scale.

Goal-directed and consistent management was judged important, but some of the requirements for effective management seemed not to be fulfilled. For instance, goals were not stated operationally; information about the system to be managed was not available or was too late and incomplete; and the condition of possessing a skill mix comparable to the complexity of the system was far from fulfilled. Because managers were very limited in their behavioral alternatives, they tended to manage too personally. There was a tendency for personality styles, rather than effective skills, to dominate the approach to managerial problems.

The most important condition for effective management is insight into the system to be managed, i.e., having some idea about what the effects of managerial actions will be. With respect to this, managers complained that they had no real "buttons to push" or "levers to pull," indicating that they were short of effective instruments for monitoring and intervening in the business.

With respect to this value, managers came up with fundamental questions, such as, "Are we really managing?" and "Can you tell me what management is or should be?"

Openness and honesty were assessed as essential as thinking and acting Telecom-wide. Managers at headquarters (all respondents did not work there) were viewed as "playing all sorts of political games." Because business was too personalized, managers tended to overreact in very personal ways, and because such personal actions tended to evoke personal reactions, the effectiveness and commitment of the organization as a whole were affected. Even communication about the introduction and progress of Perspective was not always open and honest. It was deemed important that employees realize that being open and honest works best. This implied, for instance, that it was better to refuse a task that was judged too difficult to accomplish.

Openness and honesty were identified as necessary requirements for the emerging coaching function of managers. Coaching requires that a manager be able to model the desired behavior and presupposes that the manager is able to transfer this behavior to employees.

Practical management/belief in action means doing business in a direct way, without organizational detours. This norm differentiates between the former state company and the present private-sector company. Practical management requires being direct, clear, consistent, and personal, and providing for mutual feedback. As a consequence, managers are much more actively involved in the work of employees. It is a challenge to maintain the right balance between explorative, operational, and outgoing behavior and controlling behavior.

Step 3. Commitment to Change

When managing organizational change, it is important to maintain a balance between being too open and being too tight-reined. One does not want an abdication of responsibility. During this step, it is common to find too much talking and too little real and effective action. Although a lot of communication takes place, most of the energy is devoted to circumstantial matters. A lot of time is spent in meetings. The reason for this is that at a deeper, cultural or affective level, participants fundamentally disagree, and meetings turn into a permanent state of "storming" and "norming" (Tuckman, 1965). Because managers and employees are occupied with creating a new culture and shaping new group norms, there is little time left for "performing." Team building and power plays obstruct effective performance.

A common observation was that these step-3 dynamics were much more positive within a Telecom district than between a district and other parts of the organization, e.g., business units or the head office. In the first case, a general feeling of commitment, of being a team, existed. Because this was limited to the work group or district only, team play between more distant Telecom organizational units was experienced as being "ordered about." There was no reinforcement of the values of thinking and acting Telecom-wide, commitment, and openness and honesty. Still, respondents agreed that this was a mutual phenomenon.

Step 4. Learning to Manage Interfaces

Cooperation was a crucial ability in the new organization. Working together now meant cooperating with internal and external partners (customers, employees, colleagues, suppliers, managers, etc.). Cooperation implies contract (working) and contact (together). The essence of what is to be learned in step 4 is the transition from vertical, hierarchical commandment to horizontal, mutual adjustment. Being ordered was replaced by calling on individual responsibility. Because internal and external customers are so near, the possibility of getting lost in the organization is diminished, and the relationship necessarily has to go well. Everybody knows for whom he or she is working.

> *Cooperation implies contract and contact.*

The ability to cooperate under conditions of contract and commitment is called "interface management." Managing interfaces requires being able to both disagree and negotiate (contract), and to maintain good basic relationships (contact). An additional complication is that the number of interfaces increases rapidly in today's business. Thus, interface management not only implies the shared values of commitment (contact), openness and honesty (contact), and goal-directed and consistent management (contract), but also of thinking and acting Telecom-wide. In addition to mutual acceptation (contact), interface management also is based on focus on output (contract), so the shared values of belief in action and practical management also are implied by it.

Emphasizing work results confirms standardization of output as a mechanism of work coordination. But the latter requires a clear and strong structure that answers questions such as "Where am I in the organization?," "For whom do I work?," and "Who is my customer?" At the same time that work becomes more professionalized, standardization of skills becomes a crucial coordinating instrument (Mintzberg, 1983). With interface management, work production skills themselves become output. Customers do not buy products but the way these products are produced and delivered. This is a well-known phenomenon in service marketing. But also in the domain of product marketing, added value is created by the way in which products are delivered. Therefore competition is value competition. That is why shared values constitute the core of the organization. They are not just incidental organizational "flavors," but core products and core competencies at the same time.

An example of interface management is presented by the ethnographic account by Barker (1993) of "how an organization's control system evolved...from hierarchical, bureaucratic control to concertive control in the form of self-managing teams." Actions of organizational members were controlled by "a system of value-based normative rules." Barker also stresses the possible disadvantages of a much tighter, internalized, mutual system of social or group control. In that case, social commitment and business-like contract are not in balance anymore.

Interface management also has become more important in the private domain. For instance, some recent surveys on sociocultural trends in the Netherlands demonstrated that men and women stay oriented primarily to maintaining good—especially paired—relationships (Van den Akker & Halman, 1994). In contrast to the private domain, however, learning to manage diverse interfaces in work organizations tends to be quickly mistranslated into working according to traditional hierarchical patterns. It is easy for an employee to take the role of underdog (avoiding the burden of responsibility) and for a manager to act as top dog (being in command). Unfortunately, the same kind of boss-subordinate pattern tends to be translated to relationships with customers.

Step 5. Embedding the Values in Structures and Systems

A number of system approaches were undertaken to ensure the anchoring of the new behaviors in structures and procedures. Some examples of newly developed social systems are

- Recruitment and selection: Young people with higher vocational training and university-level qualifications are recruited according to a shared-values profile and are selected with the help of assessment-center methods, in which managers participate (Jansen & Stoop, 1994).

- Management development: Employees bear responsibility for their own careers, and the company merely supports, coaches, and facilitates.

- Job-performance appraisal: Managers encourage the delegation of responsibilities. Appraisals are confined to results and outputs. Appraisals, salary adjustments, and personnel development are interconnected and reaffirm one another.

- Job content: People are not confined to boxes but are allowed to exercise their individual entrepreneurship and be judged by their performance. Job descriptions state the results that work must yield and suggest ways of achieving them. There is no interference. Each job is regarded as a business unit and each employee as an entrepreneur. The idea is to be big but small at the same time, because the company is a network of many small enterprises.

Step 6. Making Behavior Clearly Visible and Quantifiable

In addition to the interviews, the shared values were measured by a questionnaire (Bon & Jansen, 1993). A set of items was written for each value. These items were administered on a pilot basis to a random sample of 917 employees. Factor- and scale analyses revealed that the following four factors were sufficient to reproduce the observed structure of inter-item correlations:

- Thinking and acting Telecom-wide
- Job commitment: to feel oneself in one's element at work
- Goal-directed and practical management
- Openness and honesty

Thus, thinking and acting Telecom-wide and openness and honesty are reproduced, and the original scales for goal-directed and consistent management and practical management are combined into goal-directed and practical management. Finally, a new scale emerged, indicating the degree to which an employee feels in his or her element at work. It indicates job commitment, which is only a part of the shared values of commitment to the organization and the work team, as defined in Figure 1.

On a scale from one to ten (the common grading scale in the Netherlands, with "one" denoting minimal, and "ten" denoting excellent), the factor ratings were:

- Thinking and acting Telecom-wide: 6.5 (above average). There were no differences between employees working in the district sectors of finance, human resource management, logistics, commerce, and engineering.

- Job commitment: 7.4 (well above average). Respondents in the domain of human resource management rate this factor "good" (8.1).

- Goal-directed and practical management: 7.3 (well above average). Respondents working in human resource management rate this factor 8.0 (good).

- Openness and honesty: 7.0 (well above average). No work-domain differences.

These measurements, although obtained in a exploratory study, confirm the interview results. First, all rating are relatively low: above average or well above average. The values thinking and acting Telecom-wide and openness and honesty are rated relatively low. The differences between the human resource management sector and the remaining sectors of the district with respect to goal-directed and practical management and job commitment are remarkable.

Because these results stem from a pilot study, they are of a preliminary nature. At present, new and more sophisticated scales for the shared values are being developed and tested.

WHAT CAN BE LEARNED?

The literature review presented in De Jong and Jansen (1994) shows that, generally, organizational changes carry the seeds of success and failure; which prevails is dependent on the way they are implemented. Taking the step-by-step plan as a point of reference, possible and common failures result from the following:

1. Giving too much weight to contract and disregarding contact. Approaching business reorganization in a too "business-like" manner decreases commitment. It is important to develop commitment as well as stressing assigned goals and tasks.

2. Overstressing contract without devoting attention to the necessary level of employee competence (compare to Gist & Mitchell, 1992).

Formulated in a positive way, two important predictors of success in transforming organizations are commitment and a high level of competence (Locke & Latham, 1990). Thus, the third and fourth steps in implementation are crucial. They enable employees to advance in learning—to make progress in actually changing their ways of working. When this happens, learning becomes a positive experience.

In implementing organizational change, the following also should be taken into account:

1. Watch out for "unfulfilled conditions." In general, these consist of the quartet of commitment, fairness (people simply want to be treated decently), competence, and agreeableness (compare to Johnson & Ostendorf, 1993).

2. Pay attention to the "micro level" of small-group behavior of employees instead of focusing exclusively on macro organizational structures.

3. Watch out for unexpected side effects (discussed in De Jong & Jansen, 1994).

References

Barker, J.R. (1993). Tightening the iron cage: Concertive control in self-managing teams. *Administrative Science Quarterly, 38,* 408-437.

Beer, M., Eisenstat, R.A., & Spector, B. (1992). Why change programs don't produce change. *Harvard Business Review, 70.*

Bon, E.P.M., & Jansen, A.P. (1993). *Test normen en waarden model* (Test of value model). Amsterdam: O + S.

De Jong, R.D., & Jansen, P.G.W. (1994, May 16-18). *How to learn in the LO: Opportunities and pitfalls for people.* Paper presented at the International Conference on Learning Organizations—Initiatives, La Hulpe, Belgium.

Gist, M.E., & Mitchell, T.R. (1992). Self-efficacy: A theoretical analysis of its determinants and malleability. *Academy of Management Review, 17,* 183-211.

Glaser, E.M., Abelson, H.H., & Garrison, K.N. (1983). *Putting knowledge to use: Facilitating the diffusion of knowledge and the implementation of planned change.* San Francisco: Jossey-Bass.

Jansen, P.G.W., & Stoop, L.A.M. (1994). Assessment center graduate selection: Decision processes, validity, and evaluation by candidates. *International Journal of Selection and Assessment, 2*(4), 193-208.

Johnson, J.A., & Ostendorf, F. (1993). Clarification of the five-factor model with the abridged big five dimensional circumplex. *Journal of Personality and Social Psychology, 65,* 563-576.

Kotter, J.P., & Heskett, J.L. (1992). *Corporate culture and performance.* New York: The Free Press.

Kuratko, D.F., Hornsby, J.S., Naffziger, D.W., & Montagno, R.V. (1993, Winter). Implement entrepreneurial thinking in established organizations. *SAM Advanced Management Journal,* pp. 28-39.

Locke, E.A., & Latham, G.P. (1990). Work motivation: The high performance cycle. In U. Kleinbeck, H. Quast, H. Thierry, & H. Hacker (Eds.), *Work motivation.* Hillsdale, NJ: Lawrence Erlbaum.

Mintzberg, H. (1983). *Structure in fives: Designing effective organizations.* Englewood Cliffs, NJ: Prentice-Hall.

Schein, E.H. (1993, Winter). How can organizations learn faster? The challenge of entering the green room. *Sloan Management Review, 34* (2), 85-92.

Tuckman, B.W. (1965). Developmental sequence in small groups. *Psychological Bulletin, 63,* 384-399.

Van den Akker, P., & Halman, L. (1994). Attitudes in de primaire relatiesfeer: Stabiliteit of verandering? (Attitudes in the domain of primary relationships: Stability or change?). *Sociale Wetenscharpen, 37* (1), 1-29.

Paul Jansen, Ph.D., *is a professor of industrial psychology in the Department of Business Administration of the Free University, Amsterdam, The Netherlands. He also is a member of the board of the Netherlands Foundation for Management Development, chairman of the Netherlands Association for Scientific Research in Work and Organizational Psychology, member of the board of the Management Development Committee of the Netherlands Institute of Psychologists, and research fellow of the Netherlands Research Institute and Graduate School for General and Business Economics (the "Tinbergen Institute"). Dr. Jansen specializes in organizational change, assessment center methods, and management development.*

Rendel de Jong, Ph.D., *is in the psychology of work and health department at Utrecht University. His research topics are leadership and the relation between personality, stress, and organizational and professional effectiveness. He consults in the areas of management development, human resource management, and coaching.*

Transforming Organizational Cultures: Simple As ABC

Irwin M. Rubin

Abstract: This article explores the failure of some total quality management (TQM) efforts by focusing on three elements that are frequently lacking from these efforts: a definition of "culture," a consensus as to what constitutes a "good" culture, and a management information system to ensure accountability.

Day-to-day behaviors in an organization define and determine the culture of the organization. People must become aware of these behaviors and their consequences. Then, a system must be implemented that can measure and track the desired behaviors. Such a system will ensure accountability and greatly increase the chances for successful implementation of a TQM effort.

Explanations as to why total quality management (TQM) cultural-change efforts fail to live up to their transformational expectations have a common theme: Too often, the focus is on changing attitudes, not behavior, without instructions or suggestions on how to gauge that change. Accountability then falls by the wayside. Three primary reasons for the resulting demise of many a well-meaning attempt to transform an organization's culture are examined.

- Lack of focus on a pragmatic definition of the concept of culture
- Lack of essential agreement as to what constitutes a concrete image of a "good" or "better" culture
- The heretofore absence of a crucial management information system—one that empowers people to be accountable for their own behavior. Without *countability* there can be no *accountability*.

CULTURE: A PRAGMATIC PERSPECTIVE

Dictionary definitions of culture are of no pragmatic value. Words on paper give culture little if any meaning at all. Because organizations are social, not concrete, structures, actions give culture meaning. As a consequence, day-to-day behavior is both the result of and the cause of that which we call an organization's culture. Culture is something people experience concretely. No one would mistake the culture of a Madison Avenue advertising agency for that of a Swiss bank in Zurich. We know a culture when we see it and feel it.

This pragmatic perspective reduces many of the apparent complexities in approaching the transformation of organizational cultures to one simple truth and its equally simple correlate.

Truth One: All Behavior Has Consequences. If the day-to-day behavior of an organization's members is not observably (and, therefore, measurably) different at some point in the future, it is impossible to conclude that any meaningful change in organizational culture has taken place.

Truth Two: Beware the Mockery of Mimicry. Because modeling—learning by example—is the most powerful socialization agent known, a second truth follows from the first. Until such time as the senior agents of the organization—managers in positions of formal power—change their day-to-day observable (and, therefore, measurable) behavior, no change in organizational culture will become "business as usual."

Managers manage behavior, not numbers or head counts or FTEs or inventories or even objectives. And the behavior that they manage begins with their own.

BEHAVIOR: AN EXPERIENTIAL PERSPECTIVE

"All well and good!" you say. "Now all we need is a simple, behaviorally oriented template that allows us to transform our words into actions."

A variety of models are available that will allow us to talk abstractly about concrete behavior. My own approach has its early roots in the landmark research done by Neil Rackham and his colleagues. They took on the tedious and admirable challenge of *observing and audiotape recording* the behavior of managers, salespeople, and negotiators in their places of work. The researchers then spent thousands of hours analyzing, categorizing, and coding the observed experiential interactions.

Next, Rackham and his colleagues compared and studied the behavioral patterns of the "successful versus less successful." They tested training interventions designed to impart success-oriented behaviors. It was concluded that teaching managers to *code* their own and others' behaviors was key to helping people more successfully manage their own and others' behaviors.[1] Coding simply means identifying specific, concrete behaviors that are reflective of an abstract category.

It is from this simple truth that the importance of the **a**wareness of **b**ehavior and **c**onsequences—the core of Temenos' ABCs behavioral model—was derived. Without awareness (Rackham's notion of coding) of the consequences of current behavior, meaningful change becomes unlikely. Without the capacity to change behavior, no progress or improvement in consequences can take place. The management of people—oneself or others—is impossible without attention to our ABCs.

Creating a Behavioral Template Based on Experience

To create a simple, nonacademic template, we asked several thousand people, spanning many cultures and professions, the following question: "Think about an interaction you recently experienced that satisfies three criteria: (1) the task at hand was completed to the satisfaction of both parties to the interaction; (2) you walked away feeling good about your

---

[1] Rackham, N., and Morgan, T., *Behaviour Analysis in Training*, McGraw Hill, London, England, 1977.

own behavior (you knew that you were honest and fair, that you had acted with integrity); and (3) you left feeling equally good about the other person's behavior. What is a specific example of a behavior that the *other person* exhibited that you believe contributed to these outcomes?"

The first thing we noticed about people's responses was their typically vague nature. Qualities like "open-minded" or "good listening ability" are most assuredly positive. Any culture that reflected these kinds of behaviors would be judged by most people as a "good" organization for which to work or family in which to live. The problem is that at that level of abstraction, these qualities are unmeasurable and therefore unmanageable. A little prodding was all that was necessary to get to the more concrete level of the observable. An "open-minded" person became someone who, for example, "didn't argue defensively," and people with "good listening ability" became people who "didn't interrupt" or "summarized areas of agreement."

> *Managers manage behavior, not numbers or head counts or FTEs or interventions or even objectives.*

The second thing we noticed was how quickly a finite list of observable, repetitive behaviors emerged. Although the subtle nuances certainly vary across diverse relationships, the ingredients that go into the creation of what is referred to as a win-win relationship—the backbone of any excellence-oriented organizational culture—are relatively few in number.

A sample of the forty-eight behaviors that emerged from our research is presented in Figure 1. It is important to emphasize that these behaviors are "customer oriented." Recall the way the research question was phrased: "What is a specific example of a behavior that the *other person* exhibited that you believe contributed to these outcomes [win-win relationships]?" As the recipient of another person's behaviors, I am a customer.

Most important, these behaviors are observable and countable; it thus becomes both possible and justifiable to hold people accountable for exhibiting them on a regular basis. (Parenthetically—but not unimportantly—these behaviors are also highly learnable. Rackham's research documents our own experience with the power of training programs designed to extend people's awareness of behavior and consequences.)[2]

---

[2] In addition to Rackham, see also Inguagiato, Robert J., *So You're Not Paying Attention*, Honolulu, HI: Temenos®, Inc., 1994.

Item No.*	Behavior
1.	Clearly explain the bases for decisions.
10.	Tell others clearly what you want from them.
12.	Use metaphors, analogies, and vivid descriptions to heighten others' enthusiasm about possibilities.
13.	Pay careful attention without interrupting when others are trying to make a point.
30.	Ask questions like "How can I help?" and "How can I support you?"
36.	Talk from the heart about values and ideals.
41.	Admit your mistakes.
43.	Apologize for your mistakes.

*Note: There are forty-eight specific behaviors in the pool of which these eight are a sample. The forty-eight behaviors are grouped into eight distinct style clusters.

Figure 1. Sample Win-Win Behaviors

BEHAVIOR AND CULTURE: CREATING A SNAPSHOT

Using a very simple and unobtrusive tool built around these forty-eight behaviors, we have been able to help many clients avoid the second of the pitfalls mentioned in the first paragraph of this article: difficulty in developing a behaviorally specific picture of a "good" or "better" organizational culture. An overview sample of the results generated for one client by our "Organizational Excellence: A Behavioral Survey" is presented in Figure 2.

From a developmental perspective, this organization is relatively young. The cultural challenge that it faces is quite clear and straightforward: It can no longer solely rely on the entrepreneurial vision and charismatic style of its founders for continued growth and development. This is evidenced by the low delta/minus delta scores for items 12 and 36 in Figure 2. At this organization's current stage of development, more concrete behaviors like "telling one another clearly what we want from one another" (item 10 in Figure 2) must be stirred into the pot of enthusiasm and big-picture dreams that have served them so well to date.[3]

---

[3] See Rubin, Irwin M., Ph.D., and Fernandez, Dr. C. Raymond, *My Pulse Is Not What It Used to Be: The Leadership Challenges in Health Care*, Honolulu, HI: The Temenos® Foundation, 1991, for more details on the stages of development in healthcare organizations.

Sample Summary

Organizational Excellence: A Behavioral Survey

Your organization wants to achieve organizational excellence. Using the Importance Scale of 0-5, please indicate in the *left-hand* column how much importance you believe the senior management team of _____ is currently placing on the following forty-eight behaviors. In the *right-hand* column, please indicate how much importance you believe the team *should be* placing on each behavior.

Importance Scale

5 = Critical
4 = Very important
3 = Important
2 = Not very important
1 = Unimportant
0 = Irrelevant

Currently*			Should Be*	Δ**
1.	21.4%	Clearly explain the bases for our decisions.	88.1%	66.7%
10.	21.4%	State clearly what we want from one another.	88.1%	66.7%
12.	50.0%	Use metaphors, analogies, and vivid descriptions to heighten one another's enthusiasm about possibilities.	40.5%	-9.5%
13.	50.0%	Pay careful attention without interrupting when others are trying to make a point.	78.6%	28.6%
30.	33.3%	Ask questions like "How can I help?" and "How can I support you?"	83.3%	50.0%
36.	71.4%	Talk from the heart about our values and ideals.	71.4%	00.0%
41.	31.0%	Admit our mistakes.	83.3%	52.3%
43.	33.3%	Apologize for our mistakes.	81.0%	47.7%

*Note: Refers to the percent of respondents who answered "very important" (4) or "critical" (5) only.

**Note: Delta (Δ) is the *difference* between *Should Be* and *Currently*.

In other words, the greater the Δ, the greater the consensual perception of need of the behavior in the future.

Figure 2. Behavioral Survey Results

An organization's culture is *both* the cause of and the result of day-to-day behavior. A culture is—at its bottom line—the result of a series of often semiconscious agreements about how people will interact and communicate with one another. Any organizational-culture profile, therefore, is nothing more than the cumulative effects of the emotions evoked as a consequence of how people choose to behave toward one another. A language system, made up of words, music (intonation), and dance (nonverbal body movements) becomes the behavioral trademark of any culture. It is this pattern of typical "words, music, and dance" that must change to effect any change in culture.

THE MISSING LEG

Organizations are quick to invest enormous amounts of time, money, and energy in the creation and utilization of sophisticated information systems that allow the instantaneous monitoring of all manner of variables important to the bottom line. If you were ever a guest at a Ritz Carlton Hotel, all of the Ritz Carlton Hotels worldwide would know how you like your morning coffee served. Supermarkets keep track of the number of cans of soup and bags of nuts in inventory. Hospitals monitor (and bill for individually) the number of BIC® razor blades used to shave preoperative patients in the same way that they monitor the technical quality of the operations performed.

Indeed, traditional TQM efforts rest on the two legs of technical effectiveness and managerial efficiency. So what is missing? Missing from most TQM efforts to date has been a focus on the third leg of personal efficacy, the quality of day-to-day interpersonal relationships.

The Healing Power of TLC

Using the healthcare industry as an example, we can examine the effects of this third leg of personal efficacy. Empirical research confirms what common sense has known about the bottom line in healthcare organizations for centuries. People heal more quickly—and are therefore discharged more quickly—from healthcare organizations where the staff members treat *one another* with "care and respect."[4]

---

[4] Revans, R.W., *Standards for Morale: Cause and Effect in Hospitals,* Oxford University Press, London, 1964, and Rubin, Irwin M., Ph.D., *Total Quality Management: Care Dealers vs. Car Dealers,* Temenos®, Inc., Honolulu, Hawaii, USA, 1992.

Put another way, "staff infections"—that is, interpersonal toxicity of any form in the boardroom or between employees of a healthcare organization—are as potentially lethal as "staph infections" in the operating room. For example, a nurse who is continually subjected to verbal abuse by an arrogant physician will find it very difficult to maintain a "caring" bedside manner.

Information Highway's New Lane: Behavioral Quality Assurance (BQA)

Without an information system that provides user-friendly on-line real-time awareness of behavior and consequences, *total* quality management is lacking one of the legs it needs to stand on. Organizational culture change will stumble. On the other hand, with a computer-driven information system built around behaviors like those that are at the core of all win-win relationships, individuals can be empowered to manage the quality of their important "customer" relationships: at home with their families, at work with their colleagues, and in the marketplace with formal users of their products or services.

With such a system, at the stroke of a key, the two parties in a relationship can each get a picture of the quality of their relationship. Frequency patterns (how often sender and recipient experience each of the other's behaviors) and requests for change (specific behaviors each would like to see more or less of) can be made available instantaneously. As a result, people committed to improving the quality of their relationships can develop what I call behavioral quality assurance (BQA) agreements. With the technology currently available at every manager's fingertips, regular reminders of BQA agreements become as easy as "ABC."

When a computer, for example, is asked to dial a colleague's phone number, it can, at the same instant, be programmed to flash a reminder of the specific behaviors that the colleague has asked the caller to exhibit. Fiber-optics communication networks also allow the recipient of a call to know who is calling. Imagine calling a work colleague and having a digital screen help you be more aware of your behavior and its consequences while on the telephone!

Becoming Truly Customer Oriented

This same set of principles and technology can give people the power to create truly customer-oriented organizational cultures. With such a computer-driven information system, the organization can treat customers as the unique individuals they are. Current customer-service efforts ultimately may lead to insincere, almost robotic behavior. Customers get a seemingly heartfelt smile...whether they want it or not.

Imagine, in contrast, the following scenario:

> When you next visit your healthcare organization, your provider asks you for some help in updating your medical record. From a subset of the forty-eight win-win behaviors (which research studies have already identified as priorities for your age, ethnic origin, and so on), you are asked to select two or three specific behaviors. These are the behaviors you want to see exhibited by anyone with whom you come in contact in this healthcare organization. They represent the observable behaviors you need to feel "cared for" by your provider organization—in human, not technical, terms. These behaviors become a part of your "treatment plan."
>
> The next time you call for an appointment, these priority behaviors—along with all the other information currently being monitored—flashes up on the screen. The behaviors also appear on the front cover of your medical record for all of your providers to see. Because the entire organization is committed to creating a caring-oriented culture, everyone has access to the information needed to ensure awareness of behavior and consequences.

In the same way that employees at the Ritz Carlton hotels pay attention to such things as coffee preferences because a customer so "cared for" is *more likely to return and may stay for longer periods*, a customer so "cared for" by a healthcare organization is *less likely to return and may stay for shorter periods.*

THE BOTTOM LINE

The computer, used as described in this paper, may be just the tool needed to heighten the quality of the messages we send one another, despite the apparent paradox of using high-tech in the service of high-touch.

Will not the very robotic, uncaring behavior the computer is designed to reduce ensue? It will not, as Edward R. Murrow pointed out when he reminded us: "The newest computer can merely compound, at speed, the oldest problem in the relations between human beings, and in the end the communicator will be confronted with the old problem of what to say and how to say it."

Only people who are willing to accept 100-percent responsibility for the win-win healing quality of their half of every relationship will find the ability to be **a**ware of their **b**ehavior and its **c**onsequences to be of value.

Irwin M. Rubin, Ph.D., brings his knowledge of human behavior in organizations to an international audience. He has spent the past fifteen years in research-and-development efforts in public and private organizations in the United States, New Zealand, and Australia. A co-author of the standard university textbook, Organizational Psychology, *he has a Ph.D. and an M.S. in organizational psychology from Sloan School of Management, Massachusetts Institute of Technology. Dr. Rubin is a former associate professor at Sloan School of Management, lecturer at Harvard Graduate School of Education, and co-director of the Health-Care Management Program at the Massachusetts Institute of Technology. He is an honorary member of the American College of Physician Executives.*

Pfeiffer & Company

ORGANIZATION EFFECTIVENESS: BUILDING INTEGRATED CAPABILITIES AND FUNCTIONING FOR ACCOMPLISHING DESIRED RESULTS

Anthony Nathan

Abstract: Organizational effectiveness is the most fundamental and critical issue in organizations. To deal with this issue, organizations need to learn about Organization Effectiveness (OE) and use this vital strategy appropriately and competently. This chapter gives an overview of the Organization Effectiveness strategy, why it is necessary, and how it works. It offers a way to increase the probabilities of accomplishing successful change, maximizing desired results, and improving competitive position on a sustainable basis.

T he need for organizational effectiveness is driven by the increasing number, complexity, and impact of external and internal environmental changes. These include changes in macroeconomic trends, markets, customer requirements, competitors, information, industry structures, technologies, political styles, governmental regulations, investors or owners, strategy alternatives, business composition, resources, suppliers, the labor force, worker competencies, and the nature of work. The pressures on organizations and their employees to change will be far greater in the future than they are today.

A more turbulent, unpredictable, and complicated environment increases the challenges for executives. They are responding by re-thinking their strategic plans related to market positioning, customer satisfaction, product quality, employees, product development, new technologies, joint ventures, productivity, cost reduction, divestment, and so on. They are going in unfamiliar, sometimes revolutionary, directions to keep their organizations viable in a changing world.

Organizational Interventions

Executives are prompted to initiate numerous interventions, such as strategic thinking, total quality management, customer-satisfaction management, business process reengineering, benchmarking, climate surveys, culture renewal, self-managed teams, learning organizations, leadership development, technical training, adventure-learning programs, diversity management, incentive programs, and downsizing. These interventions attempt to transform organizations and help them to realize their strategic objectives.

Investing considerable resources and energy in these interventions, however, does not always ensure desired results. For example, according to Schaffer and Thomson (1992):

> The performance improvement efforts of many companies have as much impact on operational and financial results as a ceremonial rain dance has on weather. While some companies constantly improve measurable performance, in many others, managers continue to dance round and round the campfire—exuding good faith and dissipating energy. This "rain dance" is the ardent pursuit of activities that sound good, look good, and allow managers to feel good, but in fact contribute little or nothing to bottom-line performance.

The success or failure of a key organizational intervention substantially affects the organization's profitability, competitive advantage, and future. An intervention can solve problems and capitalize on opportunities or it can create solutions that are worse than the problems. It can save or waste time, effort, and resources.

The outcomes of interventions can affect the organizational climate by raising or lowering morale and trust. As Warrick (1993) observes:

> Frustration, high levels of anxiety and stress, feelings of lack of control and being out of control, break down in trust and communication, a loss of confidence in management, broken or damaged spirits all accompany mismanaged change.

The accrued impact on employee resilience may be even worse. With each passing year, as people are challenged to continually improve and contribute even more, they will remember what and how changes were made and may become conditioned to distrust or resist change. Chronic change fatigue may permeate the organization, making future changes even more difficult to implement. This is not an option for any organization that wants to thrive in a future that will become cumulatively more challenging.

With so much riding on interventions, why do so many end up mediocre, cosmetic, or short lived? One reason is that poor decisions are made about what to change. Organizations may take any of the following actions:

- Target needs that are not high strategic priorities, either inadvertently or as a result of political tradeoffs;
- Set unclear or unrealistic goals for change;
- Select interventions that are inappropriate or inadequate for accomplishing the changes required;
- "Spray and pray"—implement too many interventions at one time;
- Change direction frequently; and/or
- Fail to ensure that the interventions are congruent and integrated with other key initiatives and have a strategic focus.

Another reason is that organizations may lack integrated foundations (infrastructures) for planning, initiating, managing, supporting, sustaining, evaluating, and learning from interventions. Organizations may:

- Plunge into interventions with poor understanding, poor sponsorship, lack of commitment, and poor role definition;
- Avoid risk taking and act expediently;

- Focus on current circumstances and wallow in the status quo;
- Fail to diagnose needs and to plan interventions effectively;
- Use unskilled facilitators or inadequate change processes;
- Spread resources over too may interventions;
- Fail to develop supporting capabilities and functioning to enable and fortify changes;
- Focus on activities instead of on results;
- Fail to monitor progress and adjust as required;
- Fail to allow time for interventions to take root; and/or
- Fail to apply lessons learned from earlier interventions to new initiatives.

Unfortunately, many decision makers repeat their mistakes, influenced by old assumptions, values, and momentum. John Rollwagen, CEO of Cray Research, advises organizations to get out of their traditional comfort zones, let go of the past, and find different ways to accomplish results. He warns: "You're almost certain to get swallowed up because you're stepping off from the past and backing into the future" (Galagan, 1992).

To break out of the status quo and preempt organizational effectiveness, executives need to take a hard look at their past and future strategies and interventions. They need to ask questions such as:

- In retrospect, which strategies and interventions of the last five years fell short of expectations in terms of contribution to results? What have been the accrued costs of failure? Why did the interventions fail to achieve the expected results? What capabilities and functioning should the organization have had in place (but did not have) for supporting these interventions?

- What key strategies and interventions are planned for the next five years? What capabilities and functioning are required to support the accomplishment of these future directions? If the organization builds these supporting capabilities and functioning, what could be its actual results? If nothing is done to build these capabilities and functioning, which underlying problems would probably continue to negatively impact the plans? What would be the cumulative costs if these plans were not realized over the next five years?

- Are current organizational perspectives (thinking patterns, assumptions, mental models, paradigms) effective for dealing with these issues or are they in need of change?

Such a diagnosis may lead executives to reexamine their assumptions and values about what end results they truly desire; what changes are required to obtain those results; how to best go about accomplishing those changes; and how much ineffectiveness they are willing to tolerate.

THE MEANING OF ORGANIZATION EFFECTIVENESS

Organization Effectiveness (OE) is a philosophy and strategy for maximizing the desired results of an organization and its employees by intentionally:

- Determining the results desired;
- Developing the means for producing the results; and
- Using these means to accomplish the results on a continual basis.

Organization Effectiveness can be defined more specifically in terms of its goal, focus of change, and technology.

In terms of goal, OE aims to increase the possibility that the organization and its employees:

- Are focused on the most appropriate results;
- Are adapted to accomplishing desired results; and
- Achieve these results optimally and cumulatively.

In terms of change focus, OE works to understand, develop, and optimize the capabilities and functioning of the larger organizational system and its integrated parts, to adapt them to accomplish desired results.

In terms of technology, OE is a planned, long-range, systems and holistic approach based on technologies for realizing employee and/or organizational effectiveness on a lasting basis.

The following sections provide more information on this definition of OE.

THE PURPOSE OF OE

The purpose of OE is to maximize the accomplishment of results that are desired by the organization, its employees, and other stakeholders. In some organizations, interventions lack strategic alignment; they have taken on lives of their own and become ends in themselves. Organizations become sidetracked from their missions—critical needs and the enabling systems leading to these needs. They may even become addicted to dissipating their resources and energies in numerous activities until the outcomes are no longer relevant or valued. Such organizations have become activities-focused instead of results-focused, and that is a sure path to ineffectiveness and mediocrity.

A Results Orientation

OE develops a results orientation because it emphasizes both identifying what results are really required (OE outcome) and managing how those results are optimally accomplished (OE process). This balanced emphasis is fundamental to effectiveness. Two quotations are pertinent here: "Flawless execution does not compensate for implementing the wrong solution" (Conner, 1992) and "Even the right things done the wrong way are not likely to succeed" (Warrick, 1993). The aim is to do the right things the right way.

Desired results may be defined in terms of the ability and success of the organization in the following areas:

Creating and shaping a future for itself in which it can thrive. This relates to supporting the organization's competitive strategies, realizing its vision, and fulfilling its mission. It may include how clear and shared its strategic directions are. It also may include decisions and actions that are taken to prepare the organization for the future.

Achieving short- and long-term organizational objectives. This relates to quantitative and qualitative performance indicators of return on invested capital, revenue growth, profitability, competitive advantage, customer satisfaction, product or service quality, productivity, costs, cycle time, innovation, teamwork, empowerment, and so on. It also may include the degree to which these objectives are achieved at reasonable cost.

Doing what needs to be done to respond to organizational needs. This relates to the performance of routine tasks to specified standards and their continuous improvement. It also relates to the detection of critical problems and opportunities (current and anticipated) in the organizational environment, and dealing with these in a timely manner.

Fitting better in its environment as it battles for survival and prosperity. This relates to the generation of changes required to fine tune, transform, and renew the organization to adapt to current and potential challenges. It also includes learning from experience and other stimuli as well as building increasingly more effective and sophisticated levels of capabilities and functioning for accomplishing desired results.

Obtaining and capitalizing on resources available in its environment. This includes developing human resources, mobilizing their potential in new ways, and continually improving their performance.

Maintaining and enhancing the health of its people while on the job. This includes organizational climate, morale, and physical well being.

THE HOLISTIC AND SYSTEMS APPROACH OF OE

Organization Effectiveness focuses the systems linkages to desired results, from the strategy to the intervention levels.

The realization of an organization's desired future (e.g., the organization embraces and thrives in a turbulent environment) depends on the achievement of certain organizational goals (e.g., leaders have developed broader paradigms, "helicopter" perception and thinking, intuitive reasoning and imagination, and have applied their minds to solve problems and capitalize on opportunities in a turbulent environment). In turn, each goal is enabled by the accomplishment of intentional OE interventions (e.g., the development and implementation of strategic plans emphasizing "strategic readiness," communication of the need for strategic readiness, the recruitment of new leaders with the required thinking competencies, the implementation of management development programs to foster these thinking competencies, a revision of the performance-management system to reward leaders who apply the thinking competencies, and revision of the succession-planning system to promote leaders with the thinking competencies) as well as enabled by incidental events.

Strategies and interventions thus have to work within the cause-and-effect relationships of an "organizational systems universe." This systems universe is multidimensional and complex. The systems orientation has profound implications for how strategies and OE interventions are orchestrated. Working within this systems context increases the possibility that the organization and its employees are adapted to and do successfully accomplish their present and future goals, and, consequently, realize an appropriate future for the organization.

As a basic, it is necessary to clearly:

- Specify the end results desired in as much detail as possible;
- Study the overlapping and dynamic systems that could impact the end results, track down the systems leading (via cause-and-effect linkages) to these end results, and map out a holistic systems model of the organization;

- Identify the strategies and interventions needed to impact these organizational systems and bring about the desired results;

- Examine how the various strategies and interventions are expected to impact, and are impacted by, these systems; and

- Put the right mix of strategies and interventions into an integrated framework for accomplishing the desired results and coordinate the implementation of change.

In mapping out the different levels of successor systems, all the linkages connecting the systems with the end results must be tracked. The overall systems map portrays the order, structure, and priority of the cause-and-effect linkages leading to and from the end results. It serves as a road map for designing the necessary OE interventions. Based on this map, one can delineate the critical pathways of systems that an intervention must impact sequentially or simultaneously, thereby identifying the adjustments and additions required for the proposed interventions to work better. This map helps avoid the risk of systems forces neutralizing the interventions.

THE FOCUS OF CHANGE IN OE

Capabilities and Functioning

A key to accomplishing desired results is the degree of comprehensiveness, integration, and alignment of the capabilities and functioning of the organization and its employees.

"Capabilities" are the elements that enable the accomplishment of desired results. They include values, paradigms, culture, mission, goals, leadership, policies, structures, systems (e.g., planning, decision making, communication, learning, succession planning, performance monitoring, feedback, and reward), processes, practices, employee competencies, employee capacity, roles, equipment, and other resources.

"Functioning" is the expected operation of a capability or system of capabilities that support the accomplishment of a desired result. Capabilities and their functioning are the means for accomplishing results. They may be superstructural or infrastructural.

Superstructure

Many change interventions focus on particular systems, technologies, and practices. For example, a total quality intervention may strive to develop or apply quality function deployment planning tools, a customer focus, a quality steering committee, quality-improvement teams, a quality-oriented culture, error-free work, quantitative techniques, and a continuous improvement ethos. These capabilities and functioning form a total quality superstructure, and are used to improve product and service quality.

Superstructure is important. A larger superstructure of specific interventions must be integrated and aligned to support the organization's competitiveness strategies. Organizations must become more competent at defining what outcomes and strategies are truly required, understanding which interventions will most impact these needs, fitting the most appropriate interventions into the master plan, and leveraging these interventions optimally.

Infrastructure

However, superstructure is only half of the big picture. Superstructural capabilities and functioning, by themselves, are not sufficient to accomplish change. If specific interventions are to succeed, confronted by employee resistance and other barriers, they must be based on a solid infrastructure of supporting capabilities and functioning. This infrastructure forms the foundation on which the superstructure of specific interventions can be built. The broader and firmer the foundation, the taller the superstructure that can be constructed. As Tobin (1994) contends:

> Without solid foundations, the superstructure will bend in the wind and shake when the earth rumbles. If there is no solid base for major initiatives, the entire superstructure will eventually come crashing down or, at best, be abandoned in favor of old familiar structures of past experience.

Building on the total quality example, the success of the intervention depends largely on the availability of an infrastructure of implementation capabilities and functioning. For instance, the TQ project team could use effective change-management tools to better initiate, manage, and sustain the overall intervention. Other infrastructural capabilities may include talented project-team members, an organizational learning capacity, supportive assumptions and values, management sponsorship, an organizational planning system, project-management tools, systems thinking, an employee-involvement system, diagnostic tools, a training system, a performance-management system, an incentive system, a communications system, and so on. Without such an infrastructure, the TQ intervention will rely largely on chance, which substantially increases the possibility of failure.

Developing an Organizational Architecture

Organizations need to proactively build infrastructures from which they can launch and support their superstructural interventions. An infrastructure should integrate the necessary supporting capabilities and functioning, aligned to support the accomplishment of mission-critical interventions. This infrastructure is rarely exclusive to a specific intervention. Many of the same capabilities, including resources, can be shared among an organization's various interventions.

The architecture of infrastructure and superstructure must be developed as a package. Without superstructure, the best infrastructure is irrelevant. Without infrastructure, the superstructure is doomed to fall short of expectations. The optimal design of infrastructure and superstructure adapts the organization to accomplishing its ends. This allows change to occur by design rather than by chance.

> *Infrastructure and super-structure must be developed as a package.*

Executives must sponsor the engineering of an effective architecture of capabilities and functioning in the organization. Unfortunately, it is easier to make a case for superstructure to many executives. The long-range investment in infrastructure does not excite many short-range decision makers. We must educate decision makers about the need for a total architecture, proving to them that it works better.

Executives can use OE to transform their organizational architecture. OE examines the existing architecture of capabilities and functioning in relation to the desired results; identifies strengths and weaknesses in them; engineers an improved architecture (i.e., reinforces strengths, develops new capabilities, or reduces weaknesses); implements the various changes; and follows through to ensure that the improved architecture is effective, lasting, and continually improving. If the organization is starting from a lower base of capabilities and functioning, extraordinary efforts will have to be made to build the necessary architecture.

These changes to architecture create layers of potentialities for effectiveness in the organization. Whether the organization actually becomes effective depends on its ability and willingness to utilize the engineered architecture as it works to accomplish change.

THE TECHNOLOGIES USED IN OE

Organization Effectiveness typically applies at least three disciplines or technologies: human resource development (HRD), human performance technology (HPT), and organization development (OD). The three disciplines are interrelated. Some tools are common to all technologies (e.g., performance analysis, project planning, change management, and training). This is because HRD, HPT, and OD interventions often contain the same elements of learning, human performance, and change management.

Organization Effectiveness uses these technologies in a holistic, integrated, and nonpartisan manner. Both HPT and OD operate at the level of performance or effectiveness; HRD operates at the level of learning or potential for effectiveness. HPT has a tendency to focus on behavioral change; OD focuses on cognitive and systems change. The attractiveness of OE is that it not only transcends the identity issues surrounding HRD, OD, and HPT, it also refocuses the organization on the results it truly desires.

The three technologies can be differentiated by their specific focuses and purposes:

1. Human Resource Development (HRD). The target of HRD is the people (individuals and work groups) in an organization.

In terms of goal, HRD identifies, develops, improves, and transfers job-related learning in people. This is done to enable people to develop the competencies and repertoire of behaviors they need to optimally perform a current or future job as well as to support their personal growth. Thus, HRD aims to increase the potential for individual and group effectiveness. HRD is used to analyze, design, develop, implement, and follow up interventions for generating learning opportunities and for stimulating individual and group learning. Typical HRD interventions are training, education, development, and career development.

2. Human Performance Technology (HPT). The target of HPT is the people (individuals and work groups) in an organization. HPT diagnoses, engineers, reinforces, and improves human performance and well-being. This is done to enable people to accomplish the desired work and the organizational results in a way that also promotes their health. Thus, HPT aims to increase individual and group effectiveness, which, in turn, contributes to organizational effectiveness. HPT is used to analyze, design, develop, implement, and follow up interventions for solving problems and seizing improvement opportunities in the human-performance system (which consists of people, work, and workplace elements). Typical HPT interventions include performance analysis, job design, role definition, personnel selection, performance management, coaching, reward systems, feedback systems, job aids, expert systems, environmental engineering, and health and wellness.

3. Organization Development (OD). The targets of OD are the whole organization and its component parts (e.g., goals, strategy, outputs, functions, culture, norms, structures, processes, resources, and work groups). OD diagnoses, engineers, reinforces, and improves organizational performance, growth, and well-being. This is done to enable the organization and its people to achieve desired business results and adapt to environmental changes in a way that also promotes organizational health. Thus, OD aims to improve organizational effectiveness.

As a process, OD is used to analyze, design, develop, implement, and follow up interventions for solving problems and seizing opportunities in the capabilities and functioning of the organization and its components. These interventions help people to change and to develop and use the potential of their organizations. Typical OD interventions include developing leadership, culture renewal, strategic planning, organizational learning, quality function deployment, total quality management, change management, technological change, organizational structure redesign, business process reengineering, self-directed work teams, team building, problem-solving systems, decision-making systems, communication systems, organizational climate surveys, succession planning, diversity management, downsizing, and quality of work life.

More specifically, OD strives to:

- Understand the organization's needs, capabilities, and functioning in systemic terms;

- Change, develop, and manage the organization's capabilities and functioning to help it cope with its environment, learn, renew itself, and accomplish other desired results; and

- Ensure healthy relationships between and within groups.

The field of organizational change today may be classified into organization development (OD) and organization transformation (OT). In this context, OD focuses on fine-tuning, incremental and modest changes. OT is a second-generation evolution of OD. It focuses on fundamental, radical, large-scale, or organization-wide changes usually involving a paradigm shift about people, work, the organization, or its environment. It is a change of kind, not of degree. Interventions such as the "learning organization," total quality management, and self-directed work teams could be classified as OT interventions.

In many instances, an intervention is not exclusive to a particular technology. For example, training (which is classified under HRD) is often used in HPT and OD. A case could also be made to classify the "learning organization" (which is classified under OD because of its systemic nature) as HRD. Organizational effectiveness focuses on dealing with organizational problems and opportunities, not on the processes and tools used to deal with these issues.

Many interventions are not exclusive to a particular technology.

Proponents of HRD, OD, and HPT have tried to subsume the other disciplines as their own, creating duplication and confusion. For example, the American Society for Training and Development defines HRD as the integrated use of training and development, organization development, and career development. The National Society for Performance and Instruction claims many OD and HRD interventions as HPT. Not to be outdone, many OD professional societies consider learning and human performance issues part of OD. The lack of consensus could be due to the evolving nature of these relatively new disciplines; "product differentiation" needed to justify a professional discipline, new book, or consulting service; and/or dogmatic posturing. It may be time to review, redefine, and reclassify the three OE disciplines. Regardless, debating about the inconsistencies or being tied to any one theoretical definition does not help the work that needs to be done in an organization.

What is important is the following:

1. Defining the OE terms and model in a manner that is most appropriate to the organization's unique characteristics and situational realities.

2. Helping organizational stakeholders to clearly understand the meanings of the terms and models so that they value, support, and explain change efforts.

3. Using a common vocabulary, model, process, and analytical tools to guide OE work, given the situation in the organization.

Organization Effectiveness should be incorporated into day-to-day management practices. Furthermore, there is no reason why all levels of employees cannot learn to use an OE framework for thinking about and acting on the issues confronting their organizations. This would help to increase understanding about critical organizational issues, the most appropriate approaches for dealing with these issues, how a particular approach will work, and what is required to obtain results from an approach.

The secret to propagating the use of OE is to "think state-of-the-art common sense, simplicity and balance" (Warrick, 1993) when communicating OE concepts to the organization. Regardless, in the technical and financial aspects of their jobs, many people are required to learn far more difficult terms and conform to more complex processes. Organizations would function at a higher level if people learned about and handled OE issues with the same discipline and resoluteness expected of them in the technical, financial, and legal aspects of their jobs.

THE EFFICIENCY OF OE

The power of OE is simple: it strives to deal with organizational effectiveness in a holistic and aligned manner. Unfortunately, in many organizations, the OE function is not structured for effectiveness and efficiency. There is an assortment of separate functions that directly or indirectly deal with organizational effectiveness issues. These functions may include strategic planning, organization development, total quality management, human resource management, management development, technical training, compensation, information systems, health and wellness, communications, career development, and so on.

These segregated functions may be operating independently and not communicating, collaborating, or coordinating with one another sufficiently. There may even be turf wars or lack of alignment to organizational direction. Each OE-related function may implement its particular solution in an ad hoc manner, based on its interpretation of an organizational need it is responsible for or happens to stumble over. This is because complex organizational problems and opportunities are multicausal and multifaceted, comprising many elements that are interrelated. A narrow intervention in a vacuum often does not work. All the individual system elements need to be improved simultaneously to accomplish meaningful and sustained results.

Organizations can capitalize on the latent synergy of their OE-related functions by, at the least, coordinating them in a broader, strategic framework for dealing with organizational effectiveness issues. Executives should ensure that these functions are integrated with one another as well as aligned with the organization's and business units' strategic plans. It is imperative to find ways to ensure the complementary, aligned, efficient, and coordinated deployment of OE strategies, functions, and their interventions.

If an organization wants significant breakthroughs in organizational effectiveness, it must invest the time and effort in smarter front-end planning and coordination of OE. CD-MAP™ (Customer Driven-Mission Achievement Process) is an extremely disciplined, rigorous, and proactive positioning and planning process that can be used to systematically focus and organize all OE activities. One outcome is that OE-related functions are deployed and integrated in an aligned, comprehensive, and synergistic structure. With this umbrella structure, OE interventions can be efficiently implemented to satisfy the key requirements of customers, stakeholders, and OE practitioners.

THE OVERALL PROCESS OF OE

The OE process focuses on the organization's business landscape: defining and assessing the gap between where the organization is now, where it needs to be, and how to get there. The following process stages summarize the overall OE process. As you read it, refer to the OE diagram in the figure that follows.

1. Envision the future ideals that the organization needs to achieve. This may be a vision or business objectives related to delighted customers, preferred supplier status, industry leadership, or the embracing of a turbulent future.

2. Determine the gap between the organization's current realities (actual results) and future ideals (desired results). Diagnose the problems and opportunities underlying the results gap related to:

   - The accomplishment of the current realities and the past infrastructure and superstructure that led to these results;

   - The desired accomplishment of future ideals and the future infrastructure and superstructure necessary for generating the desired results.

   Estimate the costs if the desired results are not realized. Estimate the potential for performance improvement if the necessary architecture is built and used to support the accomplishment of desired results.

3. Given the diagnosis outcomes, consider the change options for building the architecture of infrastructure and superstructure necessary for accomplishing the organization's future ideals. Formulate a change strategy. Communicate the change strategy to the key stakeholders, educate them about it, and build their commitment for it. Integrate the change strategy into organizational plans.

4. Plan, implement, manage, institutionalize, evaluate, improve, and renew the various OE infrastructural interventions to develop and improve the necessary organizational infrastructure of capabilities and functioning.

5. Using the supporting infrastructure, plan, implement, manage, institutionalize, evaluate, improve, and renew the various OE superstructural interventions (e.g., total quality management) in an aligned, planned, and integrated manner.

CONCLUSION

Organization Effectiveness (OE) provides a powerful foundation, framework, and conduit for orchestrating the right combination of strategies and interventions to identify appropriate organizational directions; develop the necessary capabilities and functioning; use them to obtain the desired results, and realize the desired directions. OE is a strategic investment that may very well provide the greatest returns to an organization. It leverages existing strategies and interventions as well as enables the organization to pursue a whole new class of strategies and interventions for continually adding value to its assets and mobilizing their potential.

The case for OE is compelling. Escalating change is placing many organizations at breakpoint with respect to the management of employee and organizational results. As Land and Jarman (1992) state, at breakpoint the rules for success have changed so radically that continuing to use the old rules not only does not work, it also generates formidable, even insurmountable, obstacles to success.

Organization Effectiveness therefore must be managed in a more strategic, proactive, and integrated way than it has been in the past. Not dealing with this fundamental issue carries the price of being left behind competitively. It also carries the risk of painful measures when attempts eventually are made to stem organizational decline or avert obsolescence.

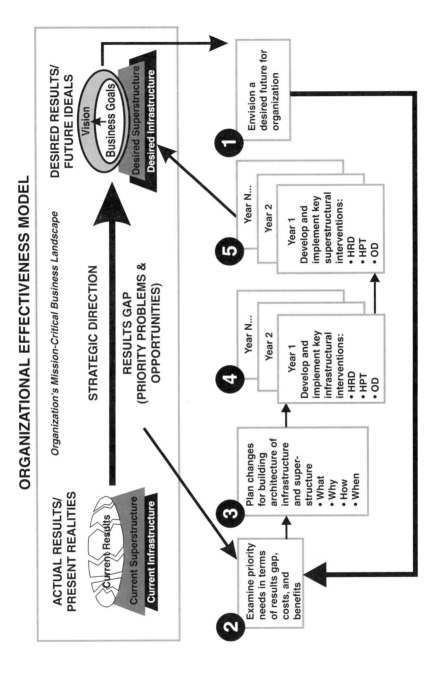

ORGANIZATIONAL EFFECTIVENESS MODEL

References

Conner, D. (1992). *Managing at the speed of change: How resilient managers succeed and prosper where others fail.* New York: Villard.

Galagan, P. (1992, November). On being a beginner. *Training and Development Journal,* p. 33.

Land, G., & Jarman, B. (1992). *Breakpoint and beyond: Mastering the future—today.* New York: Harper Collins.

Schaffer, R., & Thomson, H. (1992, January-February). Successful change programs begin with results. *Harvard Business Review,* pp. 80-89.

Tobin, D.R. (1994). *Re-educating the corporation: Foundations for the learning organization.* Essex Junction, VT: Oliver Wight Publications.

Warrick, D. (1993). What executives, managers and human resource professionals need to know about managing change. In W. French, C. Bell, & R. Zawacki (Eds.), *Organization development and transformation: Managing effective change* (4th ed.). Burr Ridge, IL: Irwin.

Anthony Nathan *is president of Anthene Consulting International, in Mississauga, Ontario, Canada. Anthene Consulting International provides consulting and training services in organizational effectiveness aimed at improving human competence, optimizing human performance, and managing change. Mr. Nathan specializes in strategic approaches to enhancing employee effectiveness, organization-wide learning, learning and development functions, human-performance management, technical learning systems, performance-improvement functions, and organizational effectiveness functions. He has assisted a variety of organizations both in Canada and internationally.*

THE EIGHT-SYSTEMS MODEL FOR IMPLEMENTING TOTAL QUALITY MANAGEMENT

Homer H. Johnson

Abstract: The failure to make total quality management "total" is the reason for its lack of success in many organizations. This article addresses this problem by proposing a model of total quality management, the eight-systems model, that may be used as a framework for designing a total-quality process. The eight systems are leadership, structure, quality planning, training, rewards and recognition, quality measurement, communication, and quality-improvement activities. The eighth system consists of the activities that actually bring about improvement, and the other systems support those improvements. As the TQM process matures, these systems should merge with the existing and ongoing organizational systems.

The implementation of total quality management (TQM) has been an elusive target in many organizations. The quality landscape seems to be littered with organizations that could never find the first step to take on the path, those that had a furious but short-lived burst of activity, and those that half-heartedly conducted quality activities that never lead anywhere.

One would think that a process that promises increased sales, increased market share, wider profit margins, higher morale, and the like could be adapted easily and quickly to most organizations. However, the contrary seems to be true.

TQM professionals know how to measure quality and have done a superb job of developing problem-solving tools and training programs to teach the tools quickly and competently. Much more difficult to develop has been the methodology to integrate the various pieces that make up TQM in an organization.

The failure to make TQM "total" seems to be the major cause of the inability of many organizations to effectively implement TQM despite its considerable advantages. Too often organizations set up quality-improvement teams, or write a quality mission statement, or establish quality goals but do these activities in isolation, unrelated to how the rest of the organization functions, so they die a quick death. In order for TQM to work, and for the organization to reap the benefits of it, the process has to be implemented "in total."

This paper is an attempt to address this problem by proposing a model of Total Quality Management, the eight-systems model, that may be used as a rough framework to design a total-quality process. A basic assumption behind the model is that total quality is (needs to be) an integrated set of activities that reaches all parts of the organization, and this is best accomplished by ensuring that the quality process is present in the key systems of the organization. Although an organization may be viewed as consisting of an integrated set of systems, the quality process also must be viewed as consisting of a similar set of systems.

The systems that define the total-quality process initially may be separate from the standard organizational systems to ensure that they receive the necessary attention. However, once the process develops, the quality system will become an important part of the regular organizational systems. For example, quality planning initially may be a separate process from that of normal business planning. However, as the total-quality process matures, quality and business planning will merge and become parts of the same planning system.

The definition of TQM used in this paper is similar to that used in the Malcolm Baldrige National Quality Award examination items.

Briefly, the underlying assumptions are:

- Quality is defined by the customer;
- The basis of quality is well-designed and well-executed systems and processes;
- The organization's operations and decisions are based on fact;
- Continuous improvement is a key part of the management of all systems and processes;
- The focus is on the prevention of all quality problems; and
- All personnel should be trained and active in quality-improvement activities.

The eight-systems model suggests that TQM can be most successfully implemented by focusing attention on eight basic management systems. These eight systems are:

1. Leadership
2. Structure
3. Quality planning
4. Training
5. Rewards and recognition
6. Quality measurement
7. Communication
8. Quality-improvement activities

This model is illustrated in Figure 1. In the model the seven outer systems are all linked to the inner system, which consists of specific activities, such as quality-improvement teams, that are designed to directly improve quality.

It is important to highlight those quality-improvement activities that directly improve quality or customer satisfaction or whatever the designated targets are in the organization. The fact that an organization has a quality policy, or has quality goals, or trains its employees in statistical process control does not reduce scrap or cycle time one bit. Improvement can come only through the employees' and managers' actually changing the ways in which the work is done or changing the design of the product or service. The quality-improvement activities are absolutely critical, and all of the other systems should be directed toward making sure that the improvement activities are occurring effectively.

Figure 1. The Eight-Systems Model for Total Quality Management

A basic assumption of the model is that in order to design an effective TQM process for an organization, the following must occur:

1. All eight systems must be "activated," i.e., the design will include all eight systems;

2. There must be a clear and specific set of activities or functions for each system; and

3. The activities of the eight systems must be integrated into a coherent total-quality process.

1. LEADERSHIP

Because total quality management includes the total organization, it is especially critical that it be led by the key executives of the organization.

Indeed, the first category of the Baldrige Award is leadership. This category is seen as the "driver" of the other categories of the award. One of the frequently cited causes of the failure to implement a TQM process is the lack of commitment or the half-hearted involvement of the senior managers.

The role of senior management, in fact of all management, is to exhibit leadership, personal involvement, and visibility in the quality-related activities of the organization. Management has a special role in creating clear quality values and ensuring that these are communicated throughout the organization and integrated into the day-to-day management and supervision of all organizational units.

> *The role of management is to exhibit leadership, personal involvement, and visibility.*

Because "quality leadership" may be new to most managers, it may be helpful to define their roles in very specific terms by listing those activities that are expected of senior managers as well as other managers.

This activity list, or behavioral-role description, may be two lists. The first list consists of those actions that a senior manager must execute to implement and maintain a TQM process, such as to form and chair a Quality Council; to make quality a part of the performance goals of his or her direct reports; to make sure that sufficient resources are provided for the quality activities; and so on.

The second list includes those activities that signal the senior manager's personal commitment to (or modeling of) the TQM process. Examples of these kinds of activities include his or her personal training of direct reports; full attendance at quality council meetings; having quality-improvement projects active in his or her office; visiting quality-improvement team meetings; writing a monthly article on quality for the company newsletter, and so on.

Similar behavioral-role descriptions should be developed for managers throughout the organization to ensure that all managers are "leading" the quality process. The Xerox Corporation (Kearns & Nadler, 1992) has used this very effectively in its "Leadership Through Quality" process in providing "Standards for a Role Model Manager" to which all managers are to adhere. Xerox managers receive feedback from employees as to the manager's conformance to these standards through an annual survey and are evaluated on these standards in the regular performance-appraisal process, and these standards are used as criteria for promotion. This provides an effective vehicle for establishing (and integrating) the "Leadership Through Quality" process throughout the organization.

2. Structure

If TQM can be viewed as a planned coordination of activities directed toward a specific goal, i.e., total customer satisfaction, then the quality "structure" can be viewed as both the division of labor and the hierarchy of authority of the coordinated activities. Thus, the quality structure tells who has the responsibility for what quality activities and defines the lines of decision-making authority.

The area of TQM design in which there is a significant danger of creating a mechanism that would compete or interfere with normal business operations is the creation of structure. There is a danger of creating a bureaucracy that could overpower the basic business processes that are key to delivering the organization's products and services.

For this reason, it seems imperative that the quality structure must have the following characteristics:

1. Closely mimic the formal structure of the organization so that it can be coordinated easily with the "normal" activities of the organization. (For example, if there is a quality council directing the quality efforts, it should consist of the members of the senior management team.)

2. Not be complex, be easy to operate, and not generate a bureaucracy of its own.

3. Eventually be merged into the "normal" structure and activities of the organization. (For example, it is difficult to see the quality activities of the Ritz-Carlton Hotel or AT&T Universal Card Services [1992 Baldrige Award winners] as anything but the normal and routine activities of these companies.)

Given all the previous provisions, Figure 2 outlines a fairly typical structure for a large corporation.

As illustrated in the figure, the quality efforts are led by senior managers who also are members of a quality council. The responsibilities of this council are to formulate quality policies and values, to formulate quality goals, to review progress on these goals, and to direct corrective actions when necessary.

The quality coordinator facilitates and coordinates quality-related activities. He or she is not responsible for quality in the organization; the managers and employees have that responsibility, with top management driving the process. This is not an "authority" position; it is one of coordination and prodding.

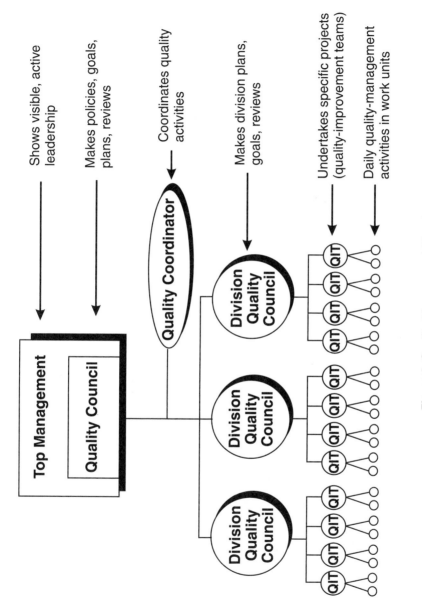

Shows visible, active leadership

Makes policies, goals, plans, reviews

Coordinates quality activities

Makes division plans, goals, reviews

Undertakes specific projects (quality-improvement teams)

Daily quality-management activities in work units

Top Management

Quality Council

Quality Coordinator

Division Quality Council

Division Quality Council

Division Quality Council

QIT

Figure 2. Quality-Management Structure

In Figure 2, each division (or plant or region) of the organization may have its own quality council, which has the same responsibilities as the council for the total organization; however, it is focused on quality-related activities of the division. It is led by the top management of the division, although the membership of the council may be broader in scope (e.g., it may include union representatives in unionized plants).

The next step in the structure is quality-improvement teams (QITs), which are assigned or choose specific quality-improvement projects. These teams are often cross-functional teams; however, they also may be within a department, or company/supplier teams, or company/customer teams.

The final activities listed in Figure 2 are those that occur as part of the daily routine of the work unit. These may include the monitoring of quality indicators, the use of statistical process control, inspection, and problem-solving activities.

The structure outlined is only one of many possibilities, and one has to design a system that best fits the organization. The important point is that there needs to be some coherent and coordinated division of labor and hierarchy of authority for quality-related activities if a total-quality process is to be successful.

3. QUALITY PLANNING

Quality planning is the process of setting quality-related objectives as well as deciding on the suitable courses of action to be taken for accomplishing those objectives.

The planning system specifies the direction that the organization will take in both the long term (five years) and the short term (one to three years) and describes the actions necessary to achieve the goals and objectives. The planning system must take into account and plan for the personnel, equipment, and training costs of the quality effort. It also should include a review-and-correction process to monitor progress on the quality plans.

As with the other systems, it is imperative that the quality-planning system be integrated with the "normal" business planning and budgeting processes of the organization. However, in the initial implementation of the quality process, a separate quality-planning process may be useful both to highlight the process and to provoke discussion of quality objectives and actions.

Pfeiffer & Company

Most quality-planning efforts in organizations in the United States are similar to, or a part of, the organization's annual management-by-objectives (MBO) process. This process includes a category for "quality objectives" together with other categories of business objectives. First, top management formulates the general objectives of the organization, then unit objectives follow in a flow-down procedure. There usually is some input and negotiation between units, divisions, and corporate headquarters as the process develops. All objectives and plans, at all levels, should support the strategic goals of the organization. Quite often, those objectives are tied in with the compensation system, so a division head's or plant manager's annual bonus is contingent on the attainment of specified objectives, including quality-related objectives.

Another planning process, more popular in Japan than in the United States, is quality policy deployment or Hoshin planning (Akao, 1991). The strategy of Hoshin planning is to focus the organization's resources on a few (three to seven) specific and important goals. These goals, chosen by the policy deployment committee, are important to the customers or the organization and allow significant progress or "break-throughs" to be made. The assumption is that it is better to make substantial progress in a few critical areas than to expend energy in a lot of areas, many of which are of minor importance.

The critical differences between the MBO process and the Hoshin process are as follows:

1. The care with which the Hoshin process targets a limited number of objectives that will have a significant impact on quality or customer satisfaction.

2. All units or persons who might contribute to those objectives are expected to do so.

For example, one of the Hoshin goals of Florida Power and Light was to eliminate or significantly reduce blackouts. Its customers had identified this as a top priority. All units that might contribute to this goal, e.g., equipment design, purchasing, customer service, and repair services, made this one of their main quality priorities.

Many organizations, including those that are active in quality improvement, do not have a formal quality-planning process. There is an expectation that all units will be engaged in a process of continuous improvement, and the units know where best to direct their efforts.

The danger with this "nonplanning" approach is that a lot of energy is spent on activities that may have little impact. There also is the danger of what Deming referred to as "suboptimizing the system," in which each unit optimizes its own area of responsibility and, in doing so, throws the larger system out of order (Walton, 1990). Some planning mechanism is necessary, one that helps coordinate quality activities around important quality goals.

4. TRAINING

The objective of the quality-training system is to provide all personnel, and sometimes suppliers and customers, with the skills to effectively perform quality-related activities. However, quality-related training is not the only type of training a manager or employee should receive. Some of the better organizations view themselves as "continuous learning" organizations, in which every person is expected to continually update and extend his or her job-related skills. Some organizations stipulate that all employees are obligated to engage in a specified number of hours of training annually. Quality also can be improved by increasing a person's competence to perform his or her job.

Quality training should be systematic and systemic. There should be several courses available for all personnel, some of which are required of everyone and some of which are restricted to those who need the specific skills.

Organizations that are beginning quality efforts should start with "quality awareness" training, with special emphasis on what TQM is, what the organization expects to gain by implementing it, and what will be expected of managers and employees as participants in the process. After the first cycle is completed with all personnel, all new hires should be given awareness training regarding the quality strategy being used in the organization and what is expected of them in the process.

Everyone in the organization also should be trained in a quality-improvement or problem-solving model—a model that is used to solve quality problems. There are several popular models, most being six-, seven-, or eight-step, structured problem-solving sequences. Some organizations train all employees in how to use the chosen model; other organizations train employees on a just-in-time basis.

Several other courses might be included in quality training. For example, courses on team skills and facilitation skills are pertinent, as much of the quality improvement occurs in teams. There could be a course on statistical process control, if the organization uses the technique, and a course on quality planning. There are other, highly specialized, courses that teach skills used by quality professionals.

The question often arises of who should do the training: the training department, outside consultants, managers, or managers and line employees? A strong case can be made for managers (or managers and line employees) providing the quality training, as they are the people most in contact with how it will be used. They also have the highest credibility. There is no better way to learn something thoroughly than by teaching it.

The flow-down method of start-up quality training used by Xerox, in which the CEO trains his direct reports and they, in turn, train their direct reports, sends a very clear signal about the commitment of managers to the quality process.

Another related issue is whether all personnel should receive two or three days of training on the quality-improvement process and the quality tools or whether the training should be done "just-in-time" by forming improvement teams around an important quality problem and training the teams as they progress. The latter approach seems to be gaining in popularity because it avoids training people who do not use their acquired skills immediately and it is less costly.

Training does not occur only in a classroom; it should be an integral part of the job. Managers and employees should be coaching and instructing one another on tools and techniques, and teams should be evaluating the processes they are using to continually increase their effectiveness.

5. REWARDS AND RECOGNITION

One of the major causes of failure of the quality process is a reward system that "endorses" quality but actually rewards something other than quality work. For example, in many organizations the only important performance criterion is meeting a production quota. Managers and employees understand what is important and what is not, and quality becomes something that is preached but not practiced.

This area elicits considerable controversy among quality professionals, particularly around the appraisal and reward aspects of the system. For example, W. Edwards Deming (the TQM "guru") was opposed to performance goals, performance appraisals, and rewarding employees based on individual performance (Walton, 1990). He argued that 85 percent of performance is caused by the design of the system, and employees have very little influence over this. Any differences that appear in employee performance are probably the results of random fluctuations.

Two additional points must be considered. The first is that managers and employees quickly learn what is important in their jobs and act accordingly. The message that quality is important must be reinforced.

Managers and their subordinates have to know that they will be rewarded in some way for producing quality products and services and that quality work is one of the expectations of the job.

A second, critical, point is that most U.S. organizations schedule annual (or quarterly) performance appraisals that determine, among other things, pay increases and promotions. Many U.S. organizations have bonus systems for executives and key managers. Whether it makes sense or not, performance appraisals and differential reward systems are part of the fabric of U.S. business.

Somehow, quality must be incorporated into performance appraisals and reward systems. One option is to do so directly. Xerox Corporation's "Leadership Through Quality" process is a good example of participation in quality improvement as a basis for raises or promotion. Other organizations have based portions (e.g., 25 percent) of executives' annual bonuses on specific improvements in quality results. Another approach is Motorola's performance-management system: a traditional MBO system is used for regular work planning (and annual pay raises), and a "Participative Management Program" has teams working on specific quality-related projects for which they receive an annual bonus, based on the results they achieve.

Although making quality a part of the appraisal and reward system is critical, surveys have indicated that employees are just as pleased with nonmonetary recognition. There are various ways of recognizing employees for their quality efforts, such as listing their names in the company newsletter; awarding them certificates, plaques, quality-recognition pins, t-shirts, movie tickets, or special parking places; placing their names on a "Quality Wall of Fame," and so on. Organizations that use Phil Crosby's TQM model (Crosby, 1979) have developed elaborate and effective programs for the recognition of individuals and teams who have excelled in quality (Johnson, 1993; Townsend, 1990). There are many ways of rewarding and recognizing people for quality work. The important thing is that a reward and recognition program for quality be in place.

6. QUALITY MEASUREMENT

An old adage states that you cannot manage what you cannot measure. The goal of the measurement system is to collect information on quality-related processes and results, to convert these data to usable formats, and to distribute the data to the appropriate user in a timely fashion.

The purpose of collecting quality-related information is to use it to improve the quality of the products/services and processes of the organization. The information is used as a "score card" to see how an organization or a unit is doing in a particular area and then to improve its processes or products.

This purpose should be very clear in an organization that is implementing the TQM process. Information should add value to the organization. The only way it can add value is in the hands of people who transform the data into action. Otherwise, the information is of no value, and collecting it is a wasteful activity.

The information that is collected in this process must have the following characteristics:

- Important to a quality-related process and to the customer; and

- Available to a person or unit who can use the information to improve the process or product or service.

A large organization may collect data on several hundred indices of quality. For example, First Chicago Corporation regularly collects data on 650 indices of quality. However, much of these data are collected only within specific units and are only of value within those units. Thus, the money transfer unit may collect data on six or eight quality indices related to its effectiveness, and the mail service may collect data on a different six to eight indices related to its effectiveness.

The types of data usually collected can be classified in four general subcategories:

1. External-Output: Data on customer satisfaction with products and services, complaint handling, product inquiries, conformance to specifications, etc.

2. External-Input: Data on quality, timeliness, etc., of suppliers' and vendors' products and service.

3. Internal-Company-wide: Data on safety, employee turnover, error rates, number of on-time shipments, employee satisfaction, etc.

4. Internal-Within Divisions or Units: Data on products or processes specific to divisions or units, e.g., statistical process control within a unit, frequency of machine breakdown, cycle time, etc.

The measurement system is critical; it is the organization's scorecard. An organization cannot know where its problems are or whether it is making progress in solving them without a good system of measuring and monitoring.

7. COMMUNICATION

As TQM becomes implemented in an organization, there is an increasing need to establish channels of communication in order to keep people informed about progress. People must be continually reminded of the purpose, goals, and activities of the quality process or they will lose interest.

One major communication need is keeping people informed about the many quality activities that are going on in the organization. Information about training activities, progress on the quality goals, the activities of each of the cross-functional quality-improvement teams; notification of coming events; and announcement of quality-award winners all are important. One effective way of disseminating this information is through a weekly or monthly quality newsletter that is distributed to all personnel. The newsletter also may include a message from the CEO and recognition of people who were helpful in the quality effort. Other communication channels are a quality bulletin board (either on a wall or via the computer), special meetings (or rallies), award ceremonies, and making quality news part of the agenda of all meetings.

A second important area of communication is the transfer of quality results. There needs to be a mechanism by which the improvements made by a quality-improvement team are dispersed for use by all relevant units. For example, one of the QITs at Florida Power and Light found that galvanized-metal power switches would corrode in salt-spray areas and subsequently fail. Changing to bronze or stainless steel switches eliminated this problem and increased service reliability. This knowledge was dispersed and is now company-wide policy (Staff, 1988). Typically, the responsibility for the transfer of results rests with the quality council and the quality coordinator.

8. QUALITY-IMPROVEMENT ACTIVITIES

This system encompasses those tasks and activities that directly affect the quality of the products, services, and processes of the organization. The words "directly affect" are key to the definition of this system. There are some activities that directly maintain and improve quality, and there are other activities that provide support for these direct activities. It is only through these direct activities that quality improvement can occur.

This distinction is critical. There are organizations that have a quality policy or a quality council, or who set quality goals, but in which there seems to be no improvement in the quality of their products and services. In such organizations, the problem often is a failure to execute.

The mechanisms designed to directly impact the quality of the products or services or processes are either nonexistent or perform poorly.

This system is the most difficult to do and to do well. It is relatively easy to write a quality policy or to set quality goals, but considerably more difficult to get quality improvement teams, quality circles, a suggestion system, and the like working effectively and delivering quality improvements on a consistent basis.

In developing this system, it is important that the activities be limited and focused, tailored to the organization, and coordinated with the quality-support systems. Too many diffuse activities are difficult to monitor, difficult to control, and difficult to keep focused on the important initiatives of the organization.

A minimal but effective system may be limited to only three basic activities:

1. A process for identifying the important quality indicators for a unit and developing a system to measure and monitor them.

2. A problem-solving and improvement process within each unit. (This could be weekly team meetings to review the key quality indicators for the unit and initiate ways of improving them, or more formal quality circles, or special project teams.)

3. A problem-solving and improvement mechanism to deal with cross-functional issues, with organization-supplier issues, and with complex problems not easily handled by a regular work team. (The most common examples of this mechanism are quality-improvement teams with cross-functional membership and which deal with cross-functional problems.)

The goal of these activities is continuous quality improvement. The teams do not wait for a problem to occur; they identify key products and processes and work to continually improve them. This is a never-ending process of focusing on a product or process, improving it, and then going on to another product or process and improving it. If this process is occurring in all units, the organization cannot help but improve its customer service and its competitive position.

A variety of other activities can be used to directly affect quality in an organization. Perhaps most common is a company-wide suggestion system in which anyone can suggest quality improvements regarding any process or product, not necessarily in their work area.

Another effective improvement mechanism is the audit team, which may be made up of customers, outside consultants, or internal personnel. The team reviews processes or products and makes recommendations for their improvement.

IMPLEMENTING AND INTEGRATING THE SYSTEM

If the total-quality process is to be successfully implemented in an organization, the eight systems must be activated and integrated in all functions of the organization.

- "Activated" means that there is a set of quality-related activities ongoing in each system.

- "Integrated" means that the activities in the eight systems support and reinforce one another.

- "In all functions" means that all units of the organization participate in the quality process.

Although there are several approaches to implementing a TQM process in an organization, one of the most common is to begin the design process by "benchmarking" several similar organizations that have implemented TQM and identifying what would work best for one's own organization. Benchmarking is the method by which members of one organization visit other organizations that are noted for their superiority in particular processes. They learn how the "best" operate and use this information as the standard in designing their own processes. For example, L.L. Bean is noted for its superiority in the distribution process and has been used as a benchmark by many firms.

The next step is for the top executives and key managers to develop a general vision of what they want the organization to become and how the quality process fits in, and then to set some general quality goals. The next step is the design of a quality structure that can facilitate the goals, including an outline of types of quality-improvement activities that are critical to achieving substantial gains in quality. This step is followed by quality-awareness training throughout the organization, then by the creation of a quality-measurement system in all units. The process continues until all eight systems are activated.

The process should be guided by a design checklist. This document lists all the major pieces that have to be in place in order for the TQM process to be fully implemented. The contents of the checklist vary, depending on the size of the organization and the approach being taken. The elements in the design of the process for a small company are different from the elements for a large corporation. As the key managers and others are benchmarking other organizations and reading about others' successes and failures, they will be gathering ideas about the elements that need to be in the TQM design of their organization. Each element should be examined, and a consensus should be reached as to which elements will be included. The final design checklist becomes the TQM implementation strategy for the organization.

The eight systems provide the framework for the design checklist. They include all the major elements that need to be activated in order to have an effective TQM process. Although the elements that make up the design may vary, all eight systems must be activated.

Figure 3 is an abbreviated outline of a design checklist. It is provided for illustrative purposes; the checklist for each organization should be developed by the organization itself, not borrowed from others. The sample checklist outlines twenty-six activities that are important to the total quality management process.

LEADERSHIP
- Top managers have investigated several leading organizations to learn of their quality plans and processes and to establish benchmarks based on their findings.
- Top managers are trained in quality principles and tools.
- Top managers are actively involved in quality-related activities.
- Top managers send clear messages through their communications and behaviors that quality is a priority in the organization.

STRUCTURE
- A quality council directs the quality activities of the organization.
- A quality coordinator has been appointed to coordinate the quality activities of the organization.
- Clear lines of responsibility, authority, and communication have been established for the quality process.
- Every unit in the organization knows that it is expected to participate in measuring and improving quality.

QUALITY PLANNING
- The organization has a quality mission statement and values statement that is understood by all personnel.
- The organization sets quality-improvement goals and has an effective mechanism for communicating the goals to all units.
- Quality goals are based on understanding and satisfying customer needs.
- There is a mechanism in place that assures that adequate resources will be available to implement the quality activities.
- The quality council periodically reviews progress on the quality goals and initiates corrective action as needed.

TRAINING
- All personnel receive quality-awareness training.
- The organization has a curriculum for training all personnel in quality principles and tools.
- All employees are trained in using a standard, continuous-improvement model.
- Quality-improvement teams receive training in how to work effectively as teams.

Figure 3. Sample Design Checklist for the TQM Process

REWARDS AND RECOGNITION

- The organization rewards employees for achieving quality goals.
- Promotion and advancement are, in part, based on achieving quality goals.
- The organization has a program that recognizes employees who have contributed to the quality process.
- The organization has a mechanism for celebrating, on a company-wide basis, quality accomplishments.

QUALITY MEASUREMENT

- The organization uses several indices to measure organization-wide quality.
- The organization regularly measures customer satisfaction with its products and services.
- Each work unit has several indices to measure the quality of its processes and output. These data are posted in the unit.
- The organization measures and monitors the quality of its suppliers.
- There are effective mechanisms for utilizing the data from the quality-measurement system to improve the quality of the organization's processes and products.

COMMUNICATION

- The quality mission and values, the goals of the quality process, and its importance to the organization are communicated to all personnel.
- The organization has an effective mechanism for informing all personnel about quality information and activities.
- Issues concerning quality, including plans and reviews of results, are regularly on the agenda of meetings.
- The organization has a mechanism for dispersing improvement results from one unit to other units.

QUALITY-IMPROVEMENT ACTIVITIES

- Quality-improvement efforts are conducted in every unit of the organization.
- Several quality-improvement teams are actively pursuing cross-functional or cross-departmental quality problems.
- A quality-improvement team is working with key suppliers to improve the quality of incoming materials.
- Quality-improvement teams are working with key customers to find ways to improve products and services.

Figure 3 (continued). Sample Design Checklist for the TQM Process

"Total" is the key word: the process must touch all systems in the organization if it is to be effective. The sample list does not include all the activities that might be part of the process. For example, important areas such as employee empowerment, employee feedback, and customer feedback are not on the list in order to keep it from being too lengthy.

Finally, there needs to be a mechanism in place that periodically reviews the effectiveness of the TQM process—whether it is achieving the desired results, what is working and what is not, what needs to be added and what needs to be dropped, and how the process can be improved to make it more effective.

It should be obvious that all of this requires a major effort on the part of the managers and employees of an organization; however, the payoffs are well worth the effort. The quality process leads to greater sales, to lower costs, to wider profit margins, and to higher morale. It is a great way to keep customers and employees satisfied and to keep the organization profitable. That is as much as one can expect from any business practice.

References

Akao, Y. (Ed.). (1991). *Hoshin kanri.* Cambridge, MA: Productivity Press.

Crosby, P.B. (1979). *Quality is free.* New York: McGraw-Hill.

Johnson, H.H. (1993). There's no more doubting Thomases here: How a small service company discovered quality. *Journal of Quality and Participation, 28,* 10-16.

Kearns, D.T., & Nadler, D.A. (1992). *Prophets in the dark.* New York: Harper Business.

Staff. (1988). Building a quality improvement program at Florida Power and Light. *Target, 4,* 1-16.

Townsend, P. (1990). *Commit to quality.* New York: John Wiley.

Walton, M. (1990). *Deming management at work.* New York: Putnam.

Homer H. Johnson, Ph.D., *is a professor of organization development in the Center for Organization Development, Loyola University, Chicago. He teaches and consults in the areas of total quality management, change management, and strategic planning. He is a member of the leadership council for the Illinois Quality Award (Lincoln Award) and is the co-chair of the Illinois Quality Award for Education. Dr. Johnson has authored several publications in the areas of quality and change management.*

FIVE LESSONS FOR INTERNAL OD CONSULTANTS

John Geirland and Marci Maniker-Leiter

Abstract: Before starting their own consulting practices, the authors spent many years as internal organization development (OD) consultants. In this article
they present the five most important lessons they have
learned about internal consulting, although all five
have applicability for external consultants as well:

    1. Establish your authority;
    2. Bring added value to the organization;
    3. Create rapport;
    4. Avoid misunderstandings; and
    5. Show courage.

One of the authors' main points is that the internal consultant's candor in expressing organizational
realities is what the job is all about; that candor is the
added value that he or she brings to the organization.
This article offers not only useful tips and several
examples from the authors' own experience, but also
a message of encouragement and motivation.

Both of us have spent many exciting and fruitful years working as internal organization development (OD) consultants. In those years we have learned—sometimes painfully—a number of lessons. In this article we summarize five of those lessons: ones that have proved particularly useful not only in our work as internal consultants, but also in subsequent work as external consultants. It is our hope that you, too, will benefit from what we discovered.

Lesson 1: Establish Your Authority

Imagine that you are an internal consultant, in a staff rather than line position, in each of the following three situations:

> *Situation 1:* Fred Breaux, senior vice president of an important division in your company, tells you that he wants to see a confidential report you wrote about the performance of Steve Stein, who works for Fred. You based the report on Steve's responses to an instrument you administered and a subsequent interview you held with him, and you assured Steve that the feedback in the report was for his eyes only. You did not count on Steve's boss's wanting a copy, and now the boss is leaning hard on you to comply.

> *Situation 2:* Sylvia Hutton, an executive vice president in your company, asks you to do a team-building intervention with her management team. After conducting confidential interviews with members of the team, you learn that one member has a drinking problem and that Sylvia is uncomfortable with confronting the individual herself. The managers believe that Sylvia wants the team-building intervention to concentrate on the drinking; in this way the managers would have to "take care of the problem for her." You know that this is precisely the wrong reason to do team building.

> *Situation 3:* Edward Pierce, a powerful executive in your company, asks you to conduct interviews with his staff members to "find out how people are feeling about things." You ask Edward if he knows of any issues of particular concern to his staff. "None that I can think of," he answers. A week later, after many

hours of interviewing, you learn that Pierce has been less than candid with you; open warfare exists between two of Pierce's managers.

What do these vignettes have in common? In each case you, as the internal consultant, are being pressured by someone with higher status and power in the organization. What authority and power you do have comes from two sources: who you know and what you are.

Who You Know

You can enhance your power through association with one or more patrons in executive management, preferably including the CEO. An executive can empower you by publicly supporting your mission in the organization. Although it is desirable to have a direct reporting relationship with a senior executive, more often than not the patronage will develop through other means, for example, a successful consulting engagement or your own efforts to market yourself internally. The challenge is for you to use the power resulting from the patronage judiciously. If you drop a patron's name frequently, whatever power you derive from it will diminish quickly. Usually it is enough for people to know that the executive supports the consultant's activities.

> *Protect visibility and usefulness by building relationships with several clients.*

One more word about patrons: Although it is helpful to have a powerful supporter in the organization, you make yourself vulnerable if you are identified to too great an extent with one person. If that executive leaves the company, transfers, passes out of favor, or is fired, you may find yourself without support. Protect your visibility and usefulness by building relationships with several clients.

An Example from Our Experience

Phil Thompson was the manager of a regional office in a company where one of us was employed. Phil's operation was thousands of miles from the home office, a fact that he relished. "We're like a ship out here, and I'm the captain," he liked to tell his people. Phil faced major challenges: high turnover, understaffing, and work-design problems. Nevertheless, he had resisted all suggestions to make changes, even when they came from his immediate supervisor.

Phil's reaction was not much different when he was contacted by phone to discuss the idea of consultant-conducted "climate interviews" with his people. He showed impatience and inflexibility. But once it was made clear that the division manager (two levels higher than Phil) was interested in the project, arrangements for a visit and subsequent intervention went smoothly.

What You Are

People who have special knowledge and skills are usually respected and often even revered. As an internal consultant, you are versed in the principles of human behavior and the technology of behavioral change. You can enhance your authority and credibility further by becoming active in professional societies and by earning degrees, certificates, and licenses in the field. By continually learning and building skills, tools, and experience, you will enhance your presence within the organization.

LESSON 2: BRING ADDED VALUE TO THE ORGANIZATION

Many people believe that human resource development professionals are not as bottom-line oriented as other professionals in the organization. To counteract this misconception and foster your own success as an internal consultant, you need to make a special effort to promote your work as contributing to the bottom line.

You must also "sell" your services internally. Although most internal consultants do not charge individual clients for consulting services, no such services are free. Clients have to invest their time, and that of their staffs, in any intervention—worth potentially hundreds or even thousands of dollars in salaries and opportunity costs. Consequently, any potential client needs to be shown that your services bring added value to the organization.

Following are some techniques for making the value of your services known:

1. *Make presentations around the company.* Hold brown-bag sessions at lunchtime, attend staff meetings, and take opportunities to give a presentation for any audience in the company.

2. *Develop a brochure.* Creating and distributing a brief brochure containing information about how your services contribute to the bottom line is an excellent idea. The brochure gives clients something to refer to long after you have concluded personal meetings or phone calls.

3. *Link your values to organizational strategies and goals.* You are more likely to be seen as making a positive contribution if your values are seen as supporting the organization's strategies and goals. Demonstrate how your services support goals such as superior customer service, high productivity, improved quality, and increasing market share.

An Example from Our Experience

A large organization based in the western U.S. was undergoing a significant downsizing. As part of this process, the company and all its employees had participated in a detailed analysis of its products and services, seeking to identify and eliminate activities that were no longer important. This self-examination took months, and during this period productivity and morale plummeted.

One of us, an internal consultant for the company at the time, developed a series of workshops on managing change to support the self-examination process and to minimize the traumatic effects. As a result of attending the workshops, employees had a greater understanding of the emotions they were feeling and developed skill in various behavioral techniques for maintaining productivity.

LESSON 3: CREATE RAPPORT

Your success as an internal consultant depends on your ability to make people feel comfortable. Remember that your clients, for the most part, are under no obligation to use your services. If people find you distant, uncaring, too pushy, or too timid, you may limit your network within the company.

Making people feel comfortable is also the first step in any OD intervention. At first, some clients may not feel comfortable in sharing all their concerns or thoughts with you. This reluctance is a form of resistance and is very common. Take the time necessary to establish rapport and discover your client's needs and concerns. Adapt yourself to the client's interpersonal style. For example, find out which of the following reflect your client's preferences:

- Numbers or anecdotes;
- Short, to-the-point meetings or chattier sessions over lunch;
- Face-to-face encounters, phone calls, or memos.

Sometimes the client is not sure why he or she has brought you in. Asking for your services may simply be in response to a gut feeling that "something doesn't feel right" or a curiosity about "how people are feeling about things." You can help the client by asking questions designed to bring the real issues to the surface. For instance, you may ask, "Was there anything that happened shortly before you contacted me?" or "At what times are you most likely to feel uneasy about things in your department? What is usually going on?" Engaging the client in an exploratory dialog not only forms the basis for the subsequent intervention, but also builds a solid working relationship.

An Example from Our Experience

The authors were brought in by an internal client who managed a large software-development project that involved almost two hundred programmers and systems analysts. "I'd like to have a stress-management program for my people," the client said. "We're having record levels of absenteeism; people are using up all their sick leave and even taking time off without pay. We know we have a challenging project here, so we need something that will help our people get through it."

At this point we could have proceeded with the planning of stress-management workshops. Instead, we guided the client through a discussion of the project and its history, a topic that was within his comfort zone. (The client was a "driver"; he preferred discussing task-related issues only.) Eventually, the client began to relax and talk about other concerns. Various issues surfaced: his working relationship with end-users, communication problems between some of the work groups on the project, and so on. Stress was not the problem, but the symptom of a larger problem—a fact that came out only after the client dropped his defenses.

LESSON 4: AVOID MISUNDERSTANDINGS

The easiest way to destroy your credibility as an internal consultant is to appear to break an understanding with a client. You can help to ensure that miscommunication is avoided by putting understandings in writing. Write a contract that clearly defines the intervention. Sit down with the client and clarify the following points, which subsequently appear in the contract:

1. *Who the client is.* Although the client's identity may appear obvious, it occasionally is not. Establish at the beginning who will receive a copy of the final report. This issue is especially important when feedback is collected on managers and that feedback turns out to be negative. If you try to identify who receives the feedback after you have already

collected it, you will run into difficulties concerning whose feedback it is and who has the right to share it.

2. *What roles and responsibilities each party assumes.* In addition to the more obvious responsibilities, you should consider tasks that may not be immediately apparent, for example, whether the client wants to delegate the handling of logistics. Another important task that the client must undertake is telling employees what to expect, which can be done in either a meeting or a memo. Providing a sample memo helps assist the client with wording, builds the consultant's credibility (because the memo is a concrete deliverable), and virtually guarantees that the employees will be appropriately informed about the pending intervention.

3. *What the client will and will not receive.* If the intervention involves gathering data (for example, through a climate survey), the client should receive a written report of the results and a verbal explanation of those results. Stating what the format of the report is to be will help avoid complaints that the report is too general or too specific, too narrow or too comprehensive.

4. *Who participates.* Voluntary participation in interventions produces more honest and, therefore, more useful results. The client may strongly urge employees to participate, but not force them to. Negative consequences can result when participation is dictated rather than freely given.

5. *What the rules of confidentiality will be.* Every employee is entitled to confidentiality. The client should know from the beginning that he or she will receive no information about who said what. Protecting people's anonymity will secure your ability to acquire useful information and to intervene effectively in the future, if necessary.

6. *What the details of follow-up will be.* You and the client should make arrangements to meet at a later date to assess the success of the intervention. If possible, set up the date of that meeting in advance so that it can be recorded in the contract. Let the client know that you will also check with him or her periodically to see how the intervention worked and to determine if you can assist further.

An Example from Our Experience

One of us was brought in to conduct an employee-opinion survey for a small department. The survey was administered, and confidential interviews were conducted. The data were analyzed, and a report was written within four weeks. There was some delay in presenting the results due to the client's "busy schedule." Several appointments were made, then canceled by the client.

Eventually the survey findings were presented and explained. The client said he was pleased with the work, and a date was set to share a summary of the findings with the department staff. Again, the meeting was canceled by the client. Additional dates were scheduled, each canceled. Eventually, six months passed before the feedback meeting was held. The client felt no need to provide people with timely feedback, but the consultant did. The issue of timely feedback to employees had not been addressed in the written contract. When the results were finally reported to all those who had participated, the data held very little credibility for employees.

LESSON 5: SHOW COURAGE

> *Rich in virtue, like an infant,*
> *Noxious insects will not sting him;*
> *Wild beasts will not attack his flesh*
> *Nor birds of prey sink claws in him.*
>
> Lao Tzu, *The Tao Te Ching*

The most important and challenging of the five lessons is to show courage. You probably will be called on to say things to your clients that they would never hear from their peers or subordinates—or even from the people they report to.

The courage to be candid may be difficult to muster in the best of times. And because the internal consultant does not usually occupy a line position, he or she is always vulnerable during periods of budget cutting and downsizing. If you find yourself in such a situation, you will be subject to the temptation to restrain your candor and avoid upsetting people.

But if you succumb to this temptation, you will limit your effectiveness and, therefore, your usefulness to the organization. Your candor in expressing organizational realities is what your job is all about; that is the added value you bring to the organization. Furthermore, many clients will sense when you are not being totally forthcoming and will not view that behavior favorably. Most clients want to hear it all. If you show fear, you damage your credibility and open yourself to pressures from others.

The best thing you can do is to cultivate a relaxed and confident attitude. Start by making yourself feel less vulnerable:

- Build up your network of contacts in other companies so that if you do lose your job, you can find out about and pursue other opportunities.

- Meet on a regular basis with your peers.

- Get active in professional societies.

- Write articles for books, journals, and newsletters in the field.

Another way to enhance your sense of security is to develop an independent consulting practice. Vacation days, weekends, and evenings can be used for consulting to other companies (not direct competitors, of course), holding workshops, or teaching evening courses at a local college. These outside activities will generate added income that can be saved for a rainy day (unemployment). By the time that rainy day rolls around, if it ever does, you will be able to find the work to support yourself between jobs or to start your own full-time practice if you choose.

Having some sense of financial independence, however modest, coupled with a belief in yourself and your profession will give you the confidence you need to ask the tough questions and convey honest feedback. Your clients will perceive your strength and respect you for it.

PARTING WORDS

Joseph Campbell, the late mythologist, said that the secret of a happy life is to "follow your bliss." He added that when you find your bliss—the work that makes you happy—everything else will flow naturally and easily. Bliss—that is, enthusiasm, energy, creativity—is the greatest asset you can have as an internal consultant. With a little effort, the rest will follow.

John Geirland, Ph.D., heads up Geirland & Associates, an organization and management consulting firm based in Studio City, California, specializing in individual and organizational assessment, team development, managing change, and organizational design. Dr. Geirland has consulted to a wide range of public and private organizations, including Amgen, U.S. West, Blue Cross/Blue Shield of Florida, General Dynamics, Great Western Bank, and the Los Angeles County Department of Mental Health, among others. He has published papers on organizational design, the impact of technology in organizations, leadership and values, and creativity. He can be reached at jgeirland@aol.com.

Marci Maniker-Leiter is a management and organization development consultant specializing in team building and managing change. Her recent clients include, among others, McDonnell Douglas Aircraft, FannieMae, Security First Insurance, and the University of California at Los Angeles. Prior to starting her consulting business, she worked for Great Western Bank, managing its Organizational Development Department, a unit that offered internal consulting. She received her Master's in organizational psychology from Columbia University.

CONTRIBUTORS

Mary Sue Barry
Principal
Full-Circle Training and Consulting
114 27th Avenue North
St. Petersburg, FL 33704
  (813) 823-3604

Howard E. Butz, Jr.
Director, Total Quality
AAI Corporation
P.O. Box 126
Hunt Valley, MD 21030
  (410) 628-3355
  fax: (410) 683-6498

Greg H. Cripple
Manager, HR Planning & Development
John Deere Credit Company
John Deere Road
Moline, IL 61265
  (309) 765-5358
  fax: (309) 765-4947

Guillermo Cuéllar, Ed.D.
Organization Development Consultant
216 Silver Lane
Sunderland, MA 01375
  (413) 665-3288

Patrick Doyle
Principal
High Impact Training Services
R.R. #2
Perth Road, Ontario K0H 2I0
Canada
  (613) 544-5400
  fax: (613) 353-6517

Maureen Wilson Dücker
Academic Adviser
Educational Policy & Leadership—
  Higher Education & Student Affairs
Ohio State University
154 West 12th Avenue
015 Enarson Hall
Columbus, OH 43210
  (614) 292-0646
  fax: (614) 292-2124
  e-mail: mducker@mgate.uvc.ohio-
    state.edu

Caela Farren, Ph.D.
President
Career Systems, Inc.
900 James Avenue
Scranton, PA 18510
  (800) 283-8839

Peter R. Garber
Manager, Teamwork Development
PPG Industries, Inc.
One PPG Place
Pittsburgh, PA 15272
  (412) 434-3417
  fax: (412) 434-3490

John Geirland, Ph.D.
President
Geirland & Associates
4335 Beck Avenue
Studio City, CA 91604
  (818) 760-4978
  fax: (818) 760-0348
  e-mail: jgeirland@aol.com

Gary Gemmill, Ph.D.
Professor Emeritus
School of Management
Syracuse University
Syracuse, NY 13244
  (315) 443-2961

Glenn Head
Leadership Team
Delaney, Inc.
Box 4488
Boulder, CO 80306
  (303) 443-6868
  fax: (303) 442-4192

Marian Head
Box 4488
Boulder, CO 80306
  (303) 440-0910
  fax: (303) 442-4192

Paul G.W. Jansen, Ph.D.
Professor of Industrial Psychology
Department of Business Administration
Free University
De Boele Laan 1105
Amsterdam 1081 HV
The Netherlands
  011-31-20-44-46126
  fax: 011-31-20-44-46005

Homer H. Johnson, Ph.D.
Professor
Center for Organization Development
Loyola University
820 North Michigan Avenue
Chicago, IL 60611
  (312) 508-3027
  fax: (312) 508-8713

M.K. Key, Ph.D.
Consultant
Quorum Health Resources, Inc.
105 Continental Place
Brentwood, TN 37027
  (615) 371-4707
  fax: (615) 371-4610

James W. Kinneer
Support Services Supervisor
Indiana Hospital
Hospital Road
Indiana, PA 15701
  (412) 357-7089
  fax: (412) 357-7241

Chuck Kormanski, Ed.D.
Career Development and Placement
  Services
Penn State Altoona Campus
3000 Ivyside Park
Altoona, PA 16601
  (814) 949-5058
  fax: (814) 949-5805

Marci Maniker-Leiter
Management and Organization
  Development Consultant
Maniker-Leiter and Associates
2333 Duxbury Circle
Los Angeles, CA 90034-1017
  (310) 559-4056

Rick Maurer
Consultant
Maurer & Associates
5653 8th Street North
Arlington, VA 22205
  (703) 525-7074
  fax: (703) 525-0183

Milan Moravec
Managing Principal
Moravec and Associates
2453 Providence Court
Walnut Creek, CA 94596-6454
  (510) 937-5461
  fax: (510) 935-1837

Pfeiffer & Company

Anthony Nathan
President
Anthene Consulting International
5289 Fallingbrook Drive
Mississauga, Ontario L5V 1N8
Canada
  (905) 567-8731
  fax: (905) 542-1105

William N. Parker
Senior Training Specialist
Virginia Power
4112 Innslake Drive
Glen Allen, VA 23060
  (804) 273-3507
  fax: (804) 273-3513

Robert C. Preziosi, D.P.A.
Professor of Management Education
School of Business and Entrepreneurship
Nova Southeastern University
3301 College Avenue
Ft. Lauderdale, FL 33314
  (305) 476-8912
  fax: (305) 370-5637

Gaylord Reagan, Ph.D.
Consultant
Reagan Consulting
5306 North 105th Plaza, #9
Omaha, NE 68134
  (402) 431-0279

Irwin M. Rubin, Ph.D.
President
Temenos®, Inc.
37 Kawananakoa Place
Honolulu, HI 96817
  (808) 528-2433
  fax: (808) 528-2434

Ernest M. Schuttenberg, Ed.D.
Professor of Education
College of Education
Cleveland State University
1860 East 22nd Street
Cleveland, OH 44115
  (216) 523-7134
  fax: (216) 687-5415

Donald T. Simpson, Ed.D.
Training and Organization Development
40 Mulberry Street
Rochester, NY 14620-2432
  (716) 442-6501
  fax: (716) 442-6501

Glenn H. Varney, Ph.D.
Professor and Director
Master of Organization Development
  Program
Bowling Green State University
546 Hillcrest Drive
Bowling Green, OH 43402
  (419) 352-7782
  fax: (419) 354-8781

Phil Ventresca
President
Advanced Management Services, Inc.
968 Washington Street
Stoughton, MA 02072
  (617) 344-1103
  fax: (617) 341-3978

Contents of the Companion Volume,
The 1996 Annual: Volume 1, Training

---

*See Experiential Learning Activities Categories, p. 5, for an explanation of the numbering system.

PRESENTATION AND DISCUSSION RESOURCES